MedikalPreneur:

The Official Guidebook for
Physicians' Success in Business

Francisco Arredondo, MD, MPH

For information about this title or to order other books
and/or electronic media, contact the publisher:

Atkins & Greenspan Writing
TwoSistersWriting.com
18530 Mack Avenue, Suite 166
Grosse Pointe Farms, MI 48236

ISBN:
978-1-956879-00-1 (Hardcover)
978-1-956879-01-8 (Paperback)
978-1-956879-02-5 (eBook)

Printed in the United States of America

Cover design: Alejandro Gonzales with Van-garde Imagery, Inc.
Interior design: Van-garde Imagery, Inc.

Dedication

This book is dedicated to the women
that I love and people I care for:

My mom: Mina Mina

My daughter: Paula

My love: Lisa

My patients: Daily engine

Our Team: Source of pride.

MedikalPreneur:

a medical professional who is an entrepreneur

Why I wrote this book

"I want to change the mentality—as well as the mythology—that physicians are lousy businesspeople. Physicians can be great entrepreneurs. They just don't know it. While their medical training provides the perfect hardware of the mind, this book can upgrade physicians' mental software, or attitude, to become the best businesspeople—with exceptional ethics in business and management—in the 21st century as MedikalPreneurs."

– Francisco Arredondo, MD, MPH

MedikalPreneur:

The Official Guidebook for
Physicians' Success in Business

Francisco Arredondo, MD, MPH

Contents

Acknowledgments

THIS BOOK IS DEDICATED to Lisa and Paula for being the counterpart to my craziness and havoc. I'm grateful that they advised me to be more patient and organized, and I'm thankful that they were always there to listen to my frustrations. Their counseling saved me from ending up in the crazy house while creating this book.

I want to give special thanks and recognition to Adrian Gonzalez for sharing his wisdom and allowing me to use his concept of the SMART/ SIMPLE Business Model.

My gratitude to Elizabeth Ann Atkins for her work ethic and being such a detail-oriented editor. For perfectly understanding the mission we established to convince and educate medical professionals of their capabilities as creative entrepreneurs.

Special thanks to Kian Razi for reading this manuscript and providing valuable feedback.

Preface

DEAR DOCTORS AND HEALTH Care Professionals:

I'm on a mission to show you how to succeed in business while maintaining a fruitful medical career. I want to help doctors and other healthcare professionals create a life and legacy that is bold, exciting, and beyond the boundaries of traditional medicine. My intention is for you to finish this book and say, "Wow, I can do this! I'm going to be an entrepreneur! Actually, I'm going to be a MedikalPreneur."

As a physician who has built 13 businesses from the ground up, I have acquired invaluable business lessons that enabled me to succeed beyond my wildest dreams. The following pages contain the lessons I've learned, and as you read this book, these same lessons will provoke a paradigm shift in your thinking as it did mine; it will provide an upgrade to your intellectual software, specifically about the limitations of a physician venturing into the business world. You will learn that yes, you can blaze new trails in business, and you will understand everything you need to know to make that happen.

To think like a physician and a businessperson, or a MedikalPreneur, as I like to call it, one must practice unconventional thinking and develop a vision unique to his or her business goals. As healthcare practitioners, it's important to avoid falling into old traps, such as the one conveyed by the Argentinian storyteller, Jorge Bucay. In *The Elephant and The Chain,*[1] a boy asks why the circus elephants don't use their power to easily escape being chained to stakes in the ground.

The adult says they're domesticated; as calves, they had repeatedly tried to pull the stakes out, but failed because they lacked strength. Convinced that they could not break free, they stopped pulling. The elephants grew up to become strong and easily escape, but they never tried because they believed they were too weak to break away.

Similarly, we healthcare providers have been mentally chained to society's misconceptions that we are incompetent business people, so we simply do not try to free ourselves from the shackles of these pre-conceived notions. This book will show you how to break those chains.

Failure Is Only Temporary Unless You Quit

By sharing my story, experiences, and data in this book, I intend to shatter the stigma that physicians are inept in business. This reputation is bol-stered by the fact that many doctors have a grandmother's heart; they're driven by a calling to help and heal, as opposed to the hardcore business pursuit of money and power. Doctors actually possess a unique combina-tion of altruism and business savvy—a powerful foundation to become a successful MedikalPreneur.

The truth is that for centuries, doctors have been operating successful businesses in the form of private medical practices, which tend to thrive for decades. Some physicians' offices even operate for generations when grown children become physicians and take over the practice upon the retirement of their parents, who often founded the medical practice, or had inherited the business from their own parents as well. Think about your family doc-tor; chances are, he or she has been operating a medical practice for many years. That is a business! How often do you hear about a physician's office going out of business? You don't! Or if you do, it's very rare.

That's because physicians make excellent entrepreneurs—as well as leaders—and I will explain exactly why and how in this book. At the same time, I intend to inspire you to become a MedikalPreneur.

Despite the many ways that physicians make excellent leaders and business people—my success as a MedikalPreneur stands as a testament to that—some leaders in the medical field attempted to stifle my mission to master business concepts.

"You're a doctor; you should not be learning things about business!" a former mentor said, admonishing me back when I was doing a Reproductive Endocrinology and Infertility Fellowship at the Hospital of the University of Pennsylvania. My mentor said this after I had asked him to sign a form allowing me to audit classes in the prestigious Wharton School of Business.

Despite his protestations, he granted permission. The business classes armed me with valuable new knowledge and instilled in me the notion that someday I could operate my own businesses.

After my fellowship, I attended the Harvard School of Public Health. While earning a master's degree there, I took many management and finance classes, including some at Harvard Business School. Later, my interest in business intensified when I worked in a hospital and conceived ideas for improving patient care. Unfortunately, I believed that my ideas could never be implemented due to the bureaucracies and conventions that asphyxiate change in large medical institutions.

While working at University Hospitals in Cleveland, my desire to improve patient care inspired me to scribble on a paper napkin my vision for how to operate my own medical practice.

"What are you doing?" asked Christine Flynn, a Registered Nurse who would ultimately work side-by-side with me for 18 years.

"I'm trying to design a practice and open a fertility center in Texas," I said. Years later, after acquiring more business know-how through books, articles, experiments, and failures, I brought the ideas scribbled on that paper napkin to life. The following pages present those concepts, as well as personal experiences that enhanced my business acumen.

Consider this book the Krav Maga[2] of business for healthcare professionals. Krav Maga is a simultaneous defense and attack fighting style that combines Karate, Judo, boxing, wrestling, and Aikido. No weapons are required, as the techniques target vulnerable body parts to disable attackers. Hungarian-Israeli martial artist Imi Lichtenfeld[3] created Krav Maga during the 1930s to help Jewish people during the Nazi occupation of Bratislava, Czechoslovakia. Then he fled to Palestine and trained Israeli Army soldiers. Krav Maga helps people fight bare-handed and win in ways reminiscent of David vs. Goliath.

Likewise, this book will make you an expert MedikalPreneur, filling you with confidence to conceive and build your own practice while in the trenches and on the front lines in the marketplace. I'm presenting everything you need to succeed in this book, so you don't need a Master's in Business Administration to excel as a MedikalPreneur. Armed with this information, you will not feel intimidated when talking with a businessperson who has an MBA, or venture capitalists, or partners in a private equity firm, or individuals with whom you're negotiating a contract. In fact, you'll feel empowered, because you'll know their strengths and weaknesses—and how to use this knowledge to your advantage.

This book is my antidote for physicians who have been too afraid and intimidated to become entrepreneurs and business leaders. I am committed to empowering health care professionals to become better businesspeople, and I hope to serve as your guide to become an excellent MedikalPreneur with fierce integrity, using your vision and innovation to transform many lives, including your own!

— Francisco "Paco" Arredondo, MD, MPH
MedikalPreneur

Chapter 1

Paco's Story: How I Became a MedikalPreneur

THE CIRCUMSTANCES OF MY birth foreshadowed my chosen career path with prescient irony. While my parents vacationed in Brussels, Belgium, my mother had accidentally left her birth control pills in a dresser drawer at the hotel in Amsterdam.

"Nothing will happen if you just miss one pill," said my father—a physician who should have known better!

That was in June of 1965. Fast forward nine months, and Paco was born in Matamoros, Mexico. When my mother told me the story, I immediately understood what Kahlil Gibran meant when he said: "Forgetfulness is a form of freedom."

My arrival as their third child was an especially joyful occasion because my parents had suffered three pregnancy losses since my brother's birth six years earlier, and my sister's arrival the year before him. The miscarriages were hard-hitting because, at the time, my father was the sole physician providing care and delivering babies in a rural town of Tamaulipas, Mexico where they lived.

His life's work was treating patients and bringing new life into the world. At home, however, he and my mother were repeatedly suffering devastating loss. Yet their love, having blossomed since their

1

introduction while my father was in medical school in Mexico City, endured the tragedies until it was time to celebrate again.

After my birth, my parents moved to Matamoros, in the northeastern Mexican state of Tamaulipas, a mere 20 miles from where he was the only practicing physician. The town rests on the southern bank of the Rio Grande, just across the border from Brownsville, Texas. Though far from my father's hometown of Saltillo in northern Mexico, and my mother's origins in the state of Chiapas near the Guatemalan border, they planted their roots in this medium-sized town.

My father, José Arredondo, MD, provided medical care in his clinic for the workers of the Mexican government by day, and ran a private practice in the evening hours. Meanwhile, my mother, Carmen Soberón-Arredondo, applied her accounting knowledge to running a local pharmacy.

In Mexico, it's traditional for a child to take on his mother's maiden name as well as his father's last name; therefore, I am Francisco Arredondo-Soberón—better known as Paco by most. To clarify the origins of the nickname Paco, let's briefly digress. There are a handful of theories, but the one that stands out posits that the nickname originated with Saint Francis of Assisi, the father of the Franciscan order. His name in Latin, according to folk etymology, was *Pater Communitatis,* which means "father of the community." Hence, Paco represents the first syllable of each word.

I witnessed my parents' industriousness and entrepreneurial success while growing up, inspiring the same qualities in me and thus setting the stage to trailblaze a life and career that have far exceeded my greatest expectations. I inherited a natural curiosity about life from my father and a strong work ethic and passion from my mother.

"I don't care what you do," my mother always said. "You can be a janitor. I just want you to try to be the best janitor in the world! You may not get there, but I want you to try and make that effort to always compete against yourself."

I was drawn to archeology and politics. At 17, I participated in the marketing team for a local mayoral campaign. My candidate lost, but the knowledge I acquired—listening to people's concerns and inspiring change—would later prove invaluable as a physician.

Meanwhile, I occasionally accompanied my father while he gave pediatric consultations in the government hospital, exposing me to the medical profession and broadening my thoughts about work, money, and creating one's own path in life. When I was 10 years old, I was sitting in the exam room with him (clearly, HIPPA did not exist in Mexico in the '70's!) and noticed that far more patients were visiting my dad in comparison to the other doctors.

"How do they pay you?" I asked.

"They give me a salary," he said.

"But you see more than the other ones. So they pay everyone the same?"

"Yes," he answered.

"That's unfair," I said. "You should propose that the government could add up the salaries of all the doctors and divide them by the number of consultations, so we can determine the cost of one consult. Then they should pay each doctor per consultation, incentivizing them to be better doctors."

My father laughed and said, "Things don't work that way, but I like the way you think." He explained how Mexico's two-tiered system of medical care enabled him to leave after four hours in the hospital to work afternoons in a clinic that he operated with several other physicians.

Young and shortsighted, I concluded incorrectly that my father was incapable of becoming a successful businessperson. It's true: he was typical of many doctors who have the heart of a grandmother—driven to help and heal everyone without regard to the money-making aspect of medicine. His altruistic calling into medicine was indeed admirable. But his inability to separate his empathy-inspired professional services from the business of operating a medical practice reinforced the doctors' reputation as unskillful businesspeople. This hinders profitability. Even in a nonprofit organization, if there is no money, there is no mission.

My observation of incongruent incentives for a physician and businessperson planted a seed in my young mind. Meanwhile, from an early age, my family exposed me to progressive thought and inspiring conversations; at age nine, I began reading the newspaper every day to deepen my understanding of the world.

"What you gain in depth, you lose in width," my father often said, meaning it was important to become a well-rounded person. This prompted me to: read a vast range of books and articles; learn languages; interact with a broad scope of people from different professions; play many sports; and learn new skills such as mountain-climbing, skydiving, cooking, and getting my bartender and mixology certification. These endeavors, I believe, helped me become a better physician and businessman.

However, this broadening of one's experiential world contradicted conventional wisdom, especially for physicians, who tend to focus only on information that enhances their performance as doctors. Later, in medical school, my peers often chuckled and questioned me for reading books that were completely unrelated to medicine. Undaunted, I read poetry, novels, and essays by authors such as Julio Cortazar, Octavio Paz, Pablo Neruda, Leon Felipe, Mario Vargas Llosa, Gabriel Garcia Marquez, Walt Whitman, Jean Paul Sartre, Michel Foucault, and Isaiah Berlin. My reading spanned human history, leading me to the most esoteric professions like wine making and soccer management. Argentinian soccer coach César Luis Menotti, once called the Philosopher of Soccer, is in my pantheon of inspiring thinkers.

Music also opened my mind to new ideas. For example, my father purchased an LP collection of 100 classical records (for Millennials, LPs are vinyl music discs that play at 33 rpm on a record player) in Mexico City. The record covers featured each composer's biography and explained how each developed his music. French composer Maurice Ravel, for example, was influenced by operas, passacaglia, New Orleans Jazz, and many musicians.

One mind-blowing revelation occurred while reading Thomas Merton's biography, *The Seven Storey Mountain.*[4] He said that music is not simply a group of sounds, but a group of sounds and *silences*, and oftentimes the silences play a more powerful role in our listening and learning experience than the actual sounds. I thought: *What you don't say is often more important than what you say.* I began to see things not only in what they could be, but also in what they could *not* be. This realization irrevocably changed me for the better.

An insatiable hunger for learning inspired me, during medical school, to join the athletic team, learn French and Italian, and continue expanding my intellectual pursuits in disparate subjects. These experiences inspired multidimensional thinking. One-dimensional thinking can result in being oblivious to the world of fascinating ideas and activities outside the scope of a typical physician's life and work. On the contrary, exposure to many ideas and topics enriches your general knowledge base and actually enhances your work as a doctor. Broad exposure to many interests boosts success, asserts David Epstein in his popular 2019 book, *Range: Why Generalists Triumph in a Specialized World.*[5]

Another powerful lesson from my parents was our home's "open door" policy, which helped my father cultivate a stellar reputation as a doctor who truly cared about his patients. At seven in the morning, the door to our home in the middle of downtown Matamoros was open to those in need, and remained open until our family went to sleep. Even on Sundays, the holiest day of the week, patients from rural areas would, for example, knock on our door to bring a sick child to see my father. He always treated them with care and never exhibited arrogance or a superior attitude that he should be placed on a pedestal because he was the doctor.

My mother was also a powerful role model. She ran the pharmacy with another doctor's wife; they worked alongside the pharmacist. My mother's work ethic inspired her to cultivate a career and contribute to our family's finances while doing the admirable work of being a homemaker.

While our home was a vibrant meeting place for friends, neighbors, and even strangers, my parents made fun outings a top priority for me and my siblings. We were among four or five families who enjoyed Saturdays camping on the beach, spending quiet time gazing up at the starry night sky, and ruminating on all the new information we continued to acquire. While camping on the beach with limited resources, we committed to making the experience fun for everyone. I learned that happiness must be shared; otherwise, it's a contradiction.

Meanwhile, my mother's free spirit and independent thinking showed how to follow my intuition and dance to the beat of my own drum. She never cared what people thought. For example, during my tenure in junior high school government, I oversaw the annual popcorn festival that raised money to improve the school's infrastructure. One day during the festival, my mother showed up disguised as a fortune teller in a tent that she had pitched nearby. Before the event, I helped this "stranger" cut horoscopes from the newspaper and paste them to the backs of cards that she pretended to read to festivalgoers.

She didn't care what anyone thought about her doing something that others might view as "beneath" or "unbecoming" of a doctor's wife, or of someone who was successful in her own right, earning respectable sums of money. Instead, my mother set an example for me to not care what people think. This freed me to flex my creativity as an entrepreneur and adventurer. This was especially true years later when I ran a half marathon dressed as a sperm and had my clinic's vehicle decorated with sperm swimming around the tires as if they were eggs.

"Don't you think being dressed as a giant sperm might undermine the professionalism of your practice?" people asked. "Why did you put cartoon sperms and eggs on your car?"

I simply shrugged and said, "That's from my mom. She couldn't care less what anyone thought." My costume and the painted vehicle inspired humorous intrigue for those less cynical, and helped grow my practice. In a later chapter, you'll learn how these unconventional tactics were extremely effective marketing tools.

Curiosity + Hard Work + Education = Success

My parents instilled in me the courage to pursue every curiosity, so I tried handball, soccer, volleyball, and Little League baseball. While attending public schools, I participated in a poetry performance group and the debate team. In middle school, I was president of the student government council.

While my mother's exuberance rubbed off on me, it contrasted with my dad's calm demeanor. He enjoyed telling jokes and was very affable, but he was introspective and had a keen ability to read people. He taught me how to observe people, read subtle cues, and trust my intuition; he demonstrated these skills during consultations that I attended with him. I also learned from my parents that it's better to try and fail, learning from one's mistakes, rather than never taking risks. One example of this occurred when they collaborated with friends to open a dry-cleaning business that epically failed.

While studying hard, I also enjoyed robust and lively social experiences at our home. My parents hosted parties every Sunday where we cooked enough paellas to feed the entire state. My task was to prepare our guests' beverages. Though I was a child, I learned to mix many drinks, including the best Cuba Libre this side of the Atlantic! I wanted to be the best, so I imitated bartenders on TV who garnished drinks with limes and fruit to make the beverages look appealing. I didn't want to create ordinary beverages; I needed them to stand out.

Medical School and Beyond

After two years of high school, my father wanted me to attend medical school in our hometown.

"No, I want to go away," I said. My goal was to attend medical school in the United States, which would be more difficult with a degree from a university in Mexico. It would also cost much more money. Fortunately, the Tecnológico de Monterrey had an exchange program with hospitals in Houston, Texas. This was my express pass to the American medical system. I did an exchange program at Baylor College of Medicine Medical Center in Houston.

At the time, I dreamed of becoming a sports doctor in the United States. I concluded my basic medical studies, graduating Summa Cum Laude and first in my class with an MD in Medicine from the Institute of Technology and Higher Studies of Monterrey in 1990. I then moved to Mexico City, a place I knew well, thanks to annual family trips during my childhood.

In Mexico, when you finish medical school, a requirement to receive your diploma mandates working for the government at a minimal salary or no salary for one year. Many medical students spend those 12 months in remote and isolated areas, often as the sole physician in town. It's a humbling experience. The alternative was to apply for one of the very few research positions available in the country.

"You got the research position!" announced a gentleman named Mr. Ramirez in the Secretary of Health's office when he phoned. "Come and pick up your documentation."

When I arrived, Mr. Ramirez was extremely nice and asked, "Oh sir, how is your Uncle Guillermo? Please tell him I said hello."

What? I was baffled. I have no Uncle Guillermo.

"Sure, Mr. Ramirez, I will," I responded, playing along amidst the thrill of being accepted into this highly coveted program to do my year of research in Mexico City in the field of reproductive biology at a very distinguished institution.

After I left Mr. Ramirez's office, it hit me! He, and presumably his staff, mistakenly believed that I was related to Secretary of Health Guillermo Soberón because he shares my mother's maiden name! This wild stroke of good luck blessed me with the opportunity to join a team of researchers who were pioneering reproductive biology research in Mexico. This was an emerging field at the time, as the world's first in vitro fertilization baby was born in the United Kingdom on July 25, 1978; the first IVF baby born in the United States was in 1981. And the first in Mexico in the city of Monterrey was in 1989, thanks to the trailblazing work of physicians such as Dr. Samuel Hernández Ayup and Dr. Pedro Galache-Vega.

I had the honor of meeting Dr. Galache-Vega, a leading authority on fertility in Monterrey, while fulfilling a rotation in Gynecology. It was then, with Dr. Galache-Vega, that a magic moment occurred. I witnessed the miracle of life for the first time as he delivered a baby; I became forever fascinated by the science of facilitating life.

"I really want to do fertility," I told Dr. Galache-Vega, who mentored me in that clinic as I learned how to do semen analysis, sperm washes, uterine inseminations, ovarian stimulation, and many procedures. The program exposed me to practices that many doctors never experience in residency, and I was still in medical school.

Specifically, Dr. Galache-Vega taught me perhaps the most important lesson about the psychology of patient interaction. He addressed his patients very respectfully and handled certain human behaviors with sensitivity and empathy, instead of judgment. He was dedicated to focusing on the psychology of the patient, not simply the disease.

Dr. Galache-Vega was a unique gynecologist, offering an uncommon approach to teaching new doctors. The usual approach did not deal with psychology or bedside manner; it was strictly clinical and often lacking warmth and compassion. He instead groomed a whole school of physicians to emulate his patient-care style. Likewise, he instilled in me one of the most important questions I continually ask myself about every endeavor in my life: "How will you differentiate yourself?"

A Long Road Ahead

Becoming a fertility specialist requires a long course of study: seven years of college and medical school, four more in gynecology, and three additional years of infertility. That meant I would officially begin my career as a fertility specialist at age 32.

After landing one of 15 research positions in Mexico City at a World Health Organization facility, I focused in contraceptive research, which maintained my connection and momentum in fertility.

New York Opportunity Beckons

During a medical conference in Monterrey, I met Dr. Benjamin Sandler, an IVF expert 12 years my senior working at Mount Sinai Hospital in New York City. As co-director of Reproductive Medicine Associates (RMA) in New York—one of the world's most celebrated infertility treatment centers—he invited me to join him for coffee.

"I passed my exams and want to do my residency in the U.S.," I told him. "Ultimately, I want to work in fertility."

"Call me next week," he said. My follow-up call led to a year-long position at Elmhurst Hospital in Queens, part of the Icahn School of Medicine at Mount Sinai. Perhaps I was not the most intellectual or skilled physician, but I was the hardest working. Very few people could beat me at work. After that, I found a position in Texas, and was very lucky that my New York internship counted as the first year of my residency. I completed the second, third, and fourth years at University of Texas Health Science Center at San Antonio, again fortunate that someone in a powerful position gave me this opportunity and more.

Dr. Carl J. Pauerstein, Chairman of the Department of Obstetrics and Gynecology at UT Health San Antonio, trained generations of physicians and earned the nickname "Mr. Fallopian Tube."

Dr. Pauerstein helped me obtain a Reproductive Endocrinology and Infertility fellowship at the prestigious Hospital of the University of Pennsylvania in Philadelphia. There I learned under the experience and expertise of yet another fertility field champion, Dr. Luigi Mastroianni, Jr., Director of the Division of Reproductive Endocrinology and Infertility at the Hospital of the University of Pennsylvania.

Unlike my residency that often meant grinding through 80- to 100-hour work weeks while seeing patients, this slower-paced fellowship allowed time to ponder the ultimate question: *How will I differentiate myself once I complete my studies?*

I understood that finance was an important aspect of running a medical practice. However, back in 1996, very few physicians had business or finance backgrounds. I saw this knowledge as a key ingredient for my future success. So I audited classes at the prestigious Wharton School of Business.

After obtaining the coveted signature from a mentor to audit classes outside of my specific field of study, I spent three days each week in a crash course on accounting, finances, strategic management, marketing, human resources, negotiation techniques, and other business topics. I viewed a strong business acumen as a way to differentiate myself from the average fertility specialist who did only fertility research and IVF, rather than learning how to run the business and create value with the services my practice would someday provide.

At the time, medical schools focused only on the medical aspect of treating patients. Concepts such as creating a powerful customer-patient focused experience and finessing the financial part of the business were simply not part of the conversation or curriculum. In fact, even mentioning the word "marketing" in medical school would cause a metaphorical heart attack in my peers: "Why do you want to deal with finances?" they asked me. "You're a doctor, not a banker!"

But they were wrong about me, and, sadly, wrong about themselves.

Heading To Harvard

While completing my fellowship, I learned that the American College of Obstetrics and Gynecologists was offering two $40,000 scholarships to complete a one-year master's degree program for either an MPH or an MBA. I applied to receive a Master of Public Health at Harvard University with a letter describing my intentions in the program and my career.

Lo and behold, this young man who had been told that my head was filled with nothing more than pipedreams earned one of the two scholarships! So here I was at one of the top educational institutions in the world—elated and grateful for the opportunity.

I enjoyed being a student and learning in a stimulating environment, without the pressure of doing clinical work. Additionally, my classmates provided a global learning experience that money could not buy. Ranging in age from 25 to 60, they came from diverse places that included Zimbabwe, Pakistan, Chile, Venezuela, Belgium, Germany, Canada, and Cyprus. Many of us lived in International House, a dormitory where we exchanged innumerable ideas and experiences while breaking bread over every international cuisine imaginable.

My visa was about to expire shortly after earning my MPH. I explored fertility opportunities in Mexico, but sadly found nothing that was conducive to my development as an elite fertility specialist with a penchant for business. At the same time, I was experiencing the joy of fertility on a personal level, as my wife—whom I married during my residency in 1995—was now pregnant.

Echoes of Homeland in Rural Kentucky

The only way I could stay in the United States was to receive a waiver to extend my visa by working in a region that was afflicted by a shortage of physicians. This opportunity took me, my then-wife, and our unborn baby to South Williamson, Kentucky, in rural Appalachia on the Kentucky-West Virginia border. During my three-year commitment, I worked at Appalachian Regional Healthcare, providing OB/GYN services, including some low-complexity fertility treatments to a poor, largely underserved population in coal mining communities.

The demographics were distinguished by heavy smokers, high teen pregnancy rates, addiction, and a general lack of education. Despite the language difference and the great proximity from where I grew up, I found an uncanny number of similarities to rural and poor Mexico that helped me relate to the people in my care as Director of Women's Health Services. These traits included family-oriented lifestyles, poverty, little education, alcoholism, magical thinking, and superstition generally associated with religious people.

Here I recalled Dr. Vega's lessons that words matter, a pillar of medicine reinforced by a later mentor, perhaps the best professor I ever had: Dr. Michael Reich. Professor Reich taught me about ethics in public health at Harvard. His teachings deepened my awareness of the power of words. I was determined to apply the importance of using language to build trust and compliance amongst patients. But how?

To find out, I conducted a study of my patients in rural Kentucky. I discovered that 80% of them smoked while pregnant, greatly increasing dangerous risks for their unborn babies. At the same time, only 20% of these women breastfed their infants (research shows that breastfeeding, when the mother is able, is the healthiest and most beneficial way to nourish a newborn, in comparison to using infant formula).

So, for example, how could I encourage new moms to breastfeed via language? I realized that instead of asking: "Would you like to breastfeed?" or "Would you like to use baby formula?" I would ask: "Would you like to use artificial infant formula, or would you like to use Mommy's milk?"

Swapping "breastfeeding" with "Mommy's milk" made the question more casual and positive, and resulted in more women choosing the best option for their babies. This had the potential to improve the health of the babies in this community who were already at a disadvantage due to exposure to cigarette smoke in the womb.

The success of manipulating language inspired other word-choice modifications that had a positive impact, namely by putting the women at ease during the sometimes difficult and high-anxiety experience of being pregnant or trying to get pregnant, often after many devastating pregnancy losses.

My study revealed that the word "vagina" triggers a less-than-positive response. I stopped saying, "We need to do a 'vaginal scan,'" and instead said, "We need to do an 'internal scan.'" And I no longer did "embryo biopsies." I conducted "embryo sampling." The term "testicular biopsy" was replaced with "sampling." And we did not "freeze" embryos; we put the embryos in "biological pause."

To enhance the experience even more, we changed "nurse" to "fertility coach." Women no longer had cysts; they had enlarged follicles. We never asked a woman, "How old are you?" We asked, "How young are you?" Positive language! These simple and subtle changes resulted in a positive patient experience that made the women and their partners feel comfortable and hopeful that their efforts would result in pregnancy and healthy babies.

While implementing all of the above practices, I was also applying many of the concepts I learned from reading the 1999 book *The Experience Economy* by B. Joseph Pine II and James H. Gilmore.[6] Updated in 2011, their book explains how the key to success in a highly competitive business world is to provide a unique and positive experience, rather than simply offering a product or service that can be obtained anywhere. Instead, you can, as an entrepreneur, attract customers and endear them to your particular business by making them feel special, pampered, and even entertained. Smart entrepreneurs no longer sell services. We sell experiences, and specifically, transformative experiences.

You can achieve this through visual, verbal, and nonverbal cues that harmonize every aspect of your service, starting with tone of voice and word choices that the patient hears when phoning your business. Enhancing a positive patient experience continues with the feelings inspired by the practice's décor, the music played softly in the background, and even the environment when a patient enters your building. However, most important is the experience you create for your patient via personal interaction with you and your staff during treatments, phone calls, emails, and follow-up care.

Meanwhile in Kentucky, my family obtained our green cards and stayed there longer than planned, earning a good salary and saving money. It was also during this time that we were blessed with the birth of our daughter, Paula, whom we playfully consider "the first Aztec Appalachian."

Moving to Cleveland

After Kentucky, I wanted to return to Texas, but the fertility division director at Case Western Reserve University in Cleveland invited me to help him develop the infertility program. So I chose to work with him while earning my Board Certification. There I noticed ways to improve the patient's experience. However, making changes without the adequate authority in a huge bureaucracy was very difficult, if not impossible. But as I've shown thus far, with the right mindset, nothing is impossible.

In Cleveland, I worked with Christine "Chris" Flynn, a Registered Nurse who witnessed my frustration and subsequent vision for a future business.

"I think he realized that all the things he wanted to do were positive," she recalled during an interview for this book. "But it would almost be impossible to make that happen in such a big institution. Once he realized that, he started thinking, 'Okay, if I can't do something to change here, I have to create my own.' That's where the inspiration for the clinic began."

Chris remembered how I first sketched out my ideas: "He retrieved a little paper napkin that you use to wipe your hands in the bathroom, and started writing on this little piece of paper, saying, 'If I ever had a clinic, this is how I would design it.'"

After four years in Cleveland, I yearned to head south, closer to my family in Matamoros. I also wanted close proximity to Monterrey, where I maintained business contacts and could generate patient referrals. San Antonio seemed the ideal locale, especially since 67% of the population was then Hispanic, and yet, unbelievably, San Antonio had no Spanish-speaking fertility specialists.

Fertility remains a small fraction of the medical industry, as only 40 to 45 fertility specialists are produced each year; that converts to one fertility specialist for every seven or eight million people! The idea was to start my practice by targeting the Hispanic community while also bringing patients from Mexico to the United States for treatment.

I visited San Antonio to interview with a group of fertility specialists that served 90% of the market in 2005. Struck by my unique upbringing, academic background, and broad interests, they offered me a position.

"What is the track for partnership?" I asked before the ink had time to dry on the contract.

"There's no such track," they said.

"I'm coming here to align with you," I said.

"No," they said, insisting that I would remain their employee with zero chance for advancement. This sobering moment inspired me to strategize how to create, own, and operate my own fertility clinic in San Antonio.

I returned to Cleveland to consult with a good friend, Ernesto Poza, a Cuban-American who wrote a book, *Family Business*. Now a professor for the Global Entrepreneurship and Family Enterprise at the Thunderbird School of Global Management, he was, back in 2006, a Case Western professor teaching entrepreneurship.

Since I did not know how to write a business plan at the time, he loaned me three MBA students who wrote my business plan as a final class project. They helped me determine that I needed $1.65 million to acquire a building and construct a lab. Armed with this knowledge, I went to Compass Bank, presented the proforma and business plans, and was approved in 48 hours for a loan for the full amount! I am forever grateful to the banker, Jeannie Bennett, who trusted me and my plan. I am also lucky that it was 2006, before the country's financial debacle of 2008.

Most of all, I am thankful to my mother who loaned me a down payment of $40,000 on the building, which I agreed to pay back with four percent interest.

Despite the significant achievement of obtaining the funds to open my business, I felt insecure about most aspects of being a medical professional and entrepreneur as I was venturing into uncharted territory. I had yet to develop the MedikalPreneur concept, but was determined to master every aspect of this marriage of two seemingly disparate professions, come hell or high water.

Virtually no information was available to guide me as a physician opening a business, so I asked for help from Dr. Benjamin Sandler, who was thriving in New York City with Reproductive Medicine Associates of New York, also known as RMA of New York.

"I have the money," I told him, "but I feel a little insecure in the lab part of the business."

Dr. Sandler promised to help me launch my company by providing a template of how to create my business. I signed a management agreement with his company and used the name RMA of Texas; our arrangement was similar to a franchise, but not entirely.

RMA of Texas is Born

What I had sketched as ideas on a paper napkin in Cleveland manifested in physical reality just a few years later. We purchased the real estate, finished the lab, and hired our staff: administrative assistant Lauralicia; medical assistant Monica; and embryologist Vicki. Our doors opened for business at Reproductive Medicine Associates of Texas in 2007. Fortunately, despite the financial crisis of 2008, our practice continued to grow exponentially and hiring expanded as we attracted new customers.

RMA of Texas expanded over the next decade into 13 extremely successful businesses. Every step and lesson helped me draw a blueprint for MedikalPreneurial success that I'm sharing with you in this book.

When we launched the company, the foundation for my entrepreneurial vision and actions were rooted in my medical education and training, as well as:

• **My father's words:** "What you gain in depth, you lose in width." All the information I acquired from vast resources throughout my life now culminated in a knowledge base that assisted in opening and growing a business. For example, my father's record collection made me very familiar with classical music, so I knew which soothing music to play in our fertility centers.

At the same time, I realized that my schoolteachers were right. Remember how your classmates always asked: "Why do we have to learn this when we will never use it in practical life?" And the teacher's wise response was, "You will never use it, however, the mental exercises will build synapses in your brain to enhance the way you think about everything else." The many things I learned growing up that were ostensibly unrelated to medicine were in fact building new synapses in my brain. I was learning about how to build a successful practice without really knowing it.

- **My mother's edict:** "Work hard and call upon internal grit to get the job done with excellence."

- **Dr. Galache-Vega's question:** "How will you differentiate yourself?"

- Finally, the perennial question all MedikalPreneurs must ask themselves: **How do I create a positive patient experience?** Here, again, I drew upon the knowledge from reading *The Experience Economy* by B. Joseph Pine II and, James H. Gilmore.[7]

Specifically, I brainstormed how my business could emulate the Disney World experience that provides a multisensory extravaganza that enchants you every step of the way, from the beautiful buildings and gardens, to the music, to the sweet smells, to the messaging on signs, to the helpful and cheerful employees, to the delicious food. Every aspect of the park created an experience of being in a wonderful place you never wanted to leave. How could I do that as a MedikalPreneur?

First, I had to gain perspective on this idea. My studies and life experience taught that no matter what you're selling—peanuts, coffee, shoe-shine services, or anything else—you can only compete with similar businesses and differentiate yourself in three areas:

Price—Unless you have a totally disruptive business model, a price war with your competitors would hurt everyone. For us, lowering our price would result in our competition—which already had the patients—simply reducing its prices and keeping the patients they had. Lowering our prices would hinder our ability to make money to operate the business.

Quality of the Product/Service—In the fertility business, the most objective measure of the quality of the product or service is the pregnancy rate for patients. Our competitors already had a very good pregnancy rate; furthermore, there are scientific and technological limitations as to how good you could be. In other words, there were constraints to successfully competing in this area.

The Customer/Patient's Experience—You can get your hair cut at any salon, but you will return to the shop where a competent stylist makes you feel the best. That "experience" enhances the delivery of quality products and services at a reasonable price. The same goes for your mission as a MedikalPreneur: You need to provide the best service at reasonable prices, while cultivating loyalty and positive health outcomes for your patients through orchestrating the best experiences for them in your offices.

Providing the best customer/patient experience offers the most opportunities to distinguish yourself against the competition.

Financial Freedom Provides Life Adventures

As a MedikalPreneur, you are your own boss charting a unique life's journey while earning enough money to live your most extravagant dreams. For me, that meant taking a month off from work every summer to spend with my daughter. We traveled the world, visited family in Spain and Mexico, and climbed Mt. Kilimanjaro. I completed my certification as a bartender and mixologist.

In 2019, I sold my businesses with the intention of embarking on an entirely new life. That included marrying my beautiful fiancé, Lisa, in Puerto Vallarta, Mexico. Our plan was to move to Paris for a year, travel throughout Europe and other continents, then return to a new home that we are building in Texas. In true entrepreneurial fashion, we had to adapt due to an unexpected pandemic.

CHAPTER 2

The MedikalPreneur's Mindset: Upgrading Your Mental Software

As a physician, you can become an extraordinary entrepreneur. But chances are, if you endorse conventional wisdom, you may not believe this. The most important step you can take toward becoming a MedikalPreneur is to shift your thinking from pessimism to optimism. From conventional to creative. From institutional to innovative. From staid to as improvisational as a street performer. Remember, the only things you can control are your thoughts, words, feelings, and actions. You have to change each of those, starting with your thoughts.

Discard the belief that you're not capable of running a medical business. Create a mindset that yes, you can, very well. I call this "upgrading your mental software to the MedikalPreneur's attitude."

Let's think of our minds as capable of obtaining an upgrade to a new and improved software that revamps thinking and behavior, just as installing a new operating system to your computer's motherboard boosts its speed and ability to process information.

Mental Power Can Do the Impossible

"It is the brain, not the heart or lungs, that is the critical organ."

— Sir Dr. Roger Bannister

Sir Dr. Roger Bannister was a medical student, a runner, and a dreamer who resisted the status quo. Bannister wanted to break the world record and run a mile in less than four minutes. He had the same two legs and lungs as other runners, but during the 1952 Olympics in Helsinki, Finland, he set a British record in the 1500 meter run. That fired him up even more to run a mile under four minutes. Even though at the time, physicians, physiologists, and exercise experts said that was impossible.

Roger Bannister believed it was possible. On May 6, 1954, he broke the world record by running one mile in three minutes and 59.4 seconds.[8] Most notable was that a New Zealander named John Landy also came under the four-minute mark just 46 days after Bannister's remarkable feat. One year later, three runners ran the mile in less than four minutes in the same race! Did the human body evolve in one year? No. Bannister upgraded the software of his mind, as well as the minds of others. He did the impossible because his body was powered by his mind.

Mahatma Gandhi said: "A man is but the product of his thoughts. What he thinks, he becomes." When you believe you can succeed as a MedikalPreneur, you can achieve that goal. Now let's do the work to boost your believing, so you can begin achieving.

Physicians Are Great Businesspeople; They Just Don't Know It!

Does the idea of a physician as an entrepreneur seem like an oxymoron?

The prevailing belief is that physicians are not good in business, wrote Arlen Meyers in a 2016 article in *The Translational Scientist*, so they should focus on patient care, and delegate business tasks to others.[9] However, Meyers said that his experience with medical professionals and scientists showed that they make excellent entrepreneurs, yet very few of America's nearly 900,000[10] actively practicing physicians have a MedikalPreneurial mindset. Meyers said those of us physicians who pioneer an entrepreneurial path can lead the way for others to follow.

Let's Look Back, Before We Look Forward

As my father and countless physicians have demonstrated, medical practices have been operating with great success for centuries. In fact, my father's practice performed far better than the average entrepreneurial endeavor, and the data proves it.

More than 20% of new businesses close after the first year in operation, according to the Business Employment Dynamics report from the U.S. Bureau of Labor Statistics.[11] By year three, 30% have gone out of business. Half of all new businesses shut their doors by year five. Even more grim: 70% of businesses fail within 10 years of opening.

In contrast, how many physicians' offices close in five years? Very few. Physicians are quite skilled at implementing and sustaining the basic elements of good business practices; this fact is our history—and our future. The same is true for leadership. However, as physicians devoted their days and years to treating patients in their practices, an erroneous belief evolved that doctors were ill-prepared to become managerial leaders.

For proof, look no further than the world's biggest and best hospital systems: The Mayo Clinic and The Cleveland Clinic. Since opening a century ago, these hospitals have thrived under the leadership of physicians serving as Chief Executive Officers. Physician leadership earned The Mayo Clinic the number-one spot on the 2019-2020 *U.S. News and World Report* ranking of hospitals,[12] with The Cleveland Clinic coming in second in 2016 and fourth on the 2019-2020 list.

Hospitals whose CEOs are physicians earn 25% higher quality scores than hospitals run by non-physician managers, according to a 2011 study that evaluated CEOs in the top 100 hospitals for *U.S. News and World Report.* The study focused on services for cancer, digestive disorders, and cardiovascular care, with the goal of discovering the link between a hospital's ranking and whether it was run by a physician or a non-medical management expert.

This impressive statistic resulted from a study by the Institute for Study of Labor, according to a December 27, 2016 article in the *Harvard Business Review* titled, "Why the Best Hospitals are Managed by Doctors," by Amanda Goodall and colleagues James K. Stoller and Agnes Baker.[13]

The article says that credibility amongst peers is a key reason that physicians make the best leaders at healthcare organizations, according to Dr. Toby Cosgrove, CEO of The Cleveland Clinic. Because doctors have worked on the front lines of treating patients, they apply their experience when making decisions at the hospital's helm. This direct experience with the daily details of healthcare delivery equips the physician executive with insights and leadership abilities that would be impossible for non-physician managers.

One MedikalPreneur Says Mindset is the Key to Success

My friend, Dr. Robert Kiltz, is one of the world's most innovative MedikalPreneurs. "Twenty-five years ago," he said during a conversation for this book, "I wrote a business plan, made an excel spreadsheet, then went to the bank and borrowed $150,000 to start a company and live my dream to run and develop my own business. Now I have 350 employees, more than $35 million in revenue, and I'm seeing clients from around the globe at six centers that we are growing into eight right now."

As Founder and Director of CNY Fertility, which is ranked among the largest fertility centers in the country, Dr. Kiltz developed innovative approaches to fertility by fusing Western medicine with Eastern healing arts. His mind-body-spirit approach "revolutionized the fertility industry by providing full-service healing arts centers where patients receive massage, acupuncture, and yoga instruction," according to his website, DoctorKiltz.com.[14]

"While I was on this journey of building my business, I had to read books on spirituality, on faith, and on business," he recalled. "I read books like, *Think and Grow Rich* by Napoleon Hill, *The Power of Positive Thinking* by Norman Vincent Peale, and *The Mind is the Master* by James Allen." He said filling his mind with these motivational books enabled him to "focus on the positives, instead of spending time on the negatives. The negatives make us fearful. Then we're stagnant and can't focus. We get angry, sad, and depressed, and can't focus on the beauty and possibilities.

"Physicians are recognizing that they have options either to be the leaders, followers, or complainers," Dr. Kiltz continued. "We doctors focus on what's wrong with medicine and what the negatives are. That's a distraction. So many of us are unhappy in medicine and what we're doing. I just met with a doc that joined a large group, but isn't happy in having a boss. When you're distracted, your mind goes into fight or flight mode and you're fighting the bureaucracy."

Resolving this conflict begins with serious soul-searching.

"Sometimes I think we've lost direction in why we became physicians," Dr. Kiltz said. "Is it to go to school, make money, and retire on a golf course?"

Dr. Kiltz said the top take-away for priming your mind to become a MedikalPreneur is to remember his core belief: "I am responsible for everything in my life. I am 100% and no one else. Being an entrepreneur is all about putting the mindset first. That's the critical part of the process. That which you think is true will unfold to be that. Everything is created through the mind."

This argument challenges doctors who are trained to make decisions based on physical evidence. "It's a hard one because we're scientists," Dr. Kiltz continued, "and in medicine, we're geared to look at the data rather than to be the dreamers. In truth, data is only developed by dreamers because everyone is only giving their dream."

When you can break away from relying only on what you can see, hear, taste, touch, and smell—fueling the creative laboratory of your mind with the same conviction that Bannister had for himself—then you will rock the world as a MedikalPreneur.

"To find the best success," Dr. Kiltz said, "you have to foster the dream that you desire. What do you want it to look like? Which way do you want it to go? The first thing is to have faith in yourself and the possibilities of the dream you desire."

Keep a vision of that in your mind. See it, feel it, know it as if it's already real.

"Belief is the foundation of everything," Dr. Kiltz said. "The opportunities of where and what you wish to do are infinite."

Be the King or Queen of the Jungle as a MedikalPreneur

As children, we learned that one animal in particular is the "king of the jungle." Understanding why provides a powerful upgrade in your mental software as a MedikalPreneur. So, which animal is it?

The lion! Is the lion the fastest animal in the jungle? No; a lion can run 50 mph, but only for short bursts, while cheetahs can sustain 58 mph for an extended period. Is the lion the strongest? No; actually, the gorilla and the elephant are stronger than the lion. Does the lion have the stronger bite? Not really; its bite is only 650 Pounds Per Square Inch (PSI), while the hippopotamus bites at 2000 PSI and crocodiles chomp down at 2500 to 4000 PSI. Is the lion the most intelligent animal? Absolutely not. The chimpanzee is several times more intelligent; the crow is significantly more intelligent than the lion. Some people say that crows have an intelligence similar to a seven-year-old human. They can think about the future, invent their own tools, and even communicate complex concepts to other crows.

So why is the lion the king of the jungle? Because its attitude is the biggest and most confident. It says, "Yes, I can eat that elephant! Yes, I can eat that hippopotamus!" When it sees a zebra, the lion decides, "There's my lunch! I might not be the strongest or the fastest, but I have the attitude that says, 'Yes, I can!'" The lion's power comes from the software of its mind.

A Step-By-Step Guide to Upgrading Your Mindset

Here are eight steps to upgrade to The MedikalPreneur's Mindset.

Step One: Boost Your Confidence—See the ICU as Your Business. When you walk into the ICU, you check the patient's blood pressure, heart rate, temperature, and other vitals. You compare his or her condition today to yesterday's. Did it improve? What is the urine output?

The input of fluids? What is the respiration rate? What is the oxygen saturation? What are the trends? What are the patterns?

"Okay," you say, "let's make a treatment plan for this individual who has been declining." Then you create a treatment plan.

Now consider walking into a business and examining its balance sheet, income, expenses, labor, and operative costs.

"Okay," you say, "let's make a business plan."

In a later chapter, you will learn how. For now, draw a parallel between the way you stride confidently into the ICU and know exactly how to treat a patient with a strategy that results in healing and wellness, and how you can walk into your own business to provide excellent products, services, and patient experiences while operating efficiently and prospering. In this way, there's no difference between the ICU and your business.

Step Two: Ignore the Naysayers. Many people—including professors, leaders in the medical field, colleagues, and others—have tried to discourage me from taking steps that ultimately led to my success as a MedikalPreneur. I acknowledged their observations and ignored their pessimism. Instead, I trusted my own intuition, which told me how to proceed. If you have no trust in yourself, who is going to trust you? If you're not capable of investing in yourself, who else will?

One of the most dramatic examples of this was when I had our company vehicle covered in a paint wrap showing sperm swimming toward the wheels as if they were eggs. People told me that was a crazy idea and a waste of money. I did it anyway, and it became one of our greatest marketing tools for attracting new patients.

Similarly, I ran a half-marathon dressed as a sperm, and to this day people remember the fierce independence that I inherited from my mother. If you weren't born with it, just practice flexing your "I'm going to do it my way" muscles. Then you'll get stronger and it will become easier to ignore the naysayers. Unfortunately, that may include your family, your mentors, and other people whose opinions you respect.

> "There are two types of people who will tell you that you cannot make a difference in this world: those who are afraid to try and those who are afraid you will succeed."
>
> —Ray Goforth

The status quo of how your peers run a medical practice can be equally discouraging, leaving some potential MedikalPreneurs to believe that the status quo is the only way to operate, and doing anything else would be too risky.

"I quit my job and started my own practice," said Dr. Angeline N. Beltsos, CEO and Chief Medical Officer of Vios Fertility Institute in Chicago, during an interview for this book. "I was managing partner of my old clinic, which was very busy. I worked with a number of men. It was the old guard. I was trying to get them to be innovative and thoughtful about how we deliver care—and not being afraid of what is possible. But my colleagues at the time couldn't imagine being risk-takers or being innovative. They really wanted to practice medicine like it's 1980. I was trying to help move this idea of thinking of the patient first."

That included abandoning the traditional gynecological practice of a sterile white room with a thin paper sheet over the exam table, metal stirrups, and a doctor holding a cold speculum while looking down on the patient. Dr. Beltsos became an observer of how we operated RMA of Texas, and created a very successful vision of how to own and operate fertility centers. She became an exceptional MedikalPreneur with several centers in Illinois, Wisconsin, Washington, and Missouri. Her group of nearly 20 physicians is changing the landscape of fertility.

What if you never attempt to live your dream? What if you play it safe, then reach the end of your life, and regret your lost potential? We usually regret what we did not do, instead of what we did and failed. Risk is better than regret. In the words of hockey superstar Wayne Gretsky: "You will miss 100% of the shots that you don't take."

Step Three: Feel the Fear and Do It Anyway. Fear is a dream-killer. Many people live their fears instead of living their dreams.

"If you want something, you must risk everything," Dr. Kiltz said. When you take a risk and succeed, you inspire others to do the same.

"Paco is a risk-taker," Dr. Beltsos said. "He's not afraid to try something new and to tell you that. Some people will do it quietly and believe, 'If we fail, nobody's watching.' It's okay to fail. That means you're trying. You have to allow that culture in your organization of trying new things and taking risks." Risks, however, do not mean allowing for medical errors. Dr. Beltsos said success grows from mistakes that provide opportunities to learn while deepening a determination to succeed.

You will never achieve that success if you allow fear to stop you. Instead, physicians who become entrepreneurs use fear as fuel to try harder, work longer, and brainstorm bigger, better ideas.

I'm about to do exactly that. I will not turn 70 years old full of regret having never lived my dream of living in Paris with my wife. The coronavirus pandemic delayed our plans, but we will prevail when it's safe. I always say shoot for the moon, because if you miss, you will be with the stars.

When you develop a business concept, it's your moonshot. Fear will tell you that you don't have the money or the time or the intelligence to succeed. But deep inside we are all lions! When you feel the fear and do it anyway, you can prove it wrong and make magic happen. The best way to accomplish this is to transform your fear and anxiety into excitement. Psychology experts present plenty of literature showing evidence that it's not wise to get rid of your negative emotions, because anxiety and fear are normal feelings. We are humans, after all.

The main objective is **not** to eliminate your anxiety and fear. The secret is to transmute the negative thoughts into excitement. A classic study by Allison Wood Brooks from the Harvard Business School was published in the *Journal of Experimental Psychology*[15] and it concludes that we must reframe the fear and anxiety as excitement. Successful athletes, such as Dr. Bannister, do this. You can increase your success by saying, "I'm excited to become a MedikalPreneur," instead of, "I'm afraid that I will fail in business."

Step Four: Be Willing to Do the Work. Dale Carnegie said, "Inaction breeds doubt and fear. Action breeds confidence and courage. If you want to conquer fear, do not sit home and think about it. Go out and get busy."

The rewards of being a MedikalPreneur may sound glamorous, but opening and operating my businesses was a round-the-clock job. I was always thinking about the moving parts to make sure everything went smoothly. And I was brainstorming new ideas 24/7.

"You have to be willing to get up at 3:30 in the morning and be the first person in the office at 4:30," Dr. Kiltz said. "You have to be willing to clean the rooms, turn the rooms over, and take personal responsibility for everything that happens in the practice. There's nothing beneath you that you will not do."

Being a MedikalPreneur is all about being a self-starter, and being motivated for yourself. "If you're not willing to do the work and take responsibility, you can't be a successful entrepreneur," Dr. Kiltz said. "You have to accept the risks, the fears, the worries, and the challenges every day. That includes meeting payroll, handling things like bank notes, insurance coverage, HR, social media, and your online reputation."

Your quest will not be easy. You will have setbacks and failures. Islands of loss exist in an ocean of successes.

Step Five: There's No Shame in Making Money in an Ethical Manner; Take Pride in It! Many physicians believe that entrepreneurship is antithetical to the Hippocratic Oath. This is untrue.

"Money is very important," Dr. Beltsos said. "Doctors need to know how to budget, how to spend it, and how to make it. You want to make as much money as you can, so you can run your business."

The problem?

"That gets doctors a little uncomfortable," she said. "They're like, 'I'm not supposed to like money, like I'm a priest.' I try to explain that [making money] is not a bad thing. You want a fiscally sound church, so it doesn't close. It needs to stay open as a place for people to get married and raise their children." Even nonprofit entities such as churches and charities will close their doors if they are not fiscally sound.

"If you don't have any money," Dr. Beltsos said, "you can't access resources."

Dr. Kiltz agreed: "If you can't make a profit, you can't help people."

"The solution," Dr. Beltsos said, "is to talk with doctors to help them think about making good money by practicing great medicine. It's extremely important in this generation of physicians to reframe the conversation around money. This particular generation has been brought up in this anti-industry atmosphere. Yet attorneys and bankers golf together. They cultivate relationships and do business together. Doctors should do the same."

There's no shame in making money in exchange for providing life-changing—and life-saving—services as a physician. You should be well-compensated for investing in a lengthy education, enduring the grueling experience of your residency, and now committing your life to the wellness of others.

A medical business requires a steady and robust stream of revenue for the overhead costs of real estate, utilities, insurance, supplies, and expenses such as marketing and advertising. You also have to pay your staff a competitive wage and provide benefits. Plus, a profitable business enables you to invest more money to enhance the patient experience that transforms their lives.

Also understand that money and success are the byproducts of your dedication, not the end products. "I never aspired to make a lot of money or to have a large practice, ever," Dr. Kiltz says. Instead, he is richly rewarded today because he followed his own vision and carved his own way.

On the flip side, the pursuit of money is not enough to sustain your satisfaction and fulfillment as a physician. Money is your servant, not your master. You can achieve ultimate well-being and happiness when you buy experiences rather than things, such as climbing Mt. Kilimanjaro, spending a month off work every year to enjoy time with your family, visiting wine country with your romantic partner, or moving to Paris. You can buy pleasurable experiences every day: a cappuccino, a manicure-pedicure, or flowers. These pleasures—big and small—make you feel good, but require money.

As a prosperous MedikalPreneur, you can practice philanthropy. Giving makes you feel better. And when you have the resources to help build a women's shelter, provide meals to the homeless, or support your favorite cancer research fund, you can make a powerful difference for countless people.

During the coronavirus pandemic, I experienced one of the best feelings ever by volunteering to give vaccination shots at the Alamodome. However, while volunteering, I saw the need to feed the volunteers and healthcare workers who were vaccinating everyone. So I created a fundraising campaign and with that money we bought food from small businesses that were struggling during the pandemic. Everyone won. Positive-sum game. The people got vaccinated, the small businesses received a little money, the volunteers felt appreciated and energized, the people who gave money felt better, and I could not have been happier to contribute in a small way to improve the health of the community I love. This is true autopoiesis, as you'll read later.

"If Money Doesn't Make You Happy, Then You Probably Aren't Spending It Right," says the title of a report by Elizabeth W. Dunn of the University of British Columbia, Daniel T. Gilbert of Harvard University, and Timothy D. Wilson of the University of Virginia.[16] They concluded that most people spend money in ways that do not buy happiness. However, they recommended that dollars can translate into joy when we: invest in experiences rather than things; give in ways that help people; and pay for small pleasures.

As a MedikalPreneur, make money with gusto, and invest it in meaningful and pleasurable experiences that enhance your business and your life.

Step Six: Be Innovative and Allow Your Authentic Self to Shine. I met Dr. Beltsos when I gave my ground-breaking talk entitled "The Patient Experience" at the American Society of Reproductive Medicine in Orlando, Florida. She was also presenting her expertise as a fertility specialist. I shared with her many innovations that we had implemented at RMA of Texas, and she ultimately applied many of the ideas to become an extraordinary and successful MedikalPreneur with a global impact.

"Paco is innovative and fun," she said. "When I met him, he's wearing this cool shirt that only really hip guys can wear. He's got this beautiful accent; he's not traditional; he's one of the most brilliant minds in our field. He's wicked smart, definitely a thought leader."

I promise I didn't pay her to say that! Dr. Beltsos was eager to learn how to shatter the mold of a traditional medical practice and find her most innovative path to success. I immediately shared many of the concepts in this book.

"He's since become my mentor and my inspiration for things I had thought about and things that had never entered my mind," she recalled. "I spent 25 years building my team and being CEO and managing partner. I found that Paco is among the handful of people I've met who understand these concepts about being a MedikalPreneur that are so vital. He absolutely is the thought leader in that because he's so innovative and authentic."

Now is the time to ask, "Am I living and practicing medicine according to the most authentic version of myself, while implementing my innovative ideas? Or am I pursuing a path that feels safe, uncontroversial, and unlikely to rouse criticism or skepticism from my family, peers, and mentors?" The answers have price tags attached. If your medical career feels incongruent with your interests and workstyle, then you'll pay a steep price for sacrificing the opportunity to craft a MedikalPreneurial strategy. Alternatively, when you flex your authenticity and innovation, you'll attract customers who appreciate your unique products and services.

Step Seven: Find Your MedikalPreneurial Sweet Spot with "Ikigai." My life as a MedikalPreneur has enabled me to travel the world, experience wild adventures, and provide an amazing life for my daughter. In fact, I take one month off every summer to spend with Paula, a pre-med student at the University of California at Los Angeles.

One year when she was 12, we went to Paris. During lunch, she ordered a bottle of water, and we were shocked that it cost $10! This inspired a profound conversation about value, passion, and purpose in the context of a young person's usual insecurities about the future. "Dad, how can I find what I'm going to be when I grow up?" she asked with the cutest tone tinged with fear. "I'm afraid I'll fail."

I shared what I had conceived in 2011 when I drew a Venn diagram to find my *raison d'etre*—my reason for being—and what makes me excited to get up every morning to live, work, and help people. While we enjoyed our meal in front of the famous Moulin Rouge theatre, I drew this diagram on my iPad:

"That is what you do in life," I said and wrote in an email to her that included the diagram. "What you love, what you are good at, and what provides funds for your needs."

Circle #1 is what you love to do. Circle #2 is your greatest skill. Circle #3 is what will help you make enough money to fulfill your desired lifestyle. The overlapping space is your sweet spot. Only years later did I discover that this intuitive guidance was actually the ancient Japanese practice of Ikigai, which means "a reason for being." Ikigai has a fourth element that I did not consider: what the world needs.

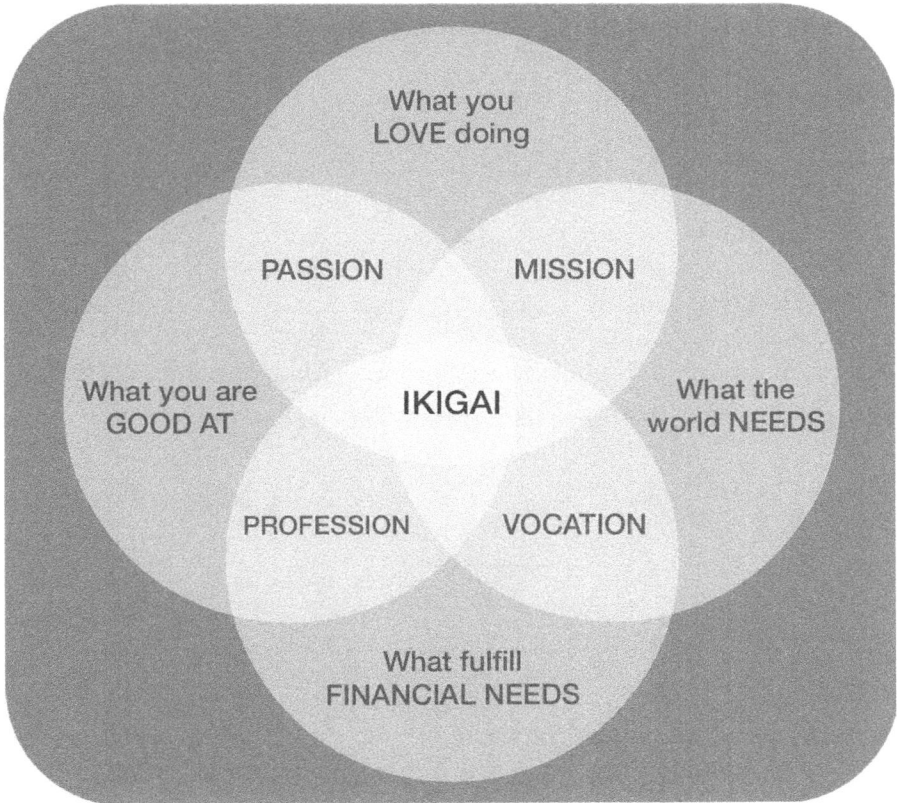

This diagram illustrates Ikigai.

This is your success secret as a MedikalPreneur—and as a human being. The concept originates from the Japanese Island of Okinawa, a Blue Zone—one of the regions in the world where people routinely live beyond 100 years old. So it's safe to say that when you spend your life doing what you love and what you are good at, and prospering from it while helping the world, you will live a longer, healthier life. Your health is your wealth. This is the best kept secret that we didn't learn in medical school.

Here's how to pinpoint your Sweet Spot:

What do you love to do? _____

What are your greatest skills? _____

What does the world need?_____

What can you be paid for: _____

How can you develop your Sweet Spot as a MedikalPreneurial? What training, financing, or other resources do you need?

_____

_____

_____

Identify a void in the market. How can you meet this need by utilizing your skills in a way that you love and makes money? Describe the product or service:

_____

_____

_____

Step Eight: Understand Three Reasons
Why You Should Be a MedikalPreneur

One: You'll Enjoy Freedom. When you open your business, you have the freedom to engineer every detail, starting with the types of products and services that you offer, as well as the architecture of your offices, the staff you hire, etc. More importantly, you'll experience freedom by living your authentic life, while doing what **you** want and not what people or society want you to do. That is freedom!

Two: You'll Have Infinite Potential for Prosperity and Helping People. You'll blaze new trails in the medical industry while you: earn money; create new products and services; create your own vision and bring it to life; allow your innovations and creativity to fly limitlessly; break the mold of conventional ways of doing things and create new, better ways to help and hire people; and leave a unique legacy for your life. All while you influence and mentor others to do extraordinary things.

Three: You Will Enjoy Life Satisfaction and Fulfillment. As your own boss, it's exciting to wake up and work in a place that you created, providing products and services exactly as you envisioned. As a MedikalPreneur, you're truly the master of your own fate; this fulfills you in ways not possible within the confines of working for a hospital, university health system, or someone else's company.

A Final Update for the Medicalpreneurial Software of the Mind

Always remember that your success is all about creating the most transformative experience for your patients or customers.

"Doctors tend to be narcissistic about wanting everything their way, from the black leather chair behind the big desk to the awards hung a certain way on the office wall," Dr. Beltsos said. "You know what? It isn't about you. It's about the person in front of you. The patient."

Chapter 3

Differentiate Yourself: Become the Best in the Business by Designing a Memorable Customer/Patient Experience

Your MedikalPreneurial mission should focus on two words: experience and transformation. In today's medical marketplace, it's not enough to simply provide a product or service that aims to solve your patient's or customer's problem.

Instead, differentiate yourself from the competition and ensure your greatest success by designing and providing an extraordinary experience that transforms the patient's life. For physicians, this usually translates into changing hurting into healing, a smoker into a nonsmoker, an obese person into a healthy person, or a diabetic into someone who is medication-free. For a fertility specialist, this means taking a patient or couple from struggling to get pregnant, to becoming a parent and building a family.

Throughout this transformational experience, the patient evolves from a complete stranger into a loyal advocate whose success story inspires him or her to become a walking, talking billboard, broadcasting praise for your business through word-of-mouth referrals, online reviews, social media posts, and positive commentary to friends, family, and colleagues. In our business, proud parents who struggled to have a family become the most influential advocates as they tell the world about how our fertility clinic helped them finally realize their dream of raising children.

This positive, firsthand press triggers a continuous cycle of new patients whose extraordinary experience and transformation make them supporters who organically send new patients to your doors.

"Welcome To The Experience Economy—It's no longer just about healing: patients want a personal transformation,"[17] said the title of an article in the September/October 2001 issue of *Health Forum Journal* by B. Joseph Pine II and James H. Gilmore. Their book, *The Experience Economy*, deeply influenced me.

The authors say that businesses beat the competition by creating a unique environment and experience, such as the Hard Rock Café restaurants that merge food and music memorabilia, and REI stores that offer 65-foot climbing walls and testing rooms that simulate rain, kayaking, walking trails, cycling, and cross-country skiing.

Another example is Jungle Roots Children's Dentistry and Orthodontics in Phoenix, where Dr. John Culp created a jungle-themed experience to inspire trust and cooperation for children receiving dental care.[18]

MedikalPreneurs are actors playing roles that set a stage starring the patient, and we speak and act in ways that provide a positive conclusion to the patient's story. Before the patient or customer enters our clinic, we script and stage interactive experiences that facilitate a transformation when they arrive.

This staging allows the MedikalPreneur to counteract patients' and customers' past experiences with physicians who lacked warmth, empathy, and good "bedside manner," leaving a cold, sterile feeling void of human connection. Sadly, because physicians are usually trained to withhold emotion—both for self-protection in high-pressure situations amidst fear and tragedy, and as a façade of professionalism—too many doctors leave patients feeling unseen, unheard, and disconnected from this medical expert whom they are trusting for life-and-death decisions. All of the above are fodder for bad patient experiences. As a result, scathing word-of-mouth criticism and online reviews where patients viciously "rate the doctor" will taint your reputation.

So how do you create a transformative experience as a MedikalPreneur? Think of your medical office as a theater. Unfortunately, some people equate words like stage, acting, performance, and theater as being inauthentic, pretending, or acting fake. Quite the contrary. This is a brilliant opportunity for you to customize every moment to make your patient or client feel special in an environment where empathy and understanding cater to their feelings and needs. Make patients feel pampered—whether that's for fertility or dermatology or physical therapy or a haircut or a car!

But the concept of physicians being trained as actors roused an uproar from doctors in 1994 after *Lancet* published an article called "Acting in Medical Practice," by Hillel Finestone MD and David Conter PhD of the University of Western Ontario.[19] The authors asserted that an acting curriculum should be added to all medical training, to teach physicians and other health care workers how to best respond to their patients' emotional needs.

My youthful experiences as a performer in grade school, and my comedic approach to life, made me fall in love with this concept. So I created a philosophy and practice comparing street theatre to the everyday workings of a doctor's office. More on that later.

For now, know that the best treatment experiences occur when patients feel that the physician empathizes with their pain and understands their point of view. The patient is seeking connection and never wants to feel like just a number. One way to cultivate empathy is to think of a time when you were a patient. Did the physician exude warmth, make eye contact, and listen to your concerns? Did the doctor speak with a caring tone and acknowledge your feelings? Also remember the eagerness you probably felt about hearing the medical professional explain your condition, the prognosis, and the treatment. Did they convey concern, or did they dictate with a cold, hard tone that felt condescending and confusing? Did the doctor sympathize with your problem or discomfort? Did the doctor make sure you understood what she/he was explaining?

It's a lie that physicians should not feel the pain of others. They should feel it, but they should also protect themselves from it.

"Don't let it hurt you," my father used to say. "You should allow your person to feel the pain without hurting you."

So how does a MedikalPreneur navigate this space to avoid being clinical and cold, while protecting your emotions and creating a memorable patient experience? By understanding that we as medical professionals are actors who perform on a stage for our patients in a theater of our clinics and offices.

As such, we provide the ultimate transformational experience when we help patients and clients achieve self-actualization through our products and services, according to Tina Mermiri, research manager of Arts & Business, in an article about the transformation economy entitled, "Beyond experience: customer, consumer, and brand."[20] She wrote that people will not engage without believing that they will receive a meaningful, emotionally gratifying experience that helps them achieve the top goal of Maslow's hierarchy of human needs: achieving one's deepest life purpose. That may sound lofty, but in fertility, for example, many women and men view starting a family as life's greatest purpose, and without our services, they could not achieve that goal.

Consumers No More: Catering to the Needs of "Prosumers"

Now in the 21st century, people who buy products, services, experiences, and transformations, are no longer called "consumers." They are "prosumers"—a portmanteau of "producer" and "consumer."[21] The new marketplace has patrons who want to be involved and participate in the design of their own consumption. They want their voices heard, their input applied, and their particular desires met in ways that feel tailored and customized. They want to be immersed in their own experiential transformation.

As a result, the paternalistic and sometimes condescending practice of medicine in which the physician is always right, has the final word, and knows everything—is extremely outdated. Prosumers will no longer submit to, or align with, anachronic treatment from a doctor or a business. Instead, the best possible outcomes occur when the patient and consumer are immersed in the process; this creates successful and sustainable results for the business. The customer is therefore the product; his or her transformation makes him/her the ultimate product of the offering. Transforming a woman who has had difficulty getting pregnant and birthing a baby—into a mother who is creating a family—is a dramatic example of this concept.

That's powerful! When you as a MedikalPreneur think about your work from this higher perspective, you'll allow your creativity and grandest visions to guide how you create your business, clinic, and/or practice. Then you'll attract "prosumers" who step into your theatre, and onto your stage, where your cast provides an experience that transforms your customers and patients for the better. This is not an object or a service that someone can purchase. It's a multi-sensory immersion into your area of expertise, providing a metamorphosis and improvement for how the patients and customers feel and live.

Create a transformative experience for your patient/customer. Think: they are *here* and are X; how can my product, service, experience take them to X+1 and *there*?

MedikalPreneurs Need Creativity and Courage

Creativity is the key ingredient to conceive and present the transformational experience for your patients. To unleash your boldest, most innovative thinking, draw on courage and ignore the naysayers, as well as the practices of the past.

Take this understanding to another level by reading two books by Rolf Jensen that were instrumental for creating and growing my businesses. First, in *The Dream Society: How the Coming Shift from Information to Imagination Will Transform Your Business*[22] Jensen asserted that we're in a "dream society" because the marketplace had evolved from a rudimental system of providing basic products and services into a marketplace where we buy into a dream concept.

For example, consider a farmer who sells eggs. Organizations and marketing campaigns raised awareness about inhumane conditions in the animal farming industry by presenting heart-wrenching images of chickens forced to lay eggs in cramped, dirty cages. Our anger and outrage inspired us to buy into the dream of chickens liberated from their cages, free to roam and lay eggs in safer, humane environments. As a result, the same dozen eggs that cost $1.50 from the farmer were labeled "free range" and cost twice the price. But we happily pay the extra money because we dream of better treatment of animals, especially those raised to produce food for humans. Therefore, we bought the dream, not the product. The product remains the same.

Restaurants also sell dreams. You can purchase coffee at many places, but Starbucks sells a specific dream with its décor, music, and unique language; it makes you feel part of an exclusive club featuring vibrant socializing in an artsy, intelligent, and hip environment. It doesn't matter whether the coffee is better, worse, or more expensive than the next café; people buy into the dream that's staged to create the Starbucks experience.

This reminds me of the roguish advice of a friend who was, let's say, very successful in the art of *amour*. This friend recommended that if you wake up one morning with a lady whose name you do not remember, take her to Starbucks for coffee, where the service is so personalized, they will write her name on the cup. To be fair, it works if you reverse the genders, too!

Likewise, in our practice, we're selling the dream of creating a family, whereas in the past, a fertility specialist was simply providing the service to help a woman get pregnant. We're not baby makers; we're family builders!

As a MedikalPreneur, it's possible to weave a dream around any product or service. If you're a dermatologist, you're selling the dream that undergoing your unique treatments and using your creams will create beautiful skin that attracts love, success, and happiness. If you're a bariatric surgeon, your patients will buy into far more than the benefits of weight loss and better health; they will invest in the dream that surgery will result in good health, confidence, and success.

This trajectory leads to Jensen's next book, *The Renaissance Society: How the Shift from Dream Society to the Age of Individual Control Will Change the Way You Do Business.*[23] Written with Mika Aaltonen, the 2013 book says we're not only selling a dream, but providing an experience that transforms the patient for the better. Today's consumer—thanks to the internet and social media—thrives on the ability to innovate and flex power to enjoy products and services that make them feel pampered and valued.

Just as during the Renaissance when influential figures such as Leonardo DaVinci mastered many subjects—such as anatomy, painting, and engineering—today's information age cultivates consumers with high standards and expectations. They demand the best. They do their homework. They comparison shop. They know your competition's pricing, services, and experiences. And they want the greatest value for entrusting you to help them heal, recover, or solve their medical problem.

The best way to attract and keep our patients is through emotion, according to Jensen. By connecting with their feelings and enhancing their mental health while educating them about their ailment or objective, we as MedikalPreneurs have limitless potential to build thriving businesses and transform lives.

Empathy Helps You Design the Best Patient Experience

For now, step into the minds and hearts of people who are seeking your expertise to solve their problem. Try to experience the patient's dilemma from their perspective. This is empathy—the ability to understand and share the feelings of another person. Empathy is one of the most important traits you can cultivate as a health care practitioner. Many of us physicians are naturally empathetic; our innate ability to feel other people's pain helps us treat them with compassion and tenacity.

However, those responses may be hindered with a patient who is difficult, vague, or unemotional. Here's where the physician can use acting skills to help the patient feel comfortable and understood. This is not being fake or inauthentic. It's about how you make the patient feel. Very importantly, "performing" and "acting" are utilized in every profession. Surely, the lawyer is playing a role to convince the jury that the client is innocent or should receive a million-dollar settlement. Teachers and professors "perform" to engage students' imaginations and inspire them to learn. A customer service professional often works from a script to ensure the best outcome for the caller and the company. Even in private encounters, men and women play roles in relationships to make their partners feel loved, protected, and affirmed.

These behaviors are motivated by a genuine desire to create the best experience for the other person. As medical professionals, this understanding helps us step beyond empathy into a whole new realm of positive outcomes for our patients and customers.

In this chapter, I'll show you how to differentiate your medical practice by taking you inside our fertility center. We invested significant resources in training our staff to create a patient experience that put people at ease and profoundly transformed their lives. This resulted in high pregnancy rates, patient satisfaction, referrals, positive reviews, and steady streams of new patients. As you read the following story, change the scenario to fit the medical practice you're designing and/or operating. Keep an open mind and consider how you can apply this patient experience to differentiate yourself as an exceptional MedikalPreneur.

* * *

Imagine you're a woman named Jenny who has endured years of struggles and financial hardship to build a family. Multiple pregnancies have ended in miscarriage, so you and your husband consult with another fertility doctor.

"He talked to us like we're stupid," your husband says, standing under harsh fluorescent lighting in the clinic's cold lobby. "I felt rushed, like this is a factory. And then that doc expects us to pay a fortune—"

"And for what!?" you say, rushing toward the door. "Did you hear the lady sobbing in the next room? The nurse was scolding her for forgetting to pick up her meds from the pharmacy and messing up her whole cycle."

Hopeless, you cringe. *Will I ever get pregnant again? Will I ever carry a baby to term? Will my husband think I'm a failure as a woman and leave me? Can we afford a different fertility specialist? Will the process bankrupt us? And will the physician and staff make it feel cold and clinical? Do we even have the emotional strength to embark on such an experience?*

Later, while driving alone, you stop at a red light. The next vehicle catches your eye in the bright sunshine of San Antonio, Texas. *Am I really seeing a car decorated with sperm? Does that wrap really look like blue and white sperms are swimming around the wheels, as if the tires are eggs waiting to be fertilized?*

A smile stops your tears and you suddenly feel optimistic. You snap a picture of the vehicle, whose door says: "RMA of Texas: World Class Fertility Care," along with a phone number 210-FERTILE. What if this is exactly what you need? A short time later, your heart pounds as you call. A pleasant voice answers: "RMA of Texas, this is Francesca, how can I make your day better?"

"Actually it is," you say, "since I saw your car decorated with sperm."

The receptionist laughs. "Well, I'm glad you called!"

"I need help," you say. "It's the anniversary of our last miscarriage. We want to try some kind of treatment."

"I'm sorry to hear that you've had miscarriages," Francesca says. "I can only imagine how awful this emotional burden must make you feel. We can definitely help you here." She asks for your name and other information to make an appointment.

You're impressed that the receptionist acknowledged your emotional burden, calling you by your name to make you feel like a human being, not a number. You feel heard. Then you visit the RMA of Texas website. It's colorful, engaging, and informative, and the company has centers in four cities. Online reviews show positive customer comments and many new parents praising the personalized service where they felt pampered throughout their successful baby quests.

A few days later, you and your husband anxiously enter the lobby.

Silver letters on the wall say RMA of Texas and: "Today you, tomorrow a family." Soft, recessed lighting illuminates warm colors and comfortable textures. Soothing music plays, and the scent of coffee and hazelnut creamer fills the air. The ceiling contains a sculpture suggesting the long journey that leads to becoming a mom. Its counter-clockwise spiral reflects how your hope for pregnancy and a family is going against your biological clock. The artwork on the wall is a mosaic of warm colors in a pattern of puzzle pieces all fitting together to create a beautiful design.

The receptionist at the front counter flashes a genuine smile that seems like it's part of her uniform. "Welcome to RMA of Texas," she says. "Please have a seat in the Welcoming Room."

"I'll take that over a waiting room," your husband adds as you sit on a plush, circular sofa. "We've been waiting long enough to have a baby. Waiting on pregnancy test results. Waiting to see if the baby will make it—"

Your husband glances around nervously. Years ago, he asked, "What if I have a low sperm count? A dude is supposed to have sperm. That's what manhood is—" His voice cracked and he left the room. *How embarrassing would it be for him now to undergo testing and discover low sperm count as the culprit for our failure to get pregnant?*

"Jenny," the receptionist says. "The doctor is taking extra time with a patient, so please help yourself to water, coffee, cappuccino, and snacks."

"Thank you."

"My pleasure," she responds.

As you wait, you realize that she did not say the doctor was running late, but was devoting attention to a patient. *If he does that for her, then surely he'll do that for me.* A short time later, as you're escorted to a consultation room by another friendly person, you pass a woman who smiles and says, "Hi, I'm Lisa Duran, the Chief Experience Officer. My job is to make sure you have the best possible experience here, from the moment you call us, to the time you take your new baby home from the hospital and beyond."

This woman's face glows with optimism and joy, as if she *knows* you'll have a successful experience here. A shiver dances up your spine. *I feel like I'm in the Disney World of fertility clinics.* At the same time, small and large paintings, murals, and other details adorned with images tell the story of the first IVF baby and the history of fertility advancements. You pass The Wall of Success, which is covered in white and yellow baby footprints and birth dates.

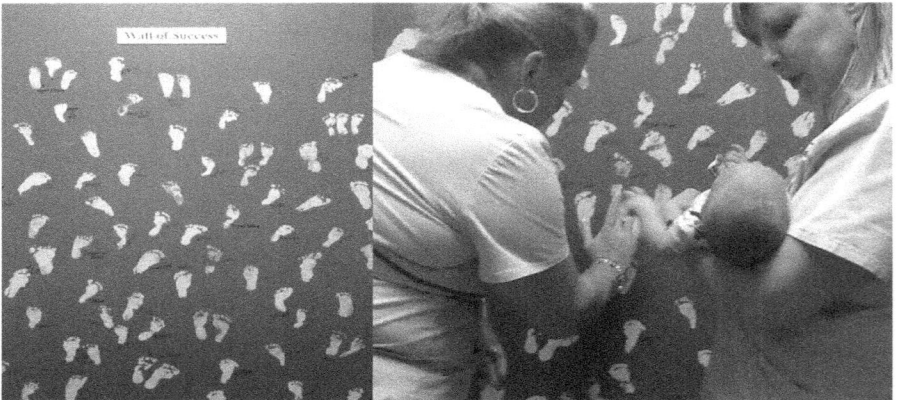

"There's such a great vibe here," you tell your husband. The hallway seems lighter at the end, thanks to a ceiling lamp symbolizing light at the end of the tunnel. Stepping into the bathroom, you notice a sperm- and egg-shaped sink. You think, *Wow, they sure have a way of making this dreadful experience feel fun and upbeat.*

In the hallway, the nurse points to a room and says, "This is the Louise Brown Room. She was the world's first test tube baby. Our rooms are named for the first test tube babies, including our first, Benjamin." The wall resembles a chalkboard. Bold letters at the top say: "I want a baby because?" Patients' stories cover the board.

"Every week, the doctor posts a picture of this on Facebook to share your hopes and dreams with the world," the nurse says. "Now let's get you started in the doctor's office." She opens a door to a softly lit room containing a simple, L-shaped desk in a corner, cozy furniture, walls painted soothing colors of teal and sunflower yellow, a bookshelf, and a small table offering a bowl of fresh fruit. On one wall hangs a big screen TV and that same puzzle-piece painting as in the lobby.

"Please, make yourselves comfortable," the nurse says, motioning toward a plush gold sofa where you and your husband sit. Anxiety zaps your energy. A few minutes later, the doctor strides in, smiling and appearing genuinely happy to see you. You and your husband rise to receive his firm handshake as he gazes directly into your eyes.

"My name is Paco," the doctor says, "and I will be in charge of the team that will help you on your journey in becoming the family you've long imagined."

The doctor wears black scrubs with his name, FRANCISCO ARREDONDO, MD, on the left chest. His black and white checkered socks suggest a fun personality. The warmth and empathy in his eyes put you and your husband at ease as you sit facing the doctor, who's on another small sofa a few feet away.

This feels personal, warm, and caring. No desk or table separate you. You are not in a cold exam room or office with harsh light. Instead, it feels like you're sitting in a living room chatting with a friend.

"Welcome to RMA of Texas," the doctor says, smiling. His charisma makes you feel encouraged. "As you read on the wall, we want you to leave here as a family. But first, tell me about yourselves, and how we can help you have some kiddos running around your house."

He turns an hourglass and says, "The hourglass measures three minutes. It's my reminder not to talk after I ask the first question, so my patients can express everything they need to say."

"Why three minutes?" you ask.

"Because studies show that doctors interrupt patients after about 18 seconds on average, and some in just 11 seconds," the doctor explains. "I read this in an article in 1984. If physicians listen until the patient completes his or her description of their problem or concern, 95% of the patients would wrap it up within two minutes."

As promised, while you and your husband tell your story, the doctor listens attentively, locking eyes with you, totally focused, like you are the only two people in the world. After you finish, he says, "I can help you. Let's start your journey toward building your family." With a clicker, he activates a slide show on the television, then enthusiastically but patiently proceeds through a presentation about the fertility process that includes the possible causes of infertility, treatments, and outcomes.

Pictured from left: Dr. Courtney Failor, Dr. Aimee Browne, Dr. Ursula Balthazar, Dr. Summer James, and Dr. Francisco "Paco" Arredondo.

"Jenny, you're 37 years young," he says, pointing to a purple and white graphic on the screen. "If we retrieve 20 eggs and freeze them, you'll have a 75% chance of getting pregnant." After several more graphics, he shows a photo of himself with four smiling women.

"We are here to deliver an EXCELLENT Patient Experience for YOU," the doctor says, echoing the words on the screen while looking at you and your husband. "We work as a TEAM. TODAY you will leave with an INDIVIDUALIZED plan." The doctor says he wants you to become familiar with everybody in the office because each person plays a critical role in the fertility process.

"You require a full team to handle your journey," he says. "This is not a haircut. This is not a salon where you say, 'If my stylist Johnny isn't here, then don't cut my hair.' Every physician is capable of handling your care. Medicine is a team sport."

While the screen says that "one in seven couples have challenges with fertility," the doctor alternates eye contact between you and your husband. "You are not alone," he says. "We're here to help."

The next slide shows a red rollercoaster. "Jenny," the doctor says, "you'll be on an emotional rollercoaster. It's normal to feel fear, frustration, anxiety, and depression during this process. You'll feel out of control, so we'll help you prepare for that."

The doctor shows colorful charts and graphs explaining the anatomy of pregnancy, as well as conception rates, how the number of eggs decreases, and how the miscarriage rate increases over a woman's lifespan. One slide explains that 30% of infertility cases result from men's semen, while 15% are caused by ovarian factors, 35% by tubal factors, and 10% by a combination of them, while 10% are unexplained.

Your husband looks anxious. "Doctor Arredondo. I mean, Paco—"

The doctor nods.

"I'm worried about whether we can afford this," your husband says.

"Since that's a top concern for many patients, we created a special financing software called Imagine Fertility to help you manage the investment that you make here in creating your family. It's so successful that centers throughout the United States are using it. It's one reason why we've helped couples like you give birth to thousands during the 13 years we've been helping make miracles for people struggling with fertility."

Your husband looks more calm as he asks, "How does this Imagine Fertility program work?"

"The same as when you buy a house," the doctor says. "You go on Zillow or another real estate app, then punch in how many bedrooms and bathrooms and other things you want. The app allows you to calculate the mortgage. Similarly, we look at the numbers, see what type of treatment you need, and calculate that with your financial status to create a monthly payment amount, just like a house note."

"Wow, I was afraid we'd have to fork over a huge chunk of change to get started," your husband says. "Plus I heard from my buddy whose wife got fertility treatments that they were buried under a mountain of bills from different labs, pharmacies, and the fertility clinic. They said it was a nightmare and almost put them under financially."

The doctor shakes his head. "We have bundle billing, so your single monthly payment covers all the expenses at once."

At the conclusion of the consultation, the doctor conveys a genuine desire to make your baby dreams come true. He gives you a business card. "Here's my cell phone number and email address. If my nurse doesn't respond, you call me directly."

You take the card. "Your cell number? I don't want to bother you—"

"It's my pleasure to serve as your doctor who helps you become a family," he says, leaving the room.

"Wow," your husband says. "What doctor says call him by his first name *and* gives you his personal number?"

You shake your head. "This experience is amazing so far. The doctor is so down to earth! The people here make you feel like your dreams matter."

"I'm convinced," your husband says. "Let's do this."

After a knock, a woman enters. Her badge says RN after her name. "Hi, I'm Janice, your Fertility Coach. Please join me at the table," she says, sitting beside you both at a curvy table. "First, please accept my deepest condolences about your losses. We want to help you look forward to the day when you celebrate bringing your new baby home from the hospital."

You and your husband flash hopeful smiles.

"How young are you?" the Fertility Coach asks, poised to type information into her computer.

"Wow, I like the way you say that! I usually feel bad when people ask, 'How old are you?' because when I say I'm 37, and they know about my struggles, they look at me with pity like I'll never have a baby."

The Fertility Coach smiles. "We'll help you change that. Now, Jenny, do you have any other concerns?"

"Yeah, I've been worried that maybe I have a *cyst*, and my doctor wanted to do a biopsy, but that sounded so scary."

"If you have an *enlarged follicle* we can simply do a *sample*," she says. You're expecting to hear a long, confusing explanation full of clinical terms, embarrassing words, and cringe-worthy procedures for poking and prodding in sensitive places. "We'll start by doing an internal scan for you, Jenny. Along the way, if we need to preserve any embryos, we can put them on biological pause."

"What does that mean?" you ask.

"The embryos can be put on biological pause in our state-of-the-art facility," the Fertility Coach says.

She hands over a book and a journal. "Now, I have some things for you. This is a workbook that Paco and a psychologist wrote. It's called *Finding You In Fertility*; it helps you understand the process by doing emotional exercises throughout the journey. And this is our *IVF Journal*, so you can write out your feelings about your experience toward having a baby. Our moms here say writing lowers their stress and helps them focus on the positive things and feel better."

You clasp the books and say, "I love to journal. This will help."

"Good. We always want you to know what to expect, and always remember that we're just a phone call away if you need help with anything. Now, here's how to apply the medications," your Fertility Coach explains while demonstrating how to deliver the meds that will prime your body for pregnancy. "You use the pen like this."

"I feel so nervous," you say.

"You mean, you feel excited, right?!" the Fertility Coach says. "Remember, Jenny, you can do this! We're rooting for you! What seems impossible, I help make possible. We're your advocates. We are your shoulder to cry on."

Crying is all you can do later, when you go to the pharmacy and pick up the bottles and boxes of medications, including shots that you have to give to yourself. You call the center, sobbing. Your Fertility Coach's soft, caring voice calms you: "Jenny, I'm here to help you. Would you like to come in so I can show you exactly which medications to take and how to take them? Or I can walk you through that over FaceTime."

"You can do that?" you ask.

"Absolutely," she says.

Another time, you call the clinic in a panic because the pharmacy failed to deliver your medication, and if you miss the doses, the entire fertility cycle will be a waste! Making matters worse, it's a Sunday. What if you can't reach anyone at the center?

"Don't worry," says RN Christine Flynn. "We'll take care of this for you."

A short time later, you're stunned and grateful when she delivers the medication to your home! You take the doses, and proceed with your in vitro fertilization cycle. (This practice was inspired by our philosophy that, *It may not be our fault, but it is our problem. If you own the problem, you own the customer.*)

Even with that problem solved, you tell your Fertility Coach: "I'm so scared that it won't work. I can't sleep and find myself crying all the time. I feel really fat and bloated, and my moods are all over the place."

Your Fertility Coach explains that you can speak with the center's mental health specialist who's an expert at counseling patients through the emotional rollercoaster of fertility treatment. That helps, and you're feeling better. You do an injection, and it's time for an egg retrieval. The problem? It's Thanksgiving Day, and the procedure requires minor surgery.

"Come in today and we will take care of it," your Fertility Coach says.

You're shocked that they're going to do this crucial step of the fertility process on a holiday when the nurses and doctors and everyone else should be eating dinner with their families. That evening, you're being prepped for surgery and your husband is with you. The doctor, embryologist, and nursing staff gather around, then proceed with retrieving eggs. The next day, while you're home resting, the doctor calls. "Hi Jenny, how are you feeling after yesterday's surgery?"

"Oh my goodness, Dr. Arredondo, I mean Paco, you actually called me?! I'm doing fine. I still can't believe you did my surgery on Thanksgiving."

"Another fertility center might have put it off a day," the doctor says, "but we always do what's right for our patients, and that meant retrieving your eggs at exactly the right time, which happened to be on Thanksgiving."

He explains that the next step is to combine your husband's sperm with your eggs in a petri dish in the laboratory. Then, during the procedure for the embryo transfer, your Fertility Coach—who long ago asked your favorite song—plays it during the procedure. Love and joy ripple through you as the embryos are implanted in your uterus, as the song sweeps you back to the magical moment of your first wedding dance. You pray that your dreams of starting a family will finally come true.

During the visit, the technician comes out of the laboratory and hands you the petri dish. "This is your embryo's first crib," she says, "and I'm your first babysitter."

Next, you have an appointment for a pregnancy test. Then you go home to eagerly await the results. Finally, the phone rings.

"Jenny, I have good news," your Fertility Coach says. "You are pregnant!"

You and your husband are overjoyed.

"Delivering good news is the reason I come to work every day," your Fertility Coach says. "Now let's schedule your repeat test in a couple of days and hopefully your first pregnancy ultrasound."

During your visits, you love how the staff seems to treat every patient and their partner like family and as equals, whether Spanish-speaking, financially challenged, or LGBTQ+.

After nine months, you birth a healthy baby! You and your husband are elated and grateful as you celebrate with the RMA staff by dipping your baby's feet in paint and pressing them to the wall.

"Your journey was my journey," your Fertility Coach says proudly. "These are my babies."

"And I am your dream maker," the doctor says proudly, looking almost as happy as your husband.

You cry tears of joy and your heart has never felt happier or more grateful.

Dissecting the Anatomy of an Excellent Patient Experience

I hope that Jenny's story illustrates how we created a unique and effective patient experience at our medical offices. Now I'll explain the reasoning behind each point, to show how you can tailor similar experiences for your particular practice, business, or product. When we created our Patient Experience, I drew from many resources that I had collected over the years, gleaning nuggets of wisdom, best practices, and psychological theories.

I also wanted expert guidance about customer service. So we invited leaders from The Ritz-Carlton Hotel Company—which is celebrated globally for first-class customer service—to visit RMA of Texas and train us on how to provide the most exquisite patient experience possible. They provided valuable insights, but we felt that we could tailor our own program to our patients with even more impact. So we held many brainstorming sessions to determine exactly how, and continued to hold monthly meetings to discuss ways to improve our patients' experience based on their feedback.

At the same time, I sponsored one of our team members to travel to Cleveland for training with The DiJulius Group, which is "recognized as the world's leading authority on Customer Service,"[24] according to their website; it says their clients include The Ritz-Carlton, Lexus, Starbucks, Nordstrom, Harley Davidson. For us, they offered a Customer Xperience Executive Academy and a Customer Service Revolution conference that provided a crash course on what we needed to learn.

In the midst of this, I attended a Spurs basketball game with my banker and his wife, Lisa Duran. She was very engaging and pleasant. "What do you do?" I asked.

"I'm a housewife and I teach my kids," she said.

"What did you do before that?"

"I was an executive trainer for Lancome cosmetics and traveled to South Africa to train executives and people in sales," Lisa said.

"I have a project for you," I said. "We have a doctor in our center who can use your skills. We've had some not positive comments about her communication style and demeanor, even though patients love her because she provides excellent medical care. I'd like for you to sit down with her and the first 20 patients and observe her words and nonverbal messages. Then please coach her about how we can create a better image for the patients."

Lisa agreed. We sponsored a trip for her and another team member, Lauralicia, to attend a program about The Experience Economy in Las Vegas, where they acquired more knowledge. Lisa did such a great job, I hired her to create our first Customer Experience Program to train our new employees. This program generated a huge buzz around town! People referred us to OB/GYN offices, who called us, wanting to know the secrets of why so many people were singing the praises of our patient experience.

Ultimately, Lisa became our Chief Experience Officer, helping improve the customer experience at RMA of Texas. From this, we created a new company, Reconceive, and she secured a contract to train the physicians and staff members at fertility centers across America and Canada.

All the while, we were pioneering new territory in the medical field, and it attracted attention. In 2010, I was invited to give the first talk in the fertility industry about The Patient Experience at the American Society of Reproductive Medicine conference in Denver, Colorado. I was excited to share my discoveries—and the success secrets at our fertility centers—with our professional peers.

"Why are you talking about customer experience?" asked many fertility specialists with a skeptical tone. "It's babies. The patient wants to get pregnant. Why focus energy on the experience rather than the results?"

I refused to let naysayers stop me from sharing these trailblazing ideas with our colleagues. So we created an extensive PowerPoint presentation about our patient experience program and titled it: "Fertility Care in the Era of Experience Economy."

The first slide showed a book that profoundly influenced me: *The Experience Economy: Work is Theatre and Every Business a Stage* by

B. Joseph Pine II and James H. Gilmore.[25] Then I presented the learning objectives for the hundreds of fertility managers and fertility specialists in attendance:

- Identify *other industries' improvements* and apply them to a fertility practice.

- Describe the *four elements to* improve the *fertility experience patient cycle.*

- Learn how the *Balance Score Card* can be used as a Strategic Management Tool in a fertility practice.

I presented the grim reality of a Bain and Company consulting firm's findings based on a survey of 362 companies.[26] They found that 80% of companies believed they provided a superior experience, but only 8% of customers described their experience as superior.

Then I shared examples of how the hotel, restaurant, and spa industries attracted and impressed customers by tailoring experiences that made patrons feel pampered, valued, and heard, in addition to the excellent products and services that each company's brand promised. I suggested that hybridization—or adopting the practices of a spa or restaurant or hotel to enhance your own products and services—would help create a positive patient experience in the fertility specialists' practices.

The remainder of the presentation described the patient care standards that we had implemented at RMA of Texas. These standards established protocols for how we talked, behaved, and guided patients through the fertility process, and created the best emotional and physical environments to deliver their desired outcome of getting pregnant and having healthy babies.

I concluded the presentation by saying that creating a positive patient experience is the way for fertility specialists to differentiate themselves from the competition in an industry where price and quality (pregnancy rates) were variables that were difficult to modify in a significant way.

"As pregnancy rates improve and equalize in many programs," I told my peers, "the quality of the patient experience will be the differentiator of our industry."

First, Understand Your Patients' Needs

Before you can create and implement the best patient experience, you need to know what your patients, clients, or customers want and need. Start by analyzing the problem you're solving for them. What are they feeling? What are their fears? What are their past negative experiences with doctors who failed to help them? What do they actually need? How can you help them achieve the best outcome? Get answers by conducting a survey of your patients and others. Then use your findings to tailor your products and services to solve the problems that your patients describe.

We did this, then compiled an 11-page PowerPoint presentation entitled, "What Patients are *Really* Asking For." We used it to teach our team members how to treat our patients as they like to be treated. Our motto was the platinum rule: *treat others how they like to be treated.* They told us, and we used our survey results and the presentation to make sure we did exactly that.

"What Patients are *Really* Asking For"

They Want Us to Acknowledge That This is Hard.

- IVF forces us to face hard truths.

- The IVF process is very emotionally stressful.

- This experience impacts our relationships with each other.

- We will do whatever it takes to have a baby.

- IVF is hard, but it's worth it.

They Want Us to Tell Them How We Will Support Them

"Support Me"

- We are on a very lonely journey.

- We depend on our personal network for support.

- Provide us a variety of options for support.

- I need the clinic's help in finding support/resources.

"Prepare Me"

- We need help evaluating our financial options.

- We want to know up front what will be happening to us emotionally, physically, and psychologically.

- We need accurate and detailed information to help us make decisions about starting IVF.

- I need a lot of information about IVF.

- I'm wary of what I find online.

"Be My Champion"

- The care our nurses provide is foundational to our experience.

- The attentiveness of the nurses gives us comfort.

- Please do not add to our pain (get skilled staff to care for us).

- We want direct and unhindered contact with our nurses.

- Reach out to us in the difficult and happy times.

"Nurture Me"

- We need privacy in the clinic during this stressful process.

- Our time is valuable.

- We need a space that offers comfort and hope.

- I want to feel comfortable in the waiting room.

"Inspire Trust"

- The clinic's reputation is important to us.

- We need a trusted partner in our care.

- We are proactive about our care.

- We rely on our doctor's skill and compassion.

- I value Dr. A's experience, commitment, and dedication to our goal.

"Make Me A Priority"

- We need a lot of attention.

- We expect our experience to remain the same (or improve) despite growth and change.

- We expect integrity and professionalism from everyone at the clinic.

- I need RMA to do what they said they would do.

"Be There For Me"

- Our relationship with the staff is a very important part of our journey.

- We need support and encouragement from the staff.

- We need consistency in our care team.

- I'm OK with different caregivers when I know them and my expectations are set.

- I would like a dedicated care team.

"Teach Me"

- Shots are hard; show us what to do.

- We need to conquer shots.

- We need to be educated about how to administer our medications.

- I need help figuring out my medications.

How do you orchestrate a transformational experience?

Follow Paco's Six-Step Formula for Differentiating Your Business:

#1. Communication—Marketing is the Gateway to the Patient Experience. Be Bold! In Jenny's story, she learned about our fertility center when our sperm-mobile caught her eye in traffic. Our telephone number emblazoned on its side enabled her to call us. This visual communication resulted in an experience that led to transformation: she finally become a mother.

Clearly, our bold marketing led to the best possible patient experience. If you fail at marketing, you won't have any patients to give them an experience. So, the gateway to the patient experience is marketing. Be daring with it!

Buck traditional thinking. Stop playing it safe. That's boring! Differentiate yourself from your competitors by doing something that others may call crazy or outlandish. They'll be talking about *you* and your unusual antics, not the doctor down the street whose nondescript marketing blends in with the other local physicians. Word-of-mouth advertising is still the most effective way to promote your business. And it's free.

So what can you do that's the equivalent of our sperm-covered car? And what will you do when you meet resistance? When you fit in, you're invisible in the crowded marketplace, and you fail as a result, asserts Seth Godin, in his 2009 book, *Purple Cow, New Edition: Transform Your Business by Being Remarkable.*[27] This is powerful! But here's where your courage as a MedikalPreneur is required, because your ideas may face ridicule and resistance.

"This is the stupidest thing you can do," our embryologist, Tony

Anderson, told me when I consulted with my staff about whether to invest in a delivery vehicle wrapped in a colorful paint job that showed sperm swimming toward the wheels as if they were eggs. "Why would you do this?" Tony said it was a waste of money to invest $15,000 in the KIA Soul car and its design.

"I thought it was crazy that he was doing that," Tony said during an interview for this book. "Until my wife saw the car, took a picture of it, and posted it on Facebook. How brilliant is that?! How many people took a picture of that car and posted it on Facebook or Instagram. Ten years later, they're still driving that car and people are still posting images of it to Facebook."

This attention may prompt people to visit your website—another powerful communication tool to showcase your products, services, and successes.

The importance of good communications comes into play again when people phone your medical practice, and the receptionist becomes your next greatest marketing tool. He or she is your human portal to the patient experience. Have you ever called an office and hung up because the receptionist was rude—or because you don't get a human voice? On the other hand, a pleasant voice with a nice greeting and eagerness to help will further achieve the goal of attracting new patients.

Words matter! I learned this from a 2008 book called *Words That Work: It's Not What You Say, It's What People Hear* by Frank Luntz.[28] He asserts that the words you use can set the tone and create a positive or a negative experience. As you saw in Jenny's story, we rescripted the way we talk with patients. We removed negative cues and used words that cultivate feelings of comfort, caring, and confidence in what we were doing.

"We put a positive spin on everything," said Chris Flynn. "It was 'our pleasure' taking care of patients, never 'no problem.' Rather than say, 'How are you doing today? I know this is a difficult process,' we asked, 'Is there anything we can help you with going through this process?'

We also made every patient feel valued by never saying, 'The doctor is running late.' Instead, we said, 'The doctor is spending extra time with a patient and will be with you shortly.' That conveyed a message to the patient that she, too, would receive extra time with the doctor when needed."

Our team also asked a lot of questions to help the patient know what she wanted and needed. When the patient asked, "Can I get pregnant?" we responded with another question: "Is that what you want?" Then I shared the "drill and hole" analogy about the guy who went into Home Depot and told an employee, "I need a quarter-inch drill."

"No, you don't need a quarter-inch drill," the employee responded. "You need a quarter-inch hole."

"Huh?" the guy was confused.

"What do you need the hole for?" the employee asked.

"Oh, to put some screws and hang some frames," the guy said.

"We have all kinds of other options to hang your frames," the employee said. "You may not even need a hole. We have this device that's Velcro, or you can use these nails, or this drill. Now that you know your options, what do you want?"

This story is important with any business. Sometimes patients and customers don't know exactly what they need. And what they know is limited. For example, if our patient said, "I want a baby!" we responded by saying, "Wait, you want to plan a family. If you want one baby and you're 25, we have time, so I can start you with a simple procedure. But if you're 38, and you want three children, then we need to freeze your embryos. Do you want a girl first, or a boy?"

Then we helped the patient understand that many options were available, depending upon her circumstances and what she wanted. Many times, the patient had not stopped to consider or learn about options beyond simply desiring a baby. An important aspect of this fact-finding conversation is watching the nonverbal cues from the patient or customer. Sometimes an expression or a gesture can speak volumes about what the patient or customer truly desires. We paid attention and asked questions accordingly. We needed to provide the choice and options they *want*, at the price they *need*, with the quality they *deserve*.

We encouraged our patients to express themselves and get in touch with their feelings and desires by providing the *IVF Journal*, inspired after I read about scriptotherapy—the therapeutic use of writing, in an article called, "The Costs and Benefits of Writing, Talking, and Thinking About Life's Triumphs and Defeats," published in the *Journal of Personality and Social Psychology* in 2006.[29]

The article described a study using three groups of 50 people, whose well-being and health were measured before and after the exercise. For six weeks—three times weekly for 15 minutes—the first group **talked**, the second group **wrote**, and the third group **thought** about their most traumatic experience. After six weeks, the people who talked and wrote had improved well-being. The people who only **thought** about their traumas did **worse**. The lesson is that talking and writing about a traumatic experience can help you let go, move on, and feel better.

Therefore, journaling enabled our patients to articulate, release, and heal the anxieties, fears, and grief of their fertility struggles, while expressing their emotions on their journeys toward getting pregnant and creating a family. We also helped our patients shift their anxiety into excitement. So when Jenny said, "I feel so nervous," her Fertility Coach responded, "You mean, you feel excited, right?!"

We adopted this practice based on evidence that elite athletes had an edge over competitors when they redirected their anxiety into excitement. I learned this in an article, "Get Excited: Reappraising Pre-Performance Anxiety as Excitement" by Alison Wood Brooks of the Harvard Business School. The article, published in the *Journal of*

Experimental Psychology[30] in 2014, inspired our team to help patients convert "negatively perceived feelings" into actual engines propelling their journey. This resulted in a much better performance for the athletes in the study, and for the aspiring moms in our fertility center.

Our team also maintained open and honest communication with our patients by always asking for feedback. Chris Flynn recalled that, "I always asked at the end, 'What could we have done better? Is there anything that you can let me know about that we can change that would be better for our patients?' Some people had some really good suggestions about how we could improve."

If a patient's answer was not "great, awesome, fabulous, excellent" and was only "fine, good, or okay," then our staff was trained to ask, "What about your experience today wasn't excellent?" We valued every complaint as a gift. While other businesses paid consultants to analyze their patients' complaints, our atmosphere of open communication inspired our patients to give us free advice that helped them, as well as our current and future patients!

#2. Environment. Have you ever been in a store where the music is loud and irritating? What if the lighting is harsh, the furniture and floors are dirty, and the aesthetics are a turn-off? Do you want to stay and shop? Certainly you've visited doctors' offices where fluorescent lighting, hard surfaces, and sterile décor created a cold and uncomfortable environment.

In Jenny's story, you saw how we designed our offices with soothing sounds, calming colors and images, comfortable textures, soft lighting, and curvy shapes suggestive of eggs and sperm. We designed an environment that appealed to all the senses while making customers feel immersed in this experience.

Your employee's code of conduct also creates an emotional environment that either enhances or hinders your patient's experience and transformation. Remember: your staff members are the voices and faces of the business, because your patients will interact with them before they ever meet you.

Your receptionist answers the phone. The nurses greet patients and prepare them for the consultation with the physician. The lab technicians draw blood, take x-rays, and perform tests. So you want to ensure that a patient's every interaction—whether by phone or in person—represents you and your business in the best possible ways. You can create the most beneficial environment for the patients, staff, and business to thrive by implementing strict Patient Care Standards. Here are examples from our office.

Non-Negotiable Standards	*Always Standards*
Never point your finger at someone or to give directions.	Escort them to the correct room or door.
On the phone, never do a blind transfer.*	Do warm transfers.*
Never say, "not a problem."	Genuinely say, "my pleasure" or "absolutely" or "certainly."
Never pass by a patient without engaging them.	Practice the "10 Feet Rule" by wearing a genuine smile as part of the uniform.
Never show frustration in public.	Focus on what you can do, not what you can't do.
Never make the customer wrong.	Own it, even if it's not your fault, and find a solution.
Never say, "I don't know."	Anticipate patient needs and/or say, "I will find out for you."
Never say, "How old are you?"	Ask, "How young are you?"
Never criticize competitors.	Respect competitors.
Never overshare with a guest.	Make casual, genuine conversation.
Never ask, "Why are you here?"	Anticipate patient needs.

Non-Negotiable Standards	*Always Standards*
Never criticize or insult other team members.	Respect your peers and anticipate teammate needs.

* A call transfer is the act of bumping a call from one user to another. We used two ways to transfer a call: cold (blind) and warm (attended). A **blind transfer** is when you transfer the customer to a ring group or another agent without speaking to the new agent first. A **warm transfer** involves you informing the next agent in your company about who's calling, what are his/her challenges, and what she/he expects of you. Then you introduce her/him to the new phone agent. This way, the customer is not forced to repeat where they're calling from, for whom, and for what reason.

Dr. Beltsos, founder of Vios Fertility Institute in Chicago, says the secret to creating a powerful patient experience is to provide an environment where the patient feels like a guest in your home.

"We have Keurig coffee makers and snacks in each patient room, which we designed like a living room with a TV, which allows us to use technology to display information that helps them understand the process," she said. "We create an atmosphere that feels like we have a guest in our home, and that makes our staff mindful that we need to show the best hospitality and kindness at all times."

#3. Accessibility. Every patient had my cell phone number and email address. A sign with a photo of me smiling, along with an invitation to call or email me at any time, hung over every desk and exit in our offices. This very unusual practice served two purposes:

First, it established a personal connection with our patients, and made them feel confident that they could contact me at any time. Did they bombard me with calls and text messages? No. I only received about one call every two weeks. Second, giving my direct number to patients helped maintain excellence amongst my staff because they knew, if they did not respond to our patients, and our patients resorted to calling me, that would be a negative strike for the employee. This accessibility creates checks and balances that help ensure customer satisfaction.

"That invites total transparency," said Dr. Beltsos. "When patients have direct access to the owner, what do you think that does to the woman sitting at the front desk? Is she going to misbehave? No, because that patient can call the doctor on his cell phone. Then he can address the employee: 'This is a problem, Angie. Sure, you were upset, I get it. You had a bad day at the office. It's okay once. But twice, you're out.' Paco's example of accessibility was a way to keep people honest and aligned with his vision. I thought that was brilliant."

Here's another way that I offered accessibility. Every time I performed a surgery, I asked my assistant to put the patient's name and phone number in my Outlook, so that at 7 p.m. it would pop up on my phone. Then I called the patient.

"Hi Jenny, this is Paco, how are you feeling from yesterday's surgery?"

"Oh doctor," Jenny exclaimed. "You called! I'm doing fine. I'm so happy you called. You are the best doctor in the world!"

Then she'd call her friends and say, "You won't believe it, the doctor called me directly to see how I'm doing!"

Then I called two other patients.

"Actually, I'm having trouble with headaches," one said.

"I'll call in a prescription for you right now," I responded. "If that doesn't solve the problem, call me at the office tomorrow."

"Oh thank you so much, doctor," she said.

"My pleasure."

Each phone call cost me 30 seconds while driving home from the office. This created a very positive perception for our doctor-patient relationship. It cultivated trust and actually prevented lawsuits, because most lawsuits have nothing to do with the outcome, but rather the quality of the interpersonal relationship. Cultivating personal relationships helps guarantee a positive, long-term outcome for both the patient and the doctor.

#4. Service Above and Beyond. We performed surgeries on holidays and saw new patients at night and on Saturdays. Many fertility doctors might refuse to do this. But we always put the patient first, and when her eggs were mature, we had to retrieve them at the most opportune time for a successful fertilization in our lab. So, when necessary, our nursing staff, our embryologist, and a doctor reported for duty in the middle of the night to take care of the patient.

ATTENTION

Covered Parking for Medical Staff ONLY

VIOLATORS WILL BE TOWED

You have to be willing to work around your customer needs, not yours. One blatant example of this occurred when I saw this signage in a medical office building. I was so appalled, I took a picture. This sign conveys the non-verbal message that, "The doctors and nurses are more important than you. Your needs are secondary!" This is unacceptable. The customers should feel special and valued, not scolded and restricted.

#5. A Patient's Problem is Our Problem to Solve. Our philosophy was, "If you own the problem, you own the patient." That means, no matter who made a mistake and caused a problem, it was our responsibility to solve it in the patient's favor. So, when training our staff, I used the following examples, which I also shared during my presentation to my peers in Denver.

- Is it our fault that despite requesting records from our competition or referral physicians, they do not send them on time? NO.

- Is it our problem? YES.

- Is it our fault that the patient was not keeping track of how much medication she had left and now it's the weekend and she needs more and no stores are open? NO.

- Is it our problem? YES.

- Is it our fault that the patient did not purchase her medication she is due to apply at midnight before her egg retrieval? NO.

- Is it our problem? YES.

You can translate this to any company or business. If you own the customer's problems, you will own that patient. In Jenny's story, when the pharmacy failed to deliver her medications that she needed that day to complete a successful IVF cycle, we did not shame, blame, or criticize her or the pharmacy. Instead, we put our energy into solving the problem, by delivering the medication to her home on a Sunday.

I have personally delivered medication to a patient at home on a weekend. The patient was so shocked and grateful that she wrote a rave review about RMA of Texas on an online website where people rate doctors. This type of genuine, online praise is the best advertising for people who are browsing for a fertility doctor.

#6. Using Harmonious Nuances to Cultivate a Positive Experience. We created a clinic where patients walked in and we knew their names and details that made them feel heard and valued.

"First, we sat and listened to the patient and looked at her," recalled our RN, Chris Flynn. "These days, our minds can be in a thousand places. So when you give someone your uninterrupted attention, with eye contact, without fidgeting with a cell phone or writing in a file, then the patient feels like you truly care. You ask questions and get to know the person, and that helps build a relationship and a positive experience for her."

We added an extra layer to this by creating something called the Secret Service.

"If you're talking to a patient and you learn they have a couple of dogs or their mother just died," Chris said, "or anything pertinent that is personal, we put it in the notes in their file, and highlighted it in green. So the next time they came in, we'd ask, 'How are your dogs?' or say, 'I'm so sorry about your mom.' It makes the patient feel connected and that you care about her."

We also deepened relationships with humor. "Dr. Arredondo always made people laugh," Chris said. "That put people at ease. You want to have that kind of relationship. His humor made it easier to break the barrier with some patients."

Funny quotes on the chalkboard under, "Why do you want to have a baby?" also helped uplift patients' emotions. The idea to cover a wall with chalkboard paint came from watching a Ted Talk.

Another way to create harmonious relationships is to find a common link with someone. "A lot of times before patients came in," Chris said, "we had information records. If they were from a different country, and if Dr. Arredondo had experience and knew anything about that country, he would share it with that patient and could make that connection. Then it's easier to have conversations and communicate to create a good experience."

Providing transparency also created a harmonious experience, and showed another example of how we borrowed from other industries—as I described in my PowerPoint presentation in Denver. In a restaurant, you feel better about eating there when you can see into the open kitchen to make sure it's clean, bright, and bustling with expert chefs using fresh food. The same goes for our laboratory. We loved that our patients were allowed to watch through a window as our technicians manipulated the eggs under a microscope, literally creating the life that would be implanted in the mom's body. When you demystify the process, and make your patients feel part of it, you engender trust and loyalty.

I learned how to do this even better while reading a 1971 book called *On Caring* by Milton Mayeroff, which *Psychology Today* suggests as "obligatory reading" because it summarizes a philosophy that enhances everything we do.[31]

On Caring was so influential, that when we were designing our fertility center, I gave the book to artist Carmen Martinez-Jover[32] and asked her to paint artwork for our centers that symbolized our mission to our patients. She started painting with the concept of an empty chair, which symbolized infertility. We hung that painting in every office; it represents the opportunity to fill the chair with human life.

Painting by Carmen Martinez-Jover

Paco's Eight Ways to Nurture Relationships with Patients

The artist created this painting to convey our promise: **"We guide patients through a transformation: Today you, tomorrow a family™."** We also pledged that: **"By combining the most advanced technology with the finest human touch, our goal is to provide World Class Fertility Care™."** To do this, we practiced Paco's Eight Ways to Nurture Relationships with Patients, which the artist presents as eight puzzle pieces on the painting, each representing one of Milton Mayeroff's tenets from *On Caring*. Here they are:

- **Patience: (upper left)** Confer patience generously to allow the patient to grow in his/her own time and own way. Give space by giving the patient "room to live," to set their own pace and participate in their own decisions. *The rocking chair calmly awaits each aspiring parent to craft the best decisions for their own circumstances.*

- **Trust: (upper middle)** Take a risk into the unknown with your patients. Patients need to trust the person providing care. *Thus, the openness of this chair, looking directly at you and the birds, displays trust.*

- **Honesty: (upper middle)** Offer sincerity to the patient's feelings and concerns. Be open to yourself and others. Be honest enough to accept our patients for who they actually are, rather than how we would like them to be. *The open, two-seated chair symbolizes that trust and honesty are intertwined. The chair represents the importance of being present to the fertility patient as a form of honesty to the moment.*

- **Hope: (upper right)** Identify all the possibilities at every step with your patient. This hope is not an idealized future at the expense of the present, but rather a present alive with a sense of the possible. *This piece characterizes the importance of keeping the faith, like a sunflower following the light and keeping the focus on what is brilliant. The dove is the spiritual aspect of the journey.*

- **Alternating Rhythms: (bottom right)** Develop the capacity to take many different viewpoints and use a broad perspective to confront the difficulties. Seek to balance attention to detail and to understand the larger context. *The swinging hammock allows you to see the same object from different angles and distances, adjusting the focus in a fluid manner.*

- **Courage: (bottom middle)** Demonstrate your determination to achieve a dream despite adverse and unknown conditions and the risk of emotional hurt. *The cushions symbolize the courage you must grasp when you experience emotionally difficult moments.*

- **Knowing: (bottom round seats)** Cultivate the willingness to deeply know your patients. Caring is to know a patient and understand their needs by responding to them. Accept patients' strengths and weaknesses. Good intentions alone do not guarantee a caring response. *Two seats—knowing a person can be **explicit**: being able to articulate information that we know about the patient, and **implicit**: sensing information that one is incapable of expressing verbally.*

- **Humility: (bottom left)** Be willing to learn from the one cared for. This requires overcoming the arrogance that exaggerates the power of the one who is caring, at the expense of the one who is being cared for. *This chair rests gently on the side, almost as a humble spectator.*

These are the elements of the *Philosophy of Care* at RMA described by philosopher Milton Mayeroff in his 1971 book, *On Caring.*

Doctors as Actors, and a Practice as a Stage for Street Theater

Every day, we perform roles where we master the emotional, physical, and intuitive powers that each requires to influence our lives and those around us in the best way.

Not convinced? Think about the tone of voice, the facial expressions, and the behaviors you exhibit when talking with your partner or spouse. You know exactly what to say and how to say it to make them feel loved, valued, heard, comforted, and secure. In the best relationships, this comes from your authentic desire to show love for that person. That authenticity is the secret sauce for a MedikalPreneur. When you can reach deep down and show the same compassion and professional desire to help your patients as you do for your family members, you'll be limitless.

As for how we play roles in life, think about the personae you present to your colleagues and your boss. It's more formal and professional with appropriate speech and behavior. Next, consider the personality that you exhibit when interacting with people at your place of worship, your child's school, your gym, and the grocery store.

We're always playing a different role, depending on the situation, or the stage. We've mastered a variety of voices, expressions, and actions—we may even walk differently and reach into a repertoire of tactics that help us achieve a goal, such as being extra polite and complimentary to the restaurant hostess who will hopefully reward you with the best table. As William Shakespeare wrote in the opening lines of *As You Like It:*[33]

All the world's a stage,

And all the men and women merely players;

They have their exits and their entrances,

And one man in his time plays many parts,

His acts being seven ages.

The seven ages refer to the phases that we experience from infant-hood to old age. One is "soldier," and I assert that, as medical professionals, we're working on the front lines of society to liberate ourselves and our patients to transform exponentially, by welcoming them into a life-changing drama.

You are the producer, director, and writer. The stage is your office. You build the set, control lighting, sound, and props. You compose the script to provide the dialogue and actions for yourself and the cast—your staff. You craft the patient's story that begins with a conflict—a health problem such as failure to get pregnant—and leads to a climax (having a baby and a starting a family), then to a positive conclusion. Your production gets rave reviews, which draw more people into your MedikalPreneurial Theatre.

My childhood background with a poetry and theatre performance group in grade school—plus my lifelong passion for making people laugh as "a clown," as I sometimes call myself—made me fall in love with these ideas! So I applied my knowledge of the different types of theater and performances, and the concept of a business as a stage, and created this template for you.

Stage Success Stories for Your Patients, Customers & Company

The MedikalPreneur on Broadway:

Presentations & Advertising

Like a Broadway show that can be performed for decades, your presentations and advertising follow the same script and never change. Like the show's writer, producer, and director, you completely control the content and performance. The audience watches and receives the information, but does not interact with its presentation.

The MedikalPreneur on Broadway:

TV & Film Productions

When you present scripted, recorded, and edited videos, automated messages, or situations/procedures that are orchestrated down to the smallest detail, you're presenting a Matching Theatre experience. You entice them with humor, emotionally appealing messaging, and even promises of adventure.

As a MedikalPreneur, you're also the writer, producer, and director, and must ensure a cohesive viewing experience for the customer or patient.

And like reviews on a performance, you're seeking five stars, which you can attain by applying customer feedback to adjust the script and how you present products and services while maintaining quality control and improving the patient/customer experience accordingly.

The MedikalPreneur's Street Theater:

Public Events & Staff Presentations

Like a street performer who's constantly adjusting to a shifting audience, and aiming to keep its attention, you follow Street Theatre format during a product launch, public meetings, and staff presentations. The audience can comment, criticize, interrupt, cheer, ask questions, and even participate in demonstrations of a product or service.

The MedikalPreneur's Street Theater:

The MedikalPreneur's Theater

Patient emergencies... power outages... an irate customer... an adverse reaction to medication. Every doctor is trained to quickly and effectively resolve medical emergencies. This is improv theater at its best; making it up as you go along, to address the situation and create the best possible outcome.

When you apply this same skill to your business, you think quickly in fast-changing and unexpected circumstances to create the best possible outcome—and even avert disaster. You can also apply this during unpredictable conversations and situations that arise when a patient or customer walks into the lobby and approaches the receptionist, or when someone calls with unique questions or solicitations.

Here are some diagrams that reinforce this concept:

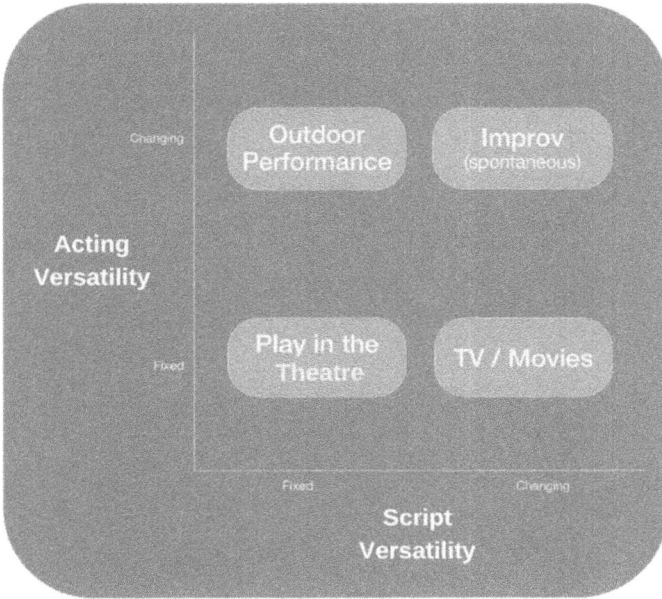

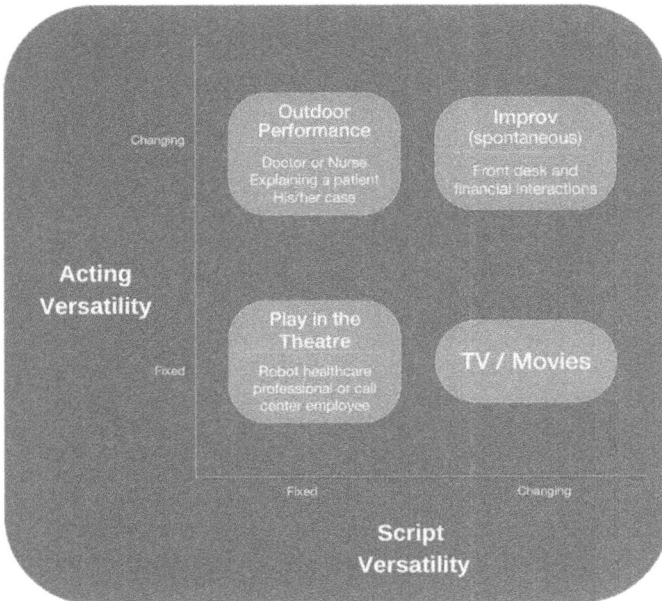

CHAPTER 4

Business Vitals: Accounting Basics for MedikalPreneurs

PRIOR TO DIVING INTO the numbers and accounting, I want to give you a simple and practical overview of the core dynamics and players in what a MedikalPreneur aims to create: a functional company.

A company is a structured legal entity that delivers value to a customer. This value could be a product, service, experience, or a transformation. The company provides resources such as: equipment, technology, human talent, or financial elements whose value converts into a product, service, experience or transformation that has *more* value than the input. This concept, exemplified in the diagram on the left, can represent any profit company.

The owners of a company are called shareholders and usually provide money (capital) to start a business, or they buy it after it's created. In return, if the company is profitable, the shareholders receive distributions or dividends for their financial risk. Other interested actors who benefit from the company's good performance are called stakeholders. They do not directly own the company as shareholders do. Stakeholders could be customers who benefit from the value added by the company; that's why the company needs to know what the customer wants.

The human talent (employees) will benefit by receiving a salary, the banks will provide loans and benefit from the revenue deposits made, and the suppliers need to be paid with money generated by the company. Also, the government and other authorities will benefit from the company's good performance because they will pay taxes as well as improve the development of the business' locale. Finally, the environment, country, culture, and attitude of the place where the business is located will have a positive or negative impact on the company's performance. In summary, the stakeholders have an interest in the company performing or not, and influence the dividends and profits that the shareholders will receive. The following diagram illustrates this point.

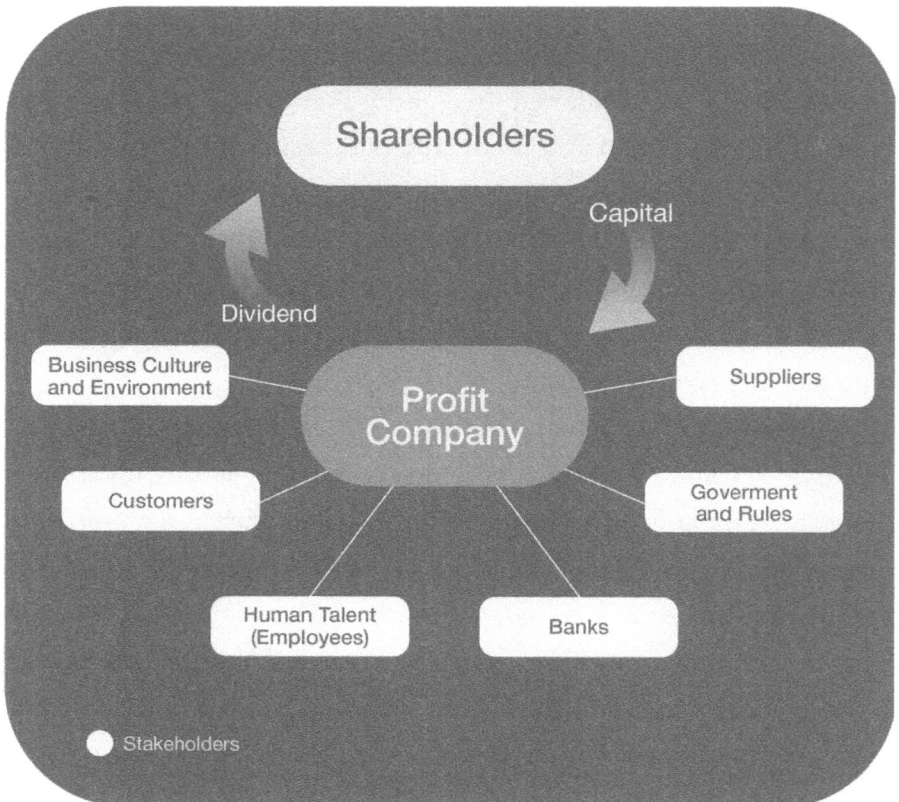

Now, let's go back to accounting. If this word short-circuits your mind—you're a physician, not an accountant, after all—then this chapter will illuminate a simple way to think about business terms as a MedikalPreneur. Accounting speaks in numbers—so do doctors! We're trained to assess the patient's conditions with numbers. We already speak this language. For example, here's how we describe a patient's health status: "BP 120 over 80, temperature 99.8, Pulse-oximeter 99, resting heart rate 65, blood sugar 113, respiratory frequency 18." This language of healthcare professionals around the world is all about the numbers.

The same is true for the financial wellness of your business. Now it's time to connect how we as physicians measure our patients' vital statistics with numbers, and how we as MedikalPreneurs assess our company's financial health with numbers.

I'll make it easy by providing a simple shift to learn accounting terms and apply the same mentality that you use for keeping a patient healthy—to owning and operating a business that thrives. And what about the math? The math required to run a company is simpler than anything you encountered in pre-med algebra and calculus courses. Accounting math is simple. You'll rarely need division or multiplication; you'll only need addition and subtraction. Furthermore, the math in accounting ALWAYS matches, and always balances.

Learn the MedikalPreneur's Accounting Lexicon

In medical school, you memorized a new vocabulary, then used these words and phrases so often during your training that they became a second language that you could probably recite in your sleep. Accounting has its own lexicon, and your success as a MedikalPreneur requires this crash course to master these concepts that comprise the golden rules of accounting. My goal is to boost your confidence and help you think, speak, and work confidently with terms that include: debit, credit, assets, liabilities, balance sheets, profit and loss, cash flow projection, cost of goods sold, income, and expenses. You will soon use these words and phrases as instinctively as you may say MRI, APGAR, or SOAP note.

Here is a diagram explaining accounting terms and how they relate to one another. I created a sentence that forms an acronym to help you remember these basic concepts that are the financial foundation of your business.

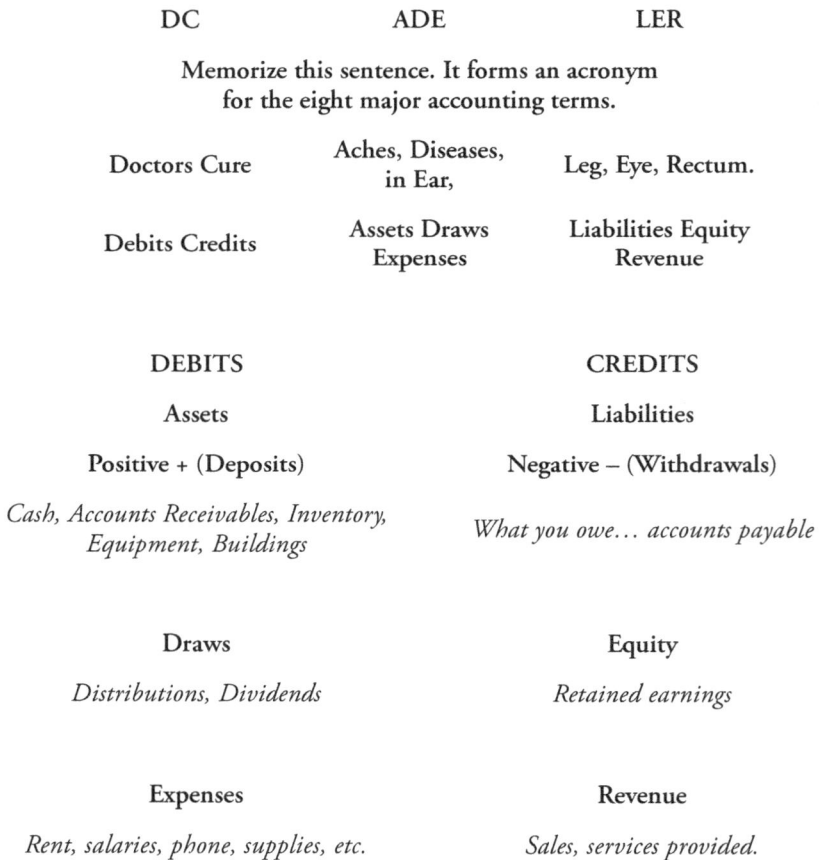

DC	ADE	LER

Memorize this sentence. It forms an acronym
for the eight major accounting terms.

Doctors Cure	Aches, Diseases, in Ear,	Leg, Eye, Rectum.
Debits Credits	Assets Draws Expenses	Liabilities Equity Revenue

DEBITS	CREDITS
Assets	Liabilities
Positive + (Deposits)	Negative − (Withdrawals)
Cash, Accounts Receivables, Inventory, Equipment, Buildings	*What you owe… accounts payable*
Draws	Equity
Distributions, Dividends	*Retained earnings*
Expenses	Revenue
Rent, salaries, phone, supplies, etc.	*Sales, services provided.*

What You Have Minus What You Owe Equals What You Own

The MedikalPreneur's Rules of Accounting are based on the mathematical fact that what you have, minus what you owe, equals what you own. So remember:

Debits always equal credits. On an accounting grid, you record a debit in the left column and a credit in the right column. The numbers are always the same, but one is positive and one is negative. This is an equal and opposite transaction: if a debit of $800 increases the balance in an account, the balance of the opposite account will decrease $800 with a credit. A **debit** adds value to an asset or expense account, or it diminishes equity, liability, or revenue accounts.[34] A **credit** enriches equity, liability, or revenue accounts, or it reduces an asset or expense account.[35] Every time you do a financial transaction, you record one number in the left column for the debit, and the same number in the right column for the credit.

Owner's Equity Equals Assets Minus Liabilities. Your **Assets** are what you own and can liquidate into cash; assets include buildings, equipment, inventory, accounts receivables, vehicles, and cash. **Liabilities**—also known as accounts payable—are your debts to other people or businesses. They are usually classified as short-term, long-term, and other liabilities. You can compute your **Equity**—or shareholders' equity or owners' equity (privately owned companies)—by subtracting your liabilities from your assets. Very simply, total assets (things your company owns) are the sum total of your equity (the value of what you own), plus your liabilities (what you owe).

Draws are withdrawals of company cash and assets by the owner for personal use. Draws can include distributions and dividends. A draw computes on the books as a credit to the cash account and a debit to the account that the owner has designated for withdrawals.

Expenses include rent, salaries, utilities, supplies, and insurance.

A **Fixed Cost**, as the name implies, is an expense that a company must pay regardless of how much money it's earning or losing. A monthly mortgage payment or rental payment are examples of fixed costs. Schedules and contracts often dictate the payments. Fixed costs are recorded on the balance sheet, income statement, and cash flow statement.

Variable Cost refers to a fluctuation in pricing when the company increases or decreases production of a product or delivery of a service. If production of the dental device that your company sells increases due to more business, then your Variable Costs will spike to cover the cost of materials required to manufacture the dental device. For example, if you spent five cents on the material to create each device you produce, and last month you manufactured 1000 pieces (1000 x $0.05 = $50.00), in this month, you have produced 2500 pieces (2500 x $0.05 = $125.00). Therefore, this $125 expense is for this month—instead of the $50 expense of the last month on the same item—equals the variable cost.

Cost of Goods Sold (COGS) are the expenses required to produce goods or services sold by the company. Examples include the supplies and salaries necessary to create the good and/or service. It does not include the expenses incurred by the sales team.

Operating Expenses are the costs not related to the direct creation of goods and/or services sold. Here we include the sales team, administrative and general expenses such as legal costs, rent, office supplies, insurance, electricity, etcetera.

Revenue is income-generated from sales and/or services provided. There are two kinds of **Profits: Gross and Net. Gross Profit** is also known as sales profit or gross income and is the surplus that a company or individual creates after taking away the costs of making and selling its products, or the costs incurred while providing its services. In general, Gross Profit excludes fixed costs. **The Formula** is Gross

Profit = Revenue − Cost of Goods Sold (COGS).

Net Profit, also known as **Net Income or Net Earnings,** is the calculation of taking the Total Sales or Revenue and taking away the COGS, operating expenses, depreciation, interest, taxes, and all other expenses. This is what investors want to see and is a marker of the company's profitability.

Depreciation describes a reduction in the value of an asset with the passage of time, due in particular to wear and tear. When you buy a car or equipment, the price for which you can sell it next year is lower. So if you bought a piece of equipment for $15,000, next year the equipment is going to cost—let's say $12,000—so you have a depreciation of $3,000. Typically, equipment is depreciated over several years, depending on what it is. The IRS will determine the timeframe. As an example, equipment, cars, and computers depreciate over five years and office furniture for seven years. Here are two diagrams that illustrate these points.

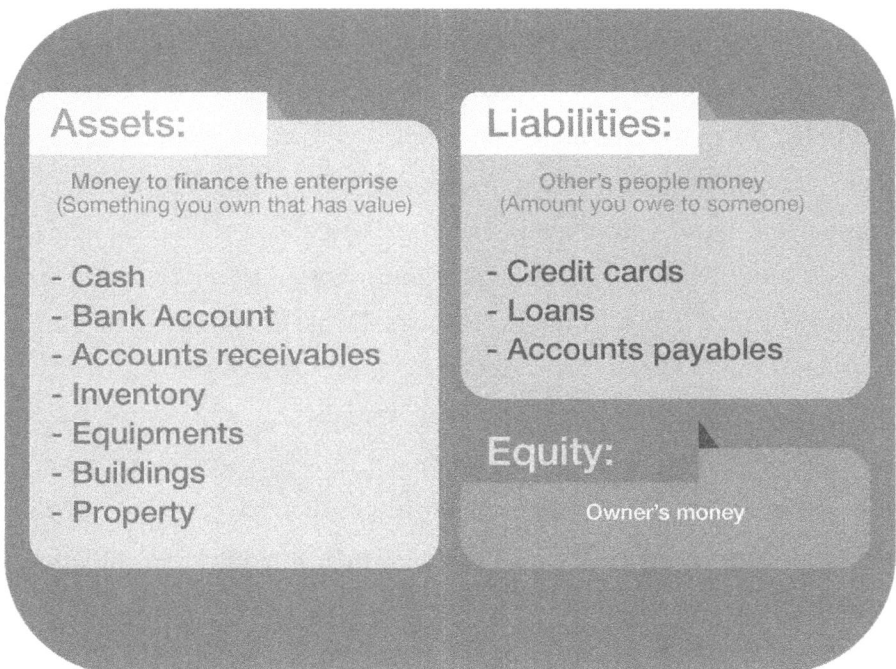

Assets:

Money to finance the enterprise
(Something you own that has value)

- Cash
- Bank Account
- Accounts receivables
- Inventory
- Equipments
- Buildings
- Property

Liabilities:

Other's people money
(Amount you owe to someone)

- Credit cards
- Loans
- Accounts payables

Equity:

Owner's money

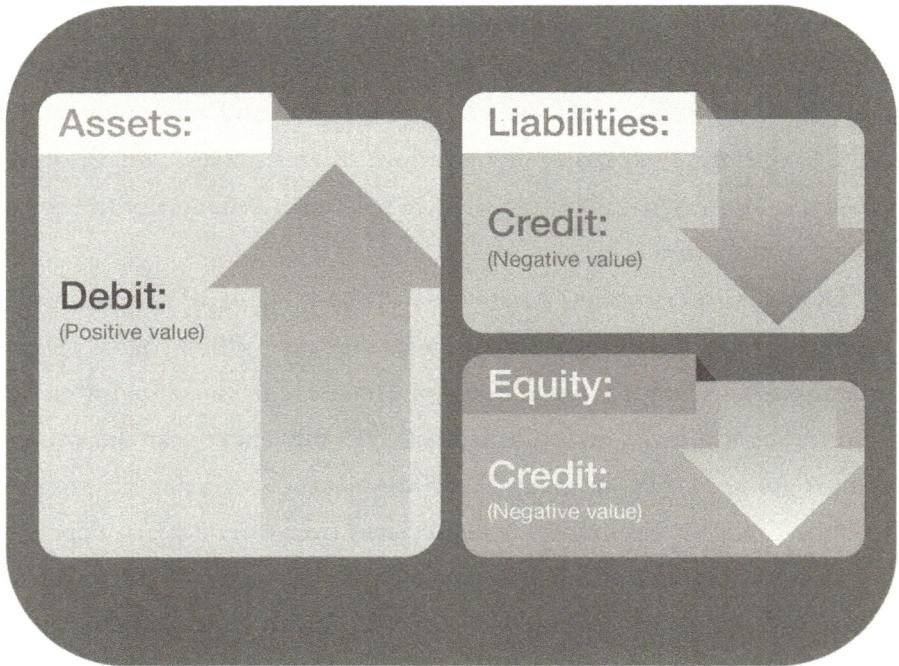

The above information is organized in three main documents that you'll use to measure, maintain, and grow your company's financial wellness. When you're treating a patient, you need to understand his past, present, and future condition; similarly, you will use the same approach for your company by using three financial statements.

It's also prudent to discern among Financial Accounting and Managerial Accounting. There are some similarities in how you obtain both and how you use them. However, there are also some significant differences. In general, the financial accounting is used for people outside the functionality of the company. The idea is to give an accurate picture of the financial health of the company for investors, creditors, and business regulators. In other words, Financial Accounting is to inform stakeholders and shareholders. These Financial Accounting reports have to follow very specific rules and policies to inform the external players. Also, the Financial Accounting describes what has happened and looks at the past. On the other hand, the Managerial Accounting is provided for the internal members of the company to make decisions and to motivate and inspire their team members of the organization. So, their use will impact the company in the future. These reports are not regulated; they are optional, not mandatory. Managerial Accounting is done much more frequently and is more detailed than the Financial Accounting. See the differences in the table.

	Management Accounting	Financial Accounting
Legality of the Reports	Optional	Mandatory
Detailing	High Level	Low level
Time Frequency	Intensive (instant, daily, weekly)	Annual or Semi-Annual
Uniformity	Varies by company	Standardized
Who uses it?	Internal players	External players
Time Perspective	Future	Past

Here's another way to see this in parallel with the example of the Intensive Care Unit. The language and detail that you use to communicate with relatives of the patient in the ICU are more general and less detailed than the report and language you use to monitor your patient and communicate with your team to manage your patient's performance in the ICU. These reports and language used to coordinate care inside the ICU are "Managerial Accounting."

The Balance Sheet, Profit & Loss Statement, and Cash Flow Projections

In the hospital, your patient's file contains all the vital information you need about past health conditions, current vitals, and future prognosis. This file is your go-to place for an immediate understanding and assessment of the patient's health. You use medical jargon to describe what's happening in the chart.

In your business, you can get an immediate understanding of your company's financial status by checking the **Balance Sheet, Profit & Loss Statement,** and **Cash Flow Projections.** These are the three pillars of a MedikalPreneur's financial success. You will use these three fundamental financial vital signs for your business, the same way that you assess the health of an individual.

1. A Balance Sheet shows the PRESENT financial figures. Balance Sheet = Today. It's a snapshot of now.

2. A Profit and Loss Statement shows the PAST financial history. It's sometimes called the Income Statement. Profit and Loss and Income Statement are the same. It involves a determined period of time.

3. The Cash Flow Projections document illustrates expected FUTURE financial trends. This is also known as Proforma. Think of this as predictions.

A simple way to remember and understand these terms is to use the analogy of a movie. The Balance Sheet is the scene we're watching right now. The Profit & Loss Statement is the past—everything that already happened in the film, and the backstory. The Cash Flow Projections predict what will happen in the rest of the movie, as well as in sequels that tell the story for years to come.

You can also use sports as an analogy for understanding these terms. The Balance Sheet is the score during the game that's happening right now. The Profit & Loss Statement is the team's past history, including this season's wins and losses, and how they're doing during this game. This provides a big picture overview that shows how the team is performing generally. Often, past performance can predict future wins and losses, unless new tactics are implemented to improve the players' performance. You can apply that to your business: if you have a losing streak, the P&L Statement can help you identify the financial drain, so you can take swift and effective action and embark on a winning trend.

The Cash Flow Projections are the analysis and predictions about how the team will do for the rest of the season and during the coming year. Keep in mind the Cash Flow Projections are only expected or hypothetical results given certain assumptions. Here's a diagram that illustrates this concept.

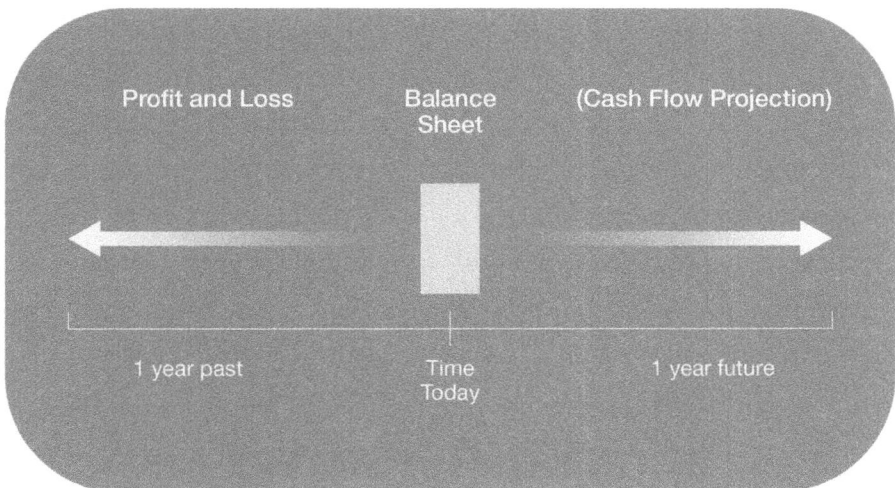

This document is called a **Balance Sheet** because it always balances. In business, because the Credits and Debits always balance to zero, and because the Assets will always be equal to Liabilities plus Equity, you will take periodic snapshots of these accounting elements on a Balance Sheet.

Viewing the accounting basics of your business through the lens of a physician in the Intensive Care Unit simplifies these concepts. In both cases, you're seeking balance and wellness. Just like when you enter the ICU and look at the patient's fluid intake and output, the levels have to match; the result must be zero. If not, the patient is either retaining fluids or losing fluids. When you use your MedikalPreneurial accounting, you're seeking a financial balance that will lead to prosperity for your business.

So let's continue the comparison to the patient in the ICU. It's very important to make this connection because the hospital is where some physicians have spent many years; it's where you feel comfortable and confident. You make decisions and you lead teams with the goal of promoting wellness for your patients. You and your medical team will be constantly monitoring her status; you will be aware of her health history prior to this medical crisis, know all the stats on her current condition, and use that information to tell the family how quickly she can recover and what the prognosis is for her future. In other words, you have a clear understanding of this patient's past, present, and future health.

In business, the three financial documents will perform this same task relating to money. First, the Balance Sheet is like taking the financial vitals of your business today—a snapshot that shows your financial status in this very moment. Compiling dollar amounts on the Balance Sheet equates to updating your ICU patient's chart right now. While doing that, understand the importance of making the numbers balance. When they don't add up, it's an alert that you need to identify the problem and find a solution. Your patient's life—and your company's viability—are at stake, so balancing these numbers is an exigent matter.

Finding an effective remedy requires the use of the **Profit & Loss Statement**, because it's like looking backwards in time to see how your "patient" has been behaving over a certain period of days, months, or years. In business, a Profit & Loss Statement can cover a quarter or an entire year. Likewise, reviewing your patient's immediate past health history enables you as the physician to design a treatment plan to help the patient recover enough to leave the ICU and embark on a journey toward full recovery. As a MedikalPreneur, you will create Cash Flow Projections to strategize how to maximize your company's greatest potential. The following compares these points.

ICU Patient Assessment as a Metaphor for the MedikalPreneur's Financial Health

		In ICU	In Business
PAST	Profit & Loss Statement	When Patient arrived, what was her status and what improvement did she have during one week in the ICU? Did the BP stabilize? Is the temperature better? Is she gaining weight? Did we get rid of all the fluids? What are all the health events relating to this ailment that have occurred until now?	What money was lost before now? Where are the most expenses occurring? What do we sell the most? What provides us better margins? How much of the operating expenses are due to rent or labor?

		In ICU	In Business
PRESENT	**Balance Sheet**	How is the Patient doing right now? What is the urgent matter that must be addressed? For example, "This patient is going to suffer and decompensate if we don't drain that fluid from the belly!"	The Balance Sheet will tell you what's happening NOW. How much money do we have? To whom do we owe money? When do we have to pay next? How much operating cash do we have? What savings opportunities are available?
FUTURE	**Cash Flow Projections**	What is the Patient's future prognosis? When do we expect the Patient to leave the ICU and begin intermediate care? Will she need physical therapy or rehabilitation? What is expected for her future quality of life and health status?	The Cash Flow Projections forecast the company's future cash flow for earnings and expenses. When are we reaching break-even? When do we predict the company will begin making a profit?

Notes:

_____

_____

_____

_____

_____

Business Vitals...

One way to look at the Balance Sheet equation is ASSETS = LIABILITIES + SHAREHOLDERS (EQUITY). Also consider the following:

1. All of the Resources and things that have value in the company (ASSETS) belong or can be claimed by somebody:

   a. An outsider of the company (Liabilities);

   b. Owners of the company (Shareholders or Equity).

Another way to look at this is to think of your house. The ASSET is your house. What you owe is your Mortgage; that is the LIABILITY. And what you have paid, your equity, is your SHAREHOLDING.

Understanding More About Your Profit & Loss Sheet

As you know now, the **Profit & Loss Sheet** covers a period of time, usually the whole year. Also known as an **Income Statement**, it shows the revenues, costs, and expenses over a specified period of time, such as a fiscal quarter or a fiscal year. A company can use this information to measure its future ability—or inability—to profit because it pinpoints where more revenue should be generated, as well as where expenses should be reduced. The P&L Sheet has two sections: Operating Expenses and Non-Operating Expenses. Here is an explanation for each.

Operating Expenses—OPEX—are the costs of running the business on a daily basis, and these costs are not related to producing products or delivering services. These expenses comprise the bulk of the company's expenses, and include: rent or mortgage payments, utilities, salaries and wages, property taxes, and business travel,[36] as well as compensation, payroll tax costs, benefits, and pension plan contributions for non-production employees. Operating Expenses also include: legal fees, property taxes, utilities, office supplies, and rent for non-production facilities. Marketing, advertising, direct mailings, travel, and literature such as brochures are also Operating Expenses.[37]

Costs of Goods Sold—COGS—is the amount of money required to provide a product or service. For example, if your clinic is providing injections, you need to calculate the cost of labor for the nurse, the price of the medicine that's being injected, the needle, the cotton balls, the alcohol wipes, the latex gloves, and any other expenses associated with delivering an injection.

If your business sells back braces, you need to compute the cost that the manufacturer charges you for each brace, the labor for the team member who does the fitting and training on how to use it, and any accessories that may be required to use the brace. If you own a spa and you specialize in massages to treat specific ailments, then you must know the compensation for your massage therapist for each service performed, as well as any oils, ointments, and other items that the service requires.

All of the previously mentioned expenses are **Direct Costs**, which are materials and salaries for your team members. You can also consider the **Indirect Costs** for each product and service, which includes the overhead expenses of mortgage or rent, utility bills, and salaries for your support staff and office administrators.[38] Once you calculate the COGS, then you can determine your mark-up to set a price for the product or service that enables you to profit.

Non-Operating Expenses account for anything you have to pay that does not relate to core business operations that you conduct on a daily basis. This can include interest payments or fees relating to international business that require currency exchanges. Other items that fit into this category can include one-time, unexpected expenses such as when you cancel a product and have inventory that you cannot use, or you're forced to radically change your operations and it incurs unexpected costs. You note these Non-Operating Expenses at the bottom of the income statement—hence, "the bottom line"—and they are subtracted from operating profits.[39]

Here are examples of an **Income Statement**.

	Jan - Dec 16
Ordinary Income/Expense Income	
Donor Egg Bank Income	210,000.00
IVF	3,873,354.32
IVF Donor	-41,600.66
Clinical	
Intrauterine Inseminations	88,070.00
Office Visits	2,269,337.78
Clinical - Other	1,529.00
Total Clinical	2,358,936.78
Lab Work	1,066.00
Sub-Rent Income	17,350.00
Office Product Sales	9,100.00
Storage Embryos	94,819.55
Total Income	6,523,025.99
Cost of Goods Sold	
Anesthesia services	92,325.00
Donor Fees	50,600.00
Gases for lab	26,544.59
Health Insurance for Donor	3,900.00
Labor	
Nursing services	52.86

Business Vitals...

			Jan - Dec 16
	Andrology		33,376.00
	Physicians		815,137.82
	Embryology		335,634.00
Nursing			474,833.42
Payroll Taxes			-124.26
Total Labor			1,658,909.84
Lab Accreditation			10,961.85
Lab Work Expense			298,609.84
Lease - Medical Equipment			161,092.68
Medical Supplies			286,370.24
Utilities - Electricity			46,104.63
Total COGS			2,635,418.67
		3,887,607.32	
Expense			
Donor Egg Bank USA			30,495.00
Advertising and Promotion			35,110.23
Alarm System Expense			1,592.88
Automobile Expense			
License & Fees		33.69	
Gas		1,859.66	
Repairs and Maintenance		794.59	
Total Automobile Expense			2,687.94
Automobile Leasing Expense			13,791.29
Bad Debts			0.00
Bank Service Charges			3,680.72

Billing Service Fees Paid		73,606.15
Bonus		
Clinical Bonus	14,475.92	
Doctor Bonus	131,748.00	
Donor Program Bonus	7,854.48	
Lab Bonus	52,725.80	
PA's Bonus	10,912.00	
Bonus - Other	266.85	
Total Bonus		217,983.05
Business Gift		3,056.44
Computer and Internet Expenses		870.47
Continuing Education		7,053.92
Collection Fee		-21.63
Credit Card Discount Fees....		
Credit Card Patients pmts	65,348.73	
CC Fee Dr Arredondo	78.54	
Total Credit Card Discount Fees....		65,427.27
Charitable Contributions		25.00
Human Resources Adv.		410.00
Depreciation Expense		25,473.00
Dues and Subscriptions		
Other-Dues	1,637.17	
DEA	731.00	
SART	2,668.00	
Local County Medical Society	1,023.00	
State Medical Assoc.	1,772.00	
CLIA (laboratory license)	300.00	

Business Vitals...

ASRM	3,550.00	
State Board of Medical Li	685.76	
AMA	710.00	
Notary	183.88	
Dues and Subscriptions - Other	450.00	
Total Dues and Subscriptions	13,710.81	
Insurance Expense		
Supp H	-301.60	
Accid	-920.66	
Critic	-1,088.64	
Disability Insurance for RMA	4,551.36	
Short Term Disability Insurance	-2,552.21	
Car Insurance	3,843.99	
General Liability Insurance	8,591.43	
Health Insurance	107,722.08	
Life and Disability Insurance	3,430.52	
Malpractice Insurance	57,724.67	
Worker's Compensation	8,921.28	
Total Insurance Expense		189,922.22
Interest Expense		481.68
Janitorial Expense		39,932.81
Lease - Administrative Eqt		38,229.21
License and Permits		325.00
Management Fee Ataraxy		319,136.54
Marketing		
Marketing Meals	33,264.70	
Marketing - Other	8,835.88	

Total Marketing		42,100.58
Meals and Entertainment		
Entertainment	704.61	
Meals	21,960.94	
Meals and Entertainment - Other	39.19	
Total Meals and Entertainment		22,704.74
Mileage		821.00
Office Supplies and Expenses		55,688.02
Parking		229.26
Payroll Expenses		
Ataraxy Management	414,437.05	
Retirement Plan	24,487.44	
Wages	247,274.43	
Payroll Tax Expense	121,796.95	
Payroll Expenses - Other		
Total Payroll Expenses		
Pest Control		
Postage and Delivery		
Printing and Reproduction		
Professional Fees		
Consultant		
Management Fees		
Donor Eligibility		
Physicians services		
Psychological Evaluations		
Payroll Fees		
Accounting		

Legal Fees

Total Professional Fees

Rent Expense

Repairs & Maint

    IVF HVAC

    Service Maintenance Agreement

    Repairs and Maintenance

    Generator

Total Repairs & Maint

Service Agreement Termination

Small Fixed Assets

    Computer Equipment Exp

Total Small Fixed Assets

Smart IVF

Software Program and Services

    Software Program

    Software Services

Total Software Program and Services

Storage

Taxes

    Franchise Tax

    Property Taxes

Total Taxes

Telephone Expense

Travel Expense

    Gas - Travel

    Meals

    Travel

Total Travel Expense

Uniforms Expenses

Uniforms	4,167.28
Laundry - Uniforms & Linens	6,137.71
Uniforms Expenses - Other	-7.96
Total Uniforms Expenses	10,297.03
Utilities	4,109.57
Total Expense	2,803,113.44
Net Ordinary Income	1,084,493.88
Other Income/Expense	
Other Income	
Other Income	50.00
Passthru Income/Loss-Smart IVF	-193,260.00
Total Other Income	-193,210.00
Other Expense	
Ask My Accountant	-982.24
Passthru N/D Exp-Smart IVF	522.00
Total Other Expense	-460.24
Net Other Income	-192,749.76
Net Income	**891,744.12**

The **Cash Flow Statement** illustrates cash increases and decreases during a specific period, which can be year-to-date, one quarter, one year, or another timespan. The document is divided into three sections for cash used for operations, investments, and finance. The Cash Flow Projection lists *anticipated* amounts of money that will flow into the company while taking into consideration the money that will flow out as expenditures. This is different than the "bottom line" for the business, because cash flow challenges can afflict a business even when it's profiting. For example, if your customers pay in advance for one month of the services you provide, and your company has a large tax bill that's also due that month, then how is your company going to pay its regular expenses and the tax bill? Although your business might make enough money next month to make up the difference and still make a profit at the end of the quarter or year, your company has immediate obligations that must be paid now.

Very importantly, the Cash Flow Statement begins with "cash and cash equivalents, beginning of period," and concludes with "cash and cash equivalents, ending of period."

Earnings Before Interest, Taxes, Depreciation, and Amortization—EBITDA—Is a Helpful Tool for The MedikalPreneur

You can measure your company's profitability with a financial measurement tool known as **EBITDA.** This is an acronym for Earnings Before Interest, Taxes, Depreciation, and Amortization. **Amortization** is the process of making regular payments to reduce or pay off a debt.

EBITDA is "a measure of a company's overall financial performance and is used as an alternative to simple earnings or net income in some circumstances,"[40] according to Investopedia. Think of EBIDTA as the money you have after net profit, which is also known as the operating income. Your EBITDA gives you buying power to expand your business, because lenders see it as strong financial leverage for your ability to profit in the future. For example, if you want to purchase a manufacturing company, and you have $1 million EBITDA, you can purchase that company for $3 million. Your EBITDA multiplies by three. The financier loans you three times your actual EBITDA because it shows your ability to wage a strong financial performance with the company that you already have. Some companies, depending on the industry, can be sold/purchased for more or less multiples of EBITDA.

It's important to distinguish Cash Flow from EBITDA. The Cash Flow Statement is a more comprehensive overview of a company's financial status when compared to EBITDA, because it shows crucial categories such as taxes, loan interest, and income from investments.[41] The amount of your company's loan interest, taxes, and investment income all impact the liquidity of the business. It's typical today to use a Cash Flow Analysis with the EBITDA to provide a clearer picture of your company's value.

Understanding Your Cash Flow Analysis (Also known as PROFORMA)

A **Proforma** or **Cash Flow Analysis** is a standard financial statement that is useful to calculate projections or future results about how your business will perform.

Here's another way to think about it as a physician. If I want my patient to lose weight and improve her blood pressure and her hemoglobin A1c/her sugar, I will say, "If you stick to this regimen for one year, you will weigh this much and your numbers will be X, Y, Z, and most likely you won't need medication for blood pressure." That's a proforma in medical terms. It's a projection for results that will occur with adherence to a strategic plan that is created to attain specific results.

A Proforma is a grid showing what I expect my revenues and costs to be—projected out typically for three to five years. It's based on presumptions and assumptions on how your business will perform. So, for example, if I sell pens, and I expect to sell 50 pens at $10 each, I can project that I will have $500. Creating a pen costs me $11, so the first year I will lose money, as I received 50 to 100. Then, say, the cost of production drops to $5, so I buy 100.

100 pens manufactured for $5 each = $500 cost to manufacture

100 pens sold for $10 each = $1,000

Subtract $500 manufacturing cost = $500 profit

When I become profitable, I'm ahead, making financial gains. That's your Proforma.

Other Important Terms for the MedikalPreneur

Should you use accrual accounting or cash-based accounting? This is an important question, and you can decide by exploring the definitions of each.

Accrual is the accumulation or increase of something over time, especially payments or benefits. Accrual refers to anticipated revenue and expenses. The concept is similar to the ICU patient whom doctors anticipate will progress to physical therapy and learn to walk again.

Cash vs. Accrual. Timing is the main difference between cash and accrual accounting. For cash accounting, revenue and expenses are recognized in real time, whereas accrual accounting refers to anticipated revenue and expenses. Typically, small businesses use cash accounting, while corporations use accrual accounting. If you have a medical practice which normally uses cash-based accounting, and you're going to sell your practice to a corporation, you ought to change your accounting to accrual so you can streamline the process, or simply put, speak apples to apples. Your accountant can help achieve this. Make sure you hire your own accountant and do not rely on someone who is working for another company.

Cost Accounting. This is a crucial aspect of business, because you need to know how much it costs to perform a procedure, purchase supplies, and conduct everyday activities. If you don't know how much it costs to provide a consult, how do you know how much to charge? Some doctors calculate it based on how much insurance is paying, or what other doctors are charging. Instead, you should ask how much it costs you. Do an analysis to learn how much a product or service costs you in terms of supplies, time, personnel, fees, and other expenses. Then say, "I want a 10% or 20% margin on top of that." You can't know how to set a price for a product or service unless you know the cost of producing it. Only then can you calculate how much of a markup is required for you to profit. If you're charging too low, and not even realizing it, you'll lose money and put your company at risk.

Break Even Point Analysis occurs when your total costs and your total revenue are equal. It means that you "break even." You don't profit and you don't lose money.

Business Vitals Thrive with Teamwork

Knowing your numbers is imperative for running a successful MedikalPreneurial business. This helps you focus only on the things that will be profitable for you, and you lead your team to exercise financial savvy with these Business Vitals.

"We always believed that you're supposed to do more with less," recalled RN Chris Flynn. "When the staff realized that we were using and discarding special sterile gloves that cost $2.50 per pair every time we entered our Operating Room, we questioned whether this was necessary. Latex gloves are really expensive items that we ordered from medical supply companies. So we asked, 'What can we use to still give the patient the best possible care, but is not quite as expensive?' We have a very clean O.R., so we asked, 'Do we really need the expensive sterile gloves every time we walk into the O.R.?' and the answer after doing a study analyzing for safety and quality was, 'No, we don't.' So this is an example of how we changed little things throughout the practice, which financially made it really successful, but did not impact the care of the patient."

Chris said the mistake occurs when medical staffs routinely order items without questioning the cost or need.

"A lot of times, you don't think about the cost," Chris said. "You just order stuff. And we did a lot of orders through our medical supply company. But then I looked at the numbers and I said, 'Dr. Arredondo, this is how much this costs, but there are alternatives. We can get it for less.' Then he said, 'What would be more comparable?' and I found less expensive items." The basic rule here is NOT to compromise safety and quality, if you find an equivalent product that saves money.

Make Accounting Best Practices
Part of Your Company's Culture

Our team valued frugality because it maintained our center's best financial health, which benefited each of us and the services we provided to so many people. When our company thrived, our success ensured our jobs and enabled us to achieve our mission of helping people start families.

Once you become adept at understanding and applying these accounting practices as a MedikalPreneur, it's imperative that you inspire your team to proceed with vigilant fiscal responsibility to conserve money. Your prosperity creates a triple win for you, your team, and the people you serve.

CHAPTER 5

How to Build the Team: Paco's 5 H's of Hiring

Your Success as a MedikalPreneur Requires a Winning Team

Becoming a medical entrepreneur may sound like a solo journey, but your success requires a team of talented people who share your vision, and who feel empowered to influence the company's success and be rewarded for it. Each person brings talents and expertise, so together you can build the business, prosper, and expand, while the team helps you orchestrate an excellent experience for every patient, client, or customer.

This chapter explains the best ways to hire your team and create a winning culture for you, the employees, and the patients. The interests of these stakeholders—shareholders, employees, suppliers and patients (customers)—need to be aligned. It's kind of like the Anna Karenina Principle, which says that a deficiency in one area guarantees failure.[42]

My philosophy is best expressed by a scene in the 2004 movie, *The Miracle.*[43] Starring Kurt Russell as head coach Herb Brooks, it's about an amateur American men's hockey team that triumphs over the undefeated Russian team in the 1980 Winter Olympics at Lake Placid, New York. Coach Brooks' unconventional methods created a hybrid coaching style as he assembled the victorious team, even in the face of criticism by those who questioned his ambitious goal. The coach simply responded that he wasn't looking for "the best players." He was looking for "the right ones."[44]

Make this your mantra as a MedikalPreneur. This is the best way to approach hiring people who will work with you. Your company's success depends on the team members you hire for every position in your office. While you're the boss, the owner, and the visionary who created the business, your staff members become the voices and faces of the company because your patients will interact with them before they ever meet you.

Your receptionist answers the phone. The nurses greet patients and prepare them for consultations with the physician. The lab technician draws blood, takes x-rays, and performs tests. In our case, the Fertility Coaches developed close relationships with patients and their partners during their journeys toward becoming pregnant and creating a family. Given the highly emotional and intimate nature of our work, it was imperative that I recruited team members who could finesse these relationships with an exquisite "bedside manner" to make the patients feel pampered, protected, and optimistic about the outcome of their procedures.

Here's why the hiring process is so important: you need to use your instincts and keen observational skills to identify the best employees who will remain loyal and help you create long-term sustainability, prosperity, and expansion. Your staff helps you achieve this during every interaction with a patient—whether by phone or in person.

At the same time, even the staff members who do not interface with patients must perform with excellence and play a positive role in the chemistry of the team; otherwise, a slacker, a gossip, or a dishonest person can wreak havoc on the office dynamics, which can hurt employee morale, cause mistakes, drive away patients, and even result in lawsuits.

It's that simple. You establish a high standard for the code of conduct in your office that creates a beneficial environment and experience for the patients, staff, and business to thrive. Anyone who is not adding and multiplying positive contributions to all of the above, does not belong there. So don't be afraid to let go of employees who are not working to maximize success. Keep searching for and interviewing people until you find the best fit. You should "hire slow and fire fast."

In sports, when players aren't scoring for the team, they're traded or their contracts are not renewed. Apply this to your business. Your reputation and financial stability—as well as the patient's health, and even survival—are at stake. So it's best to minimize your risk by recruiting the right team. If an employee is not meeting your standards, you can counsel him or her, and provide additional training. But if he or she does not improve, then use Paco's Policy of Replacement: If people do not change, change the people.

How to Recruit Employees

The current shortage of healthcare providers is predicted to worsen by 2032, according to the Association of American Medical Colleges.[45] So it may be difficult to recruit the adequate physicians, nurses, and mid-level medical professionals to work at your company. You find the right talent with innovation and creative ideas. Here are a few.

Stay connected. Build relationships with medical schools, nursing schools, and colleges that train the technicians your company requires. Attend job fairs, speak to classes, mentor students, and ask professors to recommend promising individuals whom you can hire as interns while they're still in school.[46]

Tap your contacts. Do you remember a former colleague or classmate who specialized in a skill that you need in your business? Perhaps he or she would be a good fit for your company. At the same time, you can alert people in your network that you're seeking to hire people with particular talents and experiences, and ask for referrals.

Use technology. Today's job-seekers use websites via their phones and tablets. Applying for a job is as simple as uploading a resumé once, then clicking "apply" whenever an appealing job listing appears. We posted jobs on LinkedIn, Indeed, and Craigslist.

Many websites cater to healthcare recruiters, so get familiar with them and decide which ones you will use to post your job openings. Develop a system for regularly checking for new talent as resumés are posted, and join any groups on those sites where you may connect with candidates in your specialty. The Jama Career Center at careers.jama-network.com—operated by the American Medical Association—is a good place to start.[47] You can also use an applicant tracking system (ATS), which is software that manages your recruitment process.

Differentiate yourself as an employer. In a competitive market, you can lure the best talent by offering unique perks in addition to good salaries and insurance benefits. Think about any connections or unique experiences you can provide that other MedikalPreneurs may lack, such as season tickets to your town's sports teams. You may treat your staff to an annual retreat/vacation at your cottage in the mountains or at a beachside hotel. In today's climate of high student loan debt, you could incorporate loan repayment assistance into the employee's salary. A generous maternity leave policy could also seal the deal with desirable candidates. Perhaps your office has a private workout room with a shower that employees could use. Or your office may provide an on-site cafeteria where meals and snacks are free or subsidized. Be creative!

Hire an HR professional. If you have the financial ability to hire a human resources manager, he or she can help you recruit your team by knowing exactly where and how to look for ideal candidates. This person can also help arrange and manage interviews and all the paper-work, including tax documents required when hiring employees. If you can't afford a full time HR manager, you can contract the service through temporary staffing companies.

The Best MedikalPreneurs Hire "A" People

As a MedikalPreneur, it's time to leave your ego at the door and humbly approach the hiring process. By this, I mean it's important to have the confidence to hire people who are as smart as—or even smarter!—than you. These intelligent individuals will be representing you to the patients or clients. So you want each of them to shine for the team.

When I was recruiting for my team—which grew to 80 people—I preferred to hire people who were smarter, more experienced, and more innovative than me. I loved that they brought skills that I lacked to the business, because their expertise and experience could only make our company better. And because I'm a visionary—not a detail-oriented person—I needed people to execute my ideas with the skill sets required to do so. Find people who complement your skills and fill your voids.

Herein lies the challenge for some medical professionals: ego and confidence. I was confident in my abilities; therefore, I felt no threat or intimidation by the team members who were smarter than me. I viewed their talents as assets that helped us all; our single fertility clinic expanded to a multi-million-dollar network of 13 businesses.

This practice illustrates a pattern that I've witnessed over the years amongst entrepreneurs in every field. It's common for "A" people to hire other "A" people. This combination leads to success for everyone involved. At the same time, "B" people hire "C" people. A is the best; B is average; and C is low quality.

Why wouldn't someone always hire an A? Because they feel insecure and threatened; they want to be the smartest person in the office. That is not a clever business practice. You should hire people who will add to the team and make the sum bigger than its parts. This results from healthy collaboration. The Beatles are an excellent example of this. During the 1960s, this English rock band became a global phenomenon that transformed the music industry, ranked as the best-selling music group in history, and inspired cultural shifts everywhere. When the group split, its members—John Lennon, Paul McCartney, George Harrison, and Ringo Starr—enjoyed great success. But none achieved the historic, record-breaking status that they created together as a group.

Perhaps the best example of the team being greater than the individual was demonstrated during the 2003 World Athletics Championships.[48] The French women's 100-meter relay team was the underdog, competing against top-ranked Team USA, whose four members included the world's fastest woman at the time. In contrast, the French runners each had slower running times.

But the French women's teamwork shaved time by flipping the normal order of things. The runner holding the baton deliberately slowed her personal running time to ensure the fastest hand-off to the next runner, who usually shouldered the responsibility to catch up and take the baton. This individual sacrifice resulted in a victory for the team, which won a world championship. The women also illustrated that innovation breeds success. They shifted the burden of the baton to giving rather than receiving, and that made them world champions.

Paco's Five H's for Hiring and Why They're Important

Over the years, I've devised guidelines for identifying the best people to recruit to your MedikalPreneurial team. You should also apply these guidelines when you evaluate the compatibility of potential business partners, and anyone with whom you intend to commit to a working relationship as a MedikalPreneur. Here are Paco's Five H's for Hiring. Each describes a quality you should seek in your candidates.

1. **Hungry**

2. **Humble**

3. **Happy**

4. **Honest**

5. **Human Skills**

#1 HUNGRY—You want a go-getter, a person who's not looking for an excuse to leave early, and who's willing to do the extra steps. Hungry means being eager to go above and beyond what is requested, and always wanting to do better. If you're hungry, you have grit. The book, *Grit: The Power of Passion and Perseverance* by Angela Duckworth[49] explains why this is a crucial characteristic. As the title implies, passion and persistence create "grit" that breeds success. She compiled scientific evidence to prove this point about grit, which is rooted in Ikigai. It inspires an exceptional work ethic that's driven by hunger to do your best at something you love. In business, the financial reward for this service exemplifies how hunger and hard work lead to the satisfaction of finding one's sweet spot.

As a MedikalPreneur, you can entice the best team members by offering positions that satisfy their hunger to find their sweet spot. They'll enjoy working on the team, because they're using their talents to contribute to a greater cause. They love what they're doing. And they're financially rewarded for doing so.

#2 HUMBLE—This person understands that the team is more important than the individual. He or she should know that *I'm not the* *star.* The team is the star. The company's success is about the business' name on the sign in front of the building, not the name on the employee's ID badge. Likewise, in sports, the team's name on the front of the jersey is far more important than the player's name on the back.

Being humble also means knowing that you're there to learn, and that you don't know everything. Each person should practice humility by giving credit to the team. You learn from your team members, patients, clients, and customers. In fact, a lot of people pay thousands of dollars for consultants, who tell you the same thing that your customers will tell you if you're humble enough to listen to what can improve.

Being humble means admitting to mistakes and taking action to resolve any problem that resulted—without trying to pass blame or be defensive. In fact, telling your teammates about your mistake will help them learn how to avoid repeating it in the future.

RN Chris Flynn, who directed my daily operations for 18 years, recalled that any prospective employee "really had to have humility. You can tell when you're talking with someone. You want someone warm. Sometimes it's not always the best person, but it's the right person. Not someone with 100 degrees. They can be so impersonal that they're not going to convey the feeling that we want to create here in the clinic. If someone is sitting across from me, I want them to know that if I were their sister, I would take care of them the same way. We created an environment where everybody truly, truly cares about the patient."

We hired team members who understood that our workplace had no space for big egos or renegade behaviors and decisions; everyone agreed that our mission was to put the patient first, by maintaining a cohesive way of communicating and treating patients as a team. With five physicians on our team at RMA of Texas, this was extremely important, and we succeeded with the methods described in this chapter.

#3 HAPPY—Look for people who have a sunny disposition: they smile; their eyes sparkle; they exude joy and are quick to laugh and shrug off minor annoyances; and they may even joke about it. I'm known for making jokes; humor makes everyone feel better and creates a more pleasant working environment.

"Dr. Arredondo made things fun," recalls Tony Anderson, our embryologist and lab director at RMA of Texas. "At work, he was the guy who showed up wearing a red nose in the office, playing with people. He told me that while he was growing up in Mexico, he didn't want to go to medical school. He wanted to be a comedian or a politician. Since he always wanted to be a comedian, he's got a joke for everything."

Chris Flynn added, "Dr. Arredondo was very high spirited. When you have someone with that type of spirit and inspiration around you, it inspires people to do better."

Tony said my humor proved it's possible to be a serious businessperson and physician while still creating a light-hearted environment. To paraphrase the Irish writer Thomas Moore: You have to be able to make fun of yourself. The only way to defeat the devil is to make fun of him.

My natural inclination for fun and humor establishes my preference to be around other cheerful people—especially on our team in the workplace. That's why I always hired people who genuinely exuded an upbeat attitude that uplifted everyone. That's the kind of person you want on your team. This person boosts morale for the other employees, as well as for the patients. When things go wrong and difficulties inevitably arise, this genuinely happy person will help everyone persevere with a positive outlook.

Someone with a grumpy personality will do the opposite. Beware! This is not the person to hire, despite their stellar experience and impressive degrees. You'll identify this person immediately, sensing their negativity during an interview or during a phone call. These individuals tend to complain, point blame, and express pessimistic viewpoints.

This personality type is toxic for your work environment and should be tactfully avoided. Even if you're struggling to recruit ideal candidates, do not settle for hiring a person whose negative energy will cast a gloomy cloud over your company. This mistake will hurt you in every way, such as: causing conflict between team members; driving away patients who had a bad experience with that person; and triggering angry or disappointed patients to write negative online reviews, which hurts the business by encouraging potential new patients to avoid your company.

Of course, everyone has an occasional bad day. That's when it's time to take the day off and come back tomorrow when you feel better.

Here's the attitude that I expect from our employees: If you see the glass as half full, get a smaller glass, pour the water in, and watch it overflow. I want people who can shift their thinking to perceive a positive angle where others only see a problem. Niki Lauda,[50] a Formula One driver, had a terrible accident in 1976 that burned his face and sent him into a coma. After missing two races and coming back to compete in Monza with a bandaged face after skin grafts, he was asked how he was feeling.

He responded by turning the tragedy into an advantage! He said that since the skin on half of his thigh was transplanted onto his forehead, his face and forehead had no perspiration, which is a great bonus for a race car driver! What a positive attitude! That is a person who is happy and makes fun of himself even in the most difficult of circumstances.

In fertility, and in many areas of healthcare, we're transitioning from a sick industry into a wellness industry. A good portion of our work involves being cheerleaders; we're coaches who guide our patients' transformation from sick to well, from no family to family, from obese to slim. Nothing is more important than the emotional support throughout that journey. You need positive people in your environment to encourage each other through the stress of daily operations and procedures. In addition, this team should be solid and resilient enough to withstand problems and even crises such as a power outage, storm damage, or a pandemic. Hiring happy people on your team helps you achieve the best possible outcome.

#4 HONEST—This means not taking credit from my teammates and not backstabbing anybody on the team. This means I can stand up and be firm without being obnoxious to my peers. I'm assertive. I do not steal. I give honest feedback. If I'm wrong, I want to know why. Honesty means having the courage to admit a mistake to prevent a catastrophe. It means that if you promise to do something, you actually do it.

So how can you know whether someone is honest during an interview? First, make sure the information on their resumé proves true. You can phone or email their references and ask for a detailed accounting of this person's work history, personality, and effectiveness in the workplace. Next, during the interview, listen carefully. Does their verbal story contradict their resumé, or something that they, or their references, said? Most importantly, trust your gut feelings. Your intuition will warn you if a person is being deceptive. You may simply feel that something isn't right, even if you can't pinpoint what it is. Heed that warning, as your instincts are telling you that this person may be dishonest.

In addition, use my "reading the mind in the eye test." Look the person in the eyes as they are speaking. Do they look away nervously? Can they confidently hold your gaze during the conversation? Does their body language offer clues that they're excessively nervous or afraid? Don't fear offending someone by asking questions if you discover contradictions; your business has no time or space for a dishonest person who will only hurt you in the long run.

#5 HUMAN SKILLS—Also known as "people skills," human skills involve knowing how to say good morning, smile, look someone in the eyes, exude empathy, and know when someone is hurting. Human skills also help you tune in to your colleagues' well-being. One of the most important human skills is being an active listener.

My two-minute salt clock during patient consultations helped me listen attentively and not interrupt the patient. I integrated this practice after reading a study conducted during the 1980s. It showed that the average physician who asked the patient, "How can I help you?" actually interrupted the patient, on average, within 18 seconds! When the doctor shut up and let the patient finish, he or she explained what they needed in less than two minutes. The patients felt heard, and the doctor could do the diagnosis 80% more of the time by listening. That's why we have two ears and one mouth. Listening is a very important human skill that makes an employee more effective, efficient, and personable.

Paco's Five H's for Hiring are simple guidelines that you should consider during the interview process. A candidate who scores well in this type of evaluation—and who has strong skills for the position—will serve you well. Remember, you're not looking for the best people for your team; you're looking for the right ones.

Help Wanted: Empathy Required

Empathy is one of the most important traits for healthcare providers. But how can you ensure that the people you hire for your team are empathetic to patients? You'll know by paying close attention during the interview process.

First, empathetic people are good listeners. They want to understand what the other person is feeling, so they pay attention to what's being said, along with facial expressions, tone of voice, and body language.

They're also very focused on the person who's talking.[51] They look the person in the eye and make a connection, making the talker feel seen and heard.

Watch for these cues when you're interviewing each candidate. You can also ask questions with hypothetical situations to learn how the applicant might respond to patients. If the candidate puts their own needs first, they are not empathetic. If they care more about helping the patient, then he or she is exhibiting a tendency toward empathy.

Unfortunately, many medical professionals who have excellent outcomes for their patients also have undesirable or even cold personalities that lack empathy. This is true for other employees in the business as well, and it makes a negative impression on the patients and clients.

That is bad for business, as Cleveland Clinic CEO Delos "Toby" Cosgrove, MD learned in 2005 while speaking at the Harvard Business School about a case study on Cleveland Clinic.[52] MBA student Kara Medoff Barnett raised her hand and said her family chose not to take her father to top-ranked Cleveland Clinic for mitral valve surgery because they heard the hospital lacked empathy. Then she asked, "Dr. Cosgrove, do you teach empathy at Cleveland Clinic?"[53]

Dr. Cosgrove realized that his hospital's extraordinary success rate could not stand alone to attract patients. So The Cleveland Clinic created the Office of Patient Experience and appointed its first Chief Experience Officer: Dr. James Merlino, MD, a prominent colorectal surgeon. This "CXO" was responsible for implementing policies and practices that ensured that every patient felt well cared for by nurses, physicians, surgeons, technicians, and others who exuded empathy—and a genuine desire to make every patient feel seen, heard, and nurtured.

Dr. Merlino was personally motivated to provide innovation because his own father had died at the Cleveland Clinic. Sadly, his father had felt that the nurses had been "unresponsive" and that the physicians had failed to check on him every day.[54] Dr. Merlino shared this story in a May 2013 *Harvard Business Review* article that he co-wrote with Ananth Raman called, "Health Care's Service Fanatics."[55]

This story served as a poignant example of why the hospital needed to teach empathy because its leadership had never thought about it. As a result, the Customer Experience Platform was created as an aggressive plan to improve the hospital's culture. After surveying patients and conducting studies, Dr. Cosgrove and Dr. Merlino helped create a program that trained everyone, including the janitors, on how to exude empathy and utilize practices and procedures that created a positive patient experience. All 43,000 employees had to watch a video about empathy and participate in an intensive program to learn how to incorporate empathy into every aspect of the patient experience.[56] Physicians who once only cared about a patient's medical outcome were also indoctrinated into this new mindset to practice a more empathetic bedside manner.

The program transformed the hospital from physician-centered to patient-centered. Its rankings for delivery care, quality, and safety improved in the University HealthSystem Consortium's ranking of 97 academic medical centers.[57] The Cleveland Clinic's program was so successful, it inspired a global patient experience movement.

In my practice, I conducted a study that revealed half the people choose an empathetic doctor over the top expert. As a MedikalPreneur, you must hire people in every position who understand and exude empathy.

The Ritz-Carlton Hotel Company exemplifies this with its simple credo: "We are ladies and gentlemen serving ladies and gentlemen."[58] This means that the employees treat each other with just as much kindness and empathy as they show for the guests. Herein lies the success secret for this leader in luxury hotel accommodations. Their practice builds customer loyalty, boosts employee morale, inspires workers to stay with the company, and helps the business prosper and thrive.

When You Hire the Right Team, You Can Trust Their Decisions

As a MedikalPreneur, you conceive the idea for your business and you have a vision for how to operate. Oftentimes, as a highly accomplished physician, you may have the personality trait that makes you want to control every aspect of your company. After all, you may have experienced many situations with patients whose lives depended on you taking control of every detail of their care and directing your staff to provide certain treatments and medications.

When I started RMA of Texas, I was controlling everything, including the website. That behavior was hindering our growth. Then I discovered the key to success. I designated a small team that was in charge of everything. This can be a difficult shift because as physicians, our decisions and control over a situation can be a matter of life and death. We want the patient to survive, and we feel it's our responsibility to make every important decision and control all facets of treatment.

This is not the best approach for business. And if you don't adapt your practices to foster growth, then the company will die. I liken this to sports. At first, I was playing tennis with a racket, then I found myself playing basketball with a different ball, and a different team pace. As the business grew, I was in an entirely different league, now playing football. As you grow, the rules of the game change. You have to understand when you advance to playing with a different ball with another opponent and new rules. If you don't learn those rules, and operate according to the new competition, then you will suffer losses. Even the best product or service may one day realize that there are no consumers for them.

Here's where the mindset shift is required to thrive as a MedikalPreneur. To grow your business and sustain long-term success, you need to relinquish some control of your daily operations. You can do this when you hire the most suitable people for each position in your company. Because they're experienced experts who enjoy their work, and they're committed to the culture of teamwork in your business, then you can trust them to execute their duties with the best interest of the patients and your company.

For this reason, I often say that I worked for RN Chris Flynn for 18 years. You might think it's odd or even humorous for the physician to say that he worked for the RN. However, this is the truth, and it reflects our commitment to teamwork. She had the best understanding of the daily flow of our office, and our patients, and everything that was happening. So I trusted her to guide me and give instructions on what to do each day and when. Clearly, this requires surrendering the ego and trusting your team.

However, I was not so quick to do this when I partnered with our team to run one of our fertility centers in another city. At first, I tried to control every aspect of the team, and I standardized all their decisions. But this was not the most efficient or effective way to operate. In fact, it was stifling. I realized that I had to step back and trust that this very talented team would do a great job at running the center without me trying to micromanage every detail.

In the fertility industry and in many medical practices, you cannot instill a "Catholic-style of philosophy" that restricts everyone to obey rigid rules. Instead, a "Buddhist philosophy" is more effective. This involves presenting certain principles to the team, then allowing each person to use his or her judgement on how best to apply them. Giving each team member the freedom to make good decisions—within the context of your company's best practices—is one of the greatest success secrets that I discovered during my early years in business.

Rabbits and Foxes Illustrate Teamwork

The populations of rabbits and foxes on the San Juan Islands, a chain of islands north of Seattle, can teach us about teamwork. When Spaniards settled there in 1790, they brought rabbits. The rabbit population exploded, destroying the Spaniards' vegetable gardens. The farmers needed a way to control the rabbit population, so they brought in foxes, which were not native to the land, but consumed enough rabbits to balance the population. This created equilibrium.

This story exemplifies teamwork in business. On a team with a lot of power plays and individual desires, you can maintain equilibrium and keep the ecosystem or team alive, by sometimes being a proverbial rabbit and surrendering your desires to the foxes, or by sometimes being a fox and forfeiting your power to empower the rabbits.

Architecture Rules The Ship, Not The Captain

Who is the most important person on the ship?

"The captain!" most people say.

What if you need to turn the boat 180 degrees at 10 knots in 40 yards?

If the ship is not designed to do that turn at that speed, you can have the best captain in the world, but the ship is not going to turn. Clearly, the most important person on the ship is the one who designed the boat—*the architect!*

In a business, it's the same. The framework that you construct for incentives, rewards, and punishments will determine how your business runs. If you focus only on individual performance and use metrics to reward individual performance, there will be zero desire to cooperate. We need to create rules that promote cooperation and team performance in balance with individual performance.

For example, when someone violates a company policy, you need clear-cut procedures that define the consequences. Will the person be suspended? Fined? Fired? As a MedikalPreneur, you want to have these policies and procedures in place so that you do not waste precious time, energy, and money on dealing with administrative issues that can even result in legal complaints and lawsuits filed by disgruntled employees. Every employee must learn the rules and the consequences if they are violated. In addition, the rules should be enforced equally and without favoritism. Unfair or preferential treatment can foster resentment and taint the team's cohesion.

Since the architect is more important than the captain, you should build the smartest ship that's designed to withstand storms of all sorts. An excellent example is—until now—the Constitution of the United States. For 234 years, the infrastructure of the Constitution has maintained the balance of power. The Founding Fathers designed it so that you could put someone with lackluster intelligence or even questionable ethics in the White House and the system remains protected. We hope the Founding Fathers built enough fool-proof mechanisms into the architecture of the Constitution to protect the system, regardless of which captain is sailing the ship as president.

The Japanese call these fool-proof mechanisms *poka-yokes,* and you should include them in your MedikalPreneurial architecture to prevent problems and ensure quality in as many areas as possible. At my fertility centers, one example of a *poka-yoke* was our policy to *never* process two semen samples simultaneously. Only one sample was processed at a time. This prevented any possibility of a mix-up.

Checklists provided another level of protection against mistakes. For example, when we started an IVF cycle, a checklist had to be completed, or the process could not begin. The power of this practice was reinforced within me when I read *The Checklist Manifesto: How to Get Things Right* by Atul Gawande.[59] In this 2010 book, the author explains that the simple act of creating a checklist, and following it, can help ensure errors that can cost you money, business and—for medical professionals—even lives. The airlines industry inspired this concept; a pilot cannot take off without a checklist. More than one person has to check the fuel. Two people have to check prior to take-off. The same protocol applies to nuclear reactors. The teams utilize many checklists to make sure every detail is addressed, because even a simple mistake can be deadly.

What types of checklists can you incorporate into your business? Invest the time to contemplate all plausible future scenarios and how the organization will allow for adaptation to expected and unexpected future events. As the architect of your business, you should design a framework that includes *poka-yokes* to help ensure safety and success.

Another example of a *poka-yoke* is the USB port in your computer. Can you insert the USB wrong? No; it just won't fit. It's designed so that you have to turn it exactly the right way to slide it in. Likewise, can you accidentally put your car in reverse while you're driving? No, you have to stop and put your foot on the brake. Similarly, some *poka-yokes* help prevent accidents in case a worker gets distracted. For example, a company can require two hands on each side of a machine to simultaneously push buttons to operate a metal press that in the past could have cut off fingers or even hands.

Practice Adaptation and Anticipation

The bridge to nowhere in Honduras exemplifies two important skills for the MedikalPreneur: adaptation and anticipation. It also illustrates the disaster that can result when architects fail to include *poka-yokes* in even the most technically advanced designs.

The Choluteca Bridge was celebrated for its design to survive hurricanes. It even survived Hurricane Mitch, which decimated 150 other bridges in the South American country in 1998. However, the roads around the Choluteca Bridge were swept away. Even worse, flooding re-routed the river, so water no longer flowed under the surviving stretch of bridge.[60]

Now this bridge—which has no roads connected to it and stands over dry ground—serves as a monument to planners as a metaphor for the catastrophe that can occur when you fail to consider the circumstances and structures all around your design; no matter how great it is, it can become useless when it stands alone.

This story reminds me of a quote by John Lubbock: "Earth and sky, woods and fields, lakes and rivers, the mountain and the sea, are excellent schoolmasters, and teach some of us more than we can ever learn from books."[61]

The MedikalPreneur is The Architect; The Manager Is The Captain

When Captain Sully safely landed an airplane on the Hudson River, saving the lives of 155 people on board, he was celebrated as a hero. Yes, Chesly Burnett Sullenberg III had the expertise to finesse a water landing for US Airways flight 1549 on January 15, 2009, after it took off from LaGuardia Airport.[62] But the architecture of the Airbus A-320 was also a hero, thanks to its superior engineering and design that made it the world's top-selling passenger aircraft. Both the captain's skill and the plane's architecture served to save lives.

As a MedikalPreneur, you're the architect who designs the business. This proverbial ship needs a captain. The manager is the captain, and needs to adapt in the direction of the entrepreneur, who needs to relinquish enough control for the captain to thrive. When you first open your business, you may serve as architect, captain, and manager. But as you grow, you need to delegate, and appreciate how the entrepreneur and the manager have different skill sets.

The successful entrepreneur learns that the balance of power between the entrepreneur and the manager is a delicate dance that requires committing to the common goals of providing a great customer experience and transformation, while growing and sustaining a profitable business. This synchronicity plays out in HR, marketing, accounting, daily operations, and more. From each person's perspective, a situation can appear very different. This diagram illustrates how the truth can seem absolute—until you view the object from another angle.

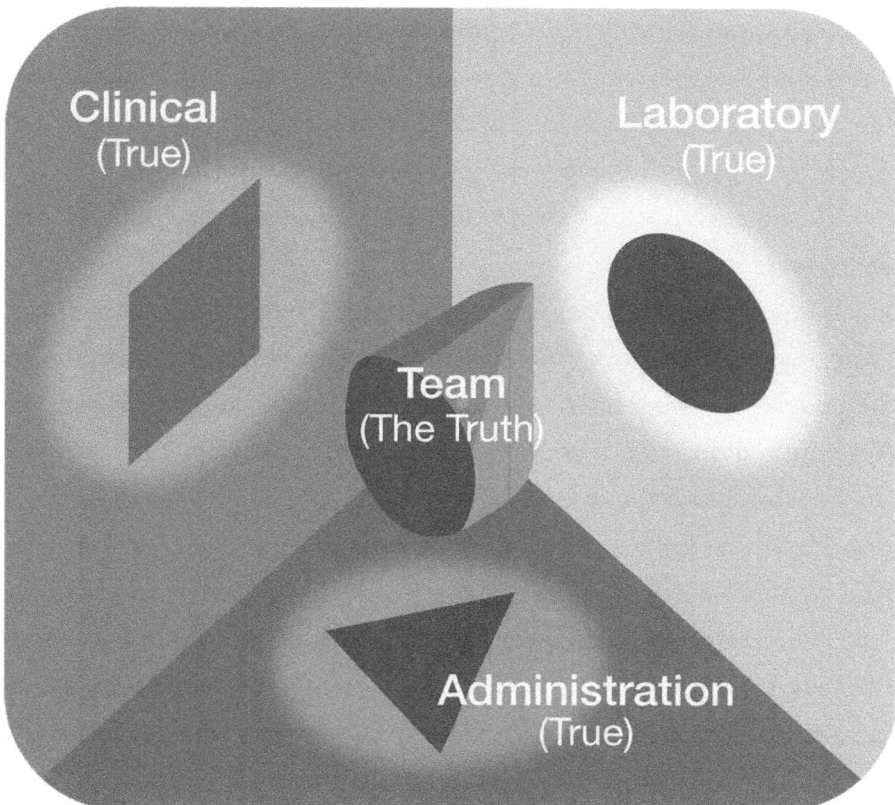

To the clinical person, the object appears as a square. Administration sees it as a triangle. And the laboratory staff sees it as a circle. Who is correct? Everyone. What is the solution? Adaptation. When you design your business model, there will be different versions of the same truth. Sometimes these truths are actually at odds with each other. Your manager must see situations from all three perspectives, and make decisions accordingly.

Empower Every Member of Your Team

As a MedikalPreneur, you can inspire your employees to perform at their best capacity when you endow them with a sense of ownership in the business. You can achieve that by including everyone and their ideas when making decisions, hiring new employees, writing policies and procedures, crafting a mission statement, and doing other tasks that affect the business.

One way to do this is to give each team member the power to veto new hires. That means everyone interviews the candidate.

"If one person vetoes the candidate, they do not get hired," Chris Flynn said.

"I interviewed with everyone in the office," recalled Tony Anderson. "There were only six other people, and I was employee number ten. All the people who were hired after me went through the same thing. Dr. Arredondo didn't care if you were Danny the cleaning guy or Tony the lab director. Everybody had an equal say. And he always listened to you. He always gave that feeling of ownership by making you feel that your opinion matters."

This is only useful when you have a small staff; when you have more employees, it becomes very difficult. As a result, we devised a system to identify applicants who were serious about working for us. We asked people to write an essay to explain, in a few hundred words, why they wanted to work for our company in particular. Only about 10 of 100 people who submitted resumés actually invested the time to research our business and write an essay. Clearly, the committed job applicant will do this, whereas the others eliminated themselves.

This practice saves you money, because the candidates have already done their research, and may require less training because they now understand your products, policies, services, and the people you serve.

Some employers, such as Amazon, actually pay employees up to $5,000 to *leave,* because they know that a happy employee is more productive and committed to the company's success.[63] Their philosophy is that they will save much more than $5,000 in the long run by getting rid of unhappy and uncommitted employees who could make costly mistakes that hurt people or trigger lawsuits.

Similarly, the software business Jellyvision discusses its "Graceful Leave Policy" with new hires on their first day, according to award-winning CEO Amanda Lannert in a January 12, 2018 article by Adam Robinson in *Inc.* magazine. The article is called "Zappos Pays Employees $2000 to Quit. This Superstar CEO Has a Different Approach," and explains five simple practices that include discussing an employee's departure on day one.[64] She said they want to hire people who are both interesting and interested, who will help the company thrive.

As a MedikalPreneur who's evaluating job candidates for your team, you can learn a lot about a person by asking which search engine they use on the internet. Are they using Internet Explorer that came loaded on their PC, or Safari that comes on a Mac? Or do they use Firefox or Google Chrome, which must be downloaded? The person who took the time to download the additional search engine(s) typically advances faster and farther in a company because he or she upgraded their browser on their own volition to improve their performance.[65] This conclusion was made by the economist Michael Housman who studied 30,000 customer service agents; his findings were included in the 2016 book *ORIGINALS: How Non-Conformists Move the World* by Adam Grant.[66]

Housman discovered that employees who used Firefox and Google Chrome stayed in their jobs 15% longer than the Safari and Explorer users. These individuals were also: less likely to miss work; happier in their jobs; and more creative when solving customers' problems. So, when you encounter Chrome and Firefox users, consider that they may be good candidates for your team.

Another example of including the entire team in important decision-making arose when we composed our mission statement and the principles that directed the company.

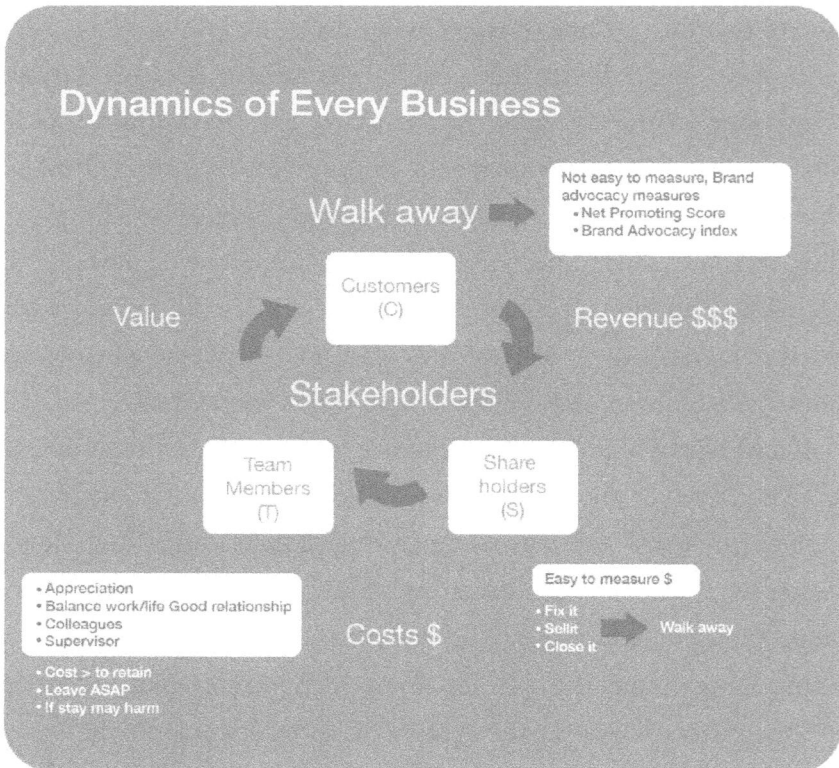

"Dr. Arredondo had everyone in the mission statement say our goals and what we wanted to offer here at RMA of Texas," Tony said. "Everybody was required to give one thing, then we narrowed it down to five principles in the mission statement. This shows that the business wasn't just about him and his vision. It was everyone's, so we could go forward with that."

Tony said empowering everyone to contribute to the company's goals and culture reflected good leadership. Even though some team members had vastly different views on issues such as politics and faith, the company's mission was a common ground that inspired cooperation and open communication.

"We're like 180 degrees from each other on everything else," Tony said, "but we are completely aligned on leadership and business. Good leaders don't say, 'It's my way or the highway.' Good leaders include everyone, and that's why we blended so well together."

At RMA of Texas, we created a system of awarding quarterly bonuses based on four elements: Volume, Quality, Cost per Case, and Customer Experience. Bonuses are a great way to motivate the team, but monetary rewards are only one tool on an important list of qualities that a company can offer to ensure employee satisfaction. Can you guess what quality that is?

Boston Consulting Group conducted one of the world's most detailed studies on this topic, by exploring 26 factors that facilitate employee happiness. Topping the list: employees want to feel appreciated for their work![67] Ranking next were: good relationships with team members; balance between one's personal and professional life; harmony with company leadership; the company's financial stability; job security; a salary that's appealing and stable; and interesting work.

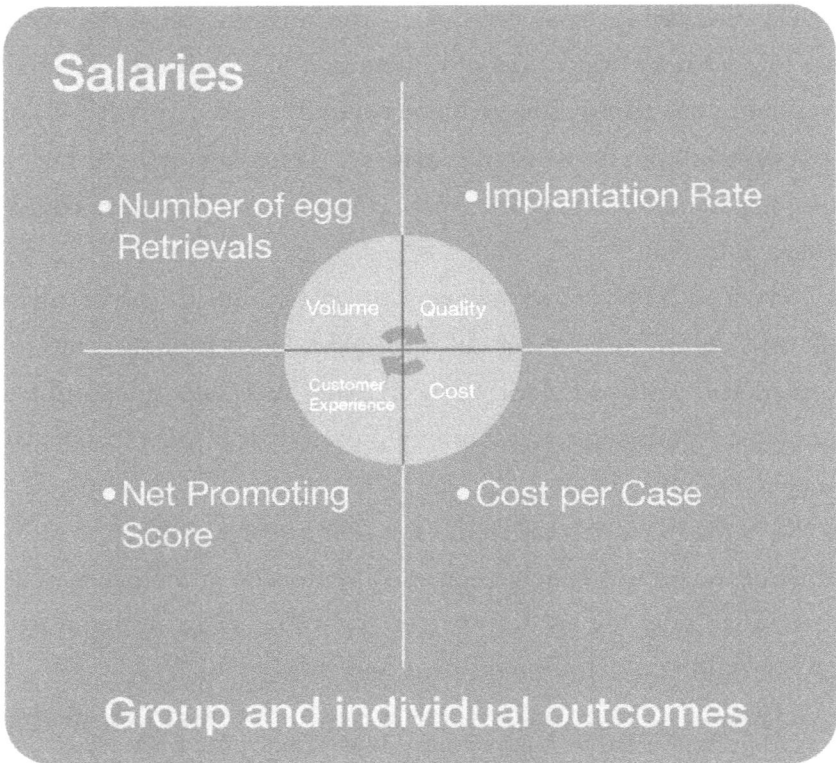

Salaries

• Number of egg Retrievals

• Implantation Rate

Volume | Quality

Customer Experience | Cost

• Net Promoting Score

• Cost per Case

Group and individual outcomes

Volume—I devised a system of bonuses for our four physicians that enabled them to select from two elements to measure the volume of services they provided. The two elements were:

1. the number of IVF cycles; or

2. the number of patients they wanted to see.

In any company, it's important to analyze the metrics of the team's performance, as well as those of each individual team member. This system enabled us to achieve that with our physicians. We had five doctors. If one brought in 20 patients, another has 30, the other has 35, and another has 35, but I only brought in 20, then the weight of the bonus is much bigger on the team than the individuals.

Avoid any system that promotes cannibalization—when doctors are fighting over patients and engaging in cut-throat competition that creates a very toxic work environment for the nurses and other staff members. This bad energy is palpable to anyone who enters your center. It's also detrimental to creating a positive patient experience that results in a transformation as dramatic as getting pregnant and creating a family. The atmosphere in the center—as with any place of healing—should be as upbeat and nurturing as possible.

Therefore, with each physician selecting how he or she prefers to measure the volume of their work, we eliminated the negative aspects of competition. That way, everyone was working for the betterment of the team, and of course, for our patients.

Quality—We measured quality by the numbers of successful implantations and pregnancy rates. When you create a bonus, think about measures that will impact your customers and that are easily measurable. In addition, the elements in the bonus system should be aligned with the interests of the employees, customers, and shareholders. By providing the best quality products and services, you help the consumer solve a problem, inspire the team members with job satisfaction, and impress the shareholders with continued profits.

Cost per Case—Team members were rewarded if they could provide a service in ways that reduced costs. This sometimes required innovative and analytical thinking, as opposed to doing things the way they were always done. Again, think in three tiers. When you transfer savings to a customer, the team member could get a raise, and the shareholder benefits financially.

For example, Chris Flynn saved money by ordering less expensive latex gloves, rather than the ones we had routinely been ordering for $2.50 per pair. Chris was motivated to examine our spending on every level of our services, and as a result discovered a way to reduce the Cost per Case. Think about how, for each patient's procedure, every member of the team would have to wear a $2.50 pair of latex gloves when they entered the OR. Spending less money for each pair of gloves could really add up on a Cost per Case basis, and for the company's annual expenses. This money-saving mindset was rewarded at bonus time.

Customer Experience—How can you know whether you're providing the best experience for your patients and clients? And how can you pinpoint where you need to improve? By asking each customer or patient to complete a survey upon completion of their treatment or use of your product or service. Positive customer experiences help ensure job security for the team member. The customer enjoys it. And the success benefits the shareholders.

You especially want to identify your weaknesses and improve them immediately. And you want to discover if any patients had an issue with a particular employee. When each employee knows that they'll receive a bigger bonus if the patients provide positive reviews, then every team member will be motivated to provide the best experience for patients.

This is why I incorporated our patient satisfaction survey by implementing the same practice that helped Enterprise Rent-A-Car cultivate customer loyalty. This practice was described in an article called, "The One Number You Need to Grow," in the December 2003 edition of *The Harvard Business Review*.[68] It explained how Enterprise Rent-A-Car used a "net promoter score" by asking customers how likely they might be to recommend their car rental service to a family member. We incorporated this question into our patient surveys to establish an architecture for each team member to perform at his or her best with every patient. Calculating each person's bonus based on patient reviews was extremely motivating because their bonuses were heavily based on whether our patients completed evaluations stating that yes, they would highly recommend RMA of Texas for relatives who needed help creating a family.

As a medical entrepreneur, you should make it a top priority to create a positive work environment for all of the above factors. When the customers, employees, and shareholders are happy, all is well—or the business will fail.

Keep Your Finger on the Pulse of Your Team

Gone are the days when the doctors retreated to a private lounge and relegated the staff to the lunchroom. As a MedikalPreneur, stay in the mix with your team, so you can observe relationship dynamics, become aware of issues, and discover problems that need resolution.

I succeeded at keeping my finger on the pulse of my businesses by orchestrating deliberate interaction with everyone. I ate lunch with my lab staff members, nurses, administrators, and doctors on a monthly basis. This was especially helpful when I suspected something personal was brewing between team members.

"Hey Nurse Jane, let's go to lunch," I'd say. Then over the meal, I'd probe to discover the problem and ask, "What can we do better?" If she identified an issue with the lab or an administrator, I would approach a lab person or administrator the next day and say, "Let's go grab lunch." Then I would get them talking and learn more about the problem and how to solve it.

Another way I cultivated communication with my team was to put only one lounge in the office, so we all worked together and took breaks together. As a result, many problems were solved there. I learned this after reading about how Apple Co-Founder Steve Jobs orchestrated interaction amongst people on every level of the company by having only one large bathroom in the whole building for men and women. This guaranteed that everyone crossed paths and exchanged ideas throughout the day.

It's also a good idea to build in mechanisms for consistent communications to discuss issues and problems as they arise. At our fertility center, we had a daily huddle at lunchtime—even if only for 10 minutes. We reviewed how many patients were scheduled that day, what were their names and status, who showed up, who was a no-show, and anything else that was happening. We followed up on whatever was discussed by calling the patients to provide updates on their care.

The huddles enabled us to address errors and near-misses, and to use them as learning experiences for everyone. You can dissect what went wrong, and together conceive new ways to prevent that particular problem from happening again in the future.

Huddles are good because: 1) you interact with each other; and 2) you plan for unexpected things. The huddle creates transparency, so everyone knows what's happening on every level of that day's operations. This can only occur if you cultivate an atmosphere of trust without shaming or blaming people. The more closely you follow Paco's 5 H's to select a great staff, the more efficient and effective your teamwork will be. This creates short-term and long-term success for your employees, your patients, and you as a MedikalPreneur.

We also provided opportunities to maintain open communications with our patients, by inviting them to an annual meeting where they shared their experiences and feedback about the care and service we provided. These meetings often included people from the community—such as a firefighter—to talk about their dedication to their work. I also cultivated good relationships with our team by hosting a few cookouts at my home for 40 people.

"Dr. Arredondo took care of us as individuals," said Chris Flynn. "He went out of his way to do nice things for us employees. Whenever he went on a trip, he would bring little trinkets back for us. Those little things made you feel like family."

The feeling of family developed among us, but I preferred not to use the word "family" when referring to employees. Starting off by referring to your employees as family is fake; you have no blood bonds. However, when you assemble a team with excellent chemistry, a family feeling evolves organically; that's when people at our center began to call each other family.

You become a tribe that shares the same goals, and you've got each other's back, just like family. That closeness will engender more success for you, your employees, and the people who benefit from your products and services.

CHAPTER 6

Marketing for MedikalPreneurs

"The best marketing doesn't feel like marketing."

—Tom Fishburne

Mastering the Art of MedikalPreneurial Marketing

As a physician, the idea of sales and marketing may make you feel uncomfortable; it may even make you cringe. After all, you went to medical school to become a doctor. And unless you attended business school, you probably have little understanding of—or interest in—the world of sales and marketing. People earn entire degrees in that field, and that simply wasn't your focus.

Now it must be.

You will only succeed as a MedikalPreneur when you master the art of marketing. I'm going to help you shift your mindset to make marketing a less bitter pill to swallow, so to speak. And if you already enjoy marketing, then I hope this chapter will inspire you to conceive and implement innovative and bold ways to attract patients and clients.

First, let's define marketing. A simplistic explanation is being in the right place at the right time with the right product or service. However, it's rarely that simple. You can stay focused on your intention by remembering the "why" of your Mission Statement: the *reason* you're in business. Make this your guiding light so you never veer off course.

For example, Amazon's mission statement explains that it strives to constantly improve its standards for the customer experience by utilizing the internet and technology to help shoppers access any product while helping businesses and content creators to thrive. It also says, "We aim to be Earth's most customer centric company."[69] This doesn't describe *how* Amazon markets. But it explains *why* they're in business, and *what* they're doing, and they convey this in their marketing messages.

Knowing your "why"—and keeping it top of mind—will powerfully fuel your mission in business. For example, perhaps you lost your spouse to colon cancer, and now you're on a mission to save other families from that tragedy. This is the "why" that inspired you to become a MedikalPreneur and perhaps invent a screening procedure and diet for colon health and cancer prevention. Remembering this "why" will motivate you to build your business, and propel you through challenging times. In a poignant YouTube video, Business Coach Rich Allen shares his why, which was inspired by watching his father fail to achieve his entrepreneurial dreams.[70]

Explore your *why* by studying the teachings of Simon Sinek, author of the global bestseller, *Start With Why: How Great Leaders Inspire Everyone to Take Action.* His 2009 Ted Talk about WHY has more than 56 million views and is subtitled in 48 languages.[71]

Marketing is the Rx for MedikalPreneurial Success!

Marketing is everything a company does to promote and sell products or services to customers,[72] according to Investopedia. Similarly, the American Marketing Association says marketing includes the company's processes for innovating, expressing, and delivering offerings that provide value for customers and clients.[73] This concept expands into "The Four P's of Marketing:"

Product—This is the product or service that you sell as a MedikalPreneur. Emphasize that you offer a unique experience that transforms the buyer's life, and convince the customer or patient to purchase this experience from you by differentiating yourself from the competition. Your branding and packaging can enhance the marketability and appeal of your offerings.

Price—Your price should be competitive and on par with the market. When you differentiate your product, service, and results as superior to the competition, you can justify raising the price. Points to consider are whether you offer discounts, coupons, customer rewards, and financing.

Place—Where is your product or service provided? What channels are used to promote and sell it? And how is it distributed?

Promotion—What advertising and publicity will you use?

Create A Marketing Plan

Benjamin Franklin said, "If you fail to plan, you are planning to fail."

That's why you need a Marketing Plan, which Entrepreneur.com defines as a written document detailing your plans to advertise and market for the next 12 months; this includes descriptions of your marketing circumstances, your target markets, and your strategies to reach your goals.[74] The many parts of a Marketing Plan include:

Your Mission Statement—What is your mission as a MedikalPreneur? Staying focused on *why* you went into business and what you intend to accomplish will inspire the best marketing messages and strategies.

Your Vision Statement—Stephen Covey suggests in his book, *The Seven Habits of Highly Effective People,*[75] that you envision your final destination before embarking on your journey to get there. This is your Vision Statement. It describes the end goal of your mission as a

MedikalPreneur. What do you want to accomplish by providing your product or service? At RMA of Texas, our vision was to help every woman who desired to start a family, achieve that.

Your Vision Statement can be simple, yet powerful. For example, the Alzheimer's Association aims to create "A world without Alzheimer's and all other dementia.™"[76] Similarly, Microsoft's Vision Statement began as: "A computer on every desk and in every home."[77] As you craft your Vision Statement, think big, bold, and long-term.

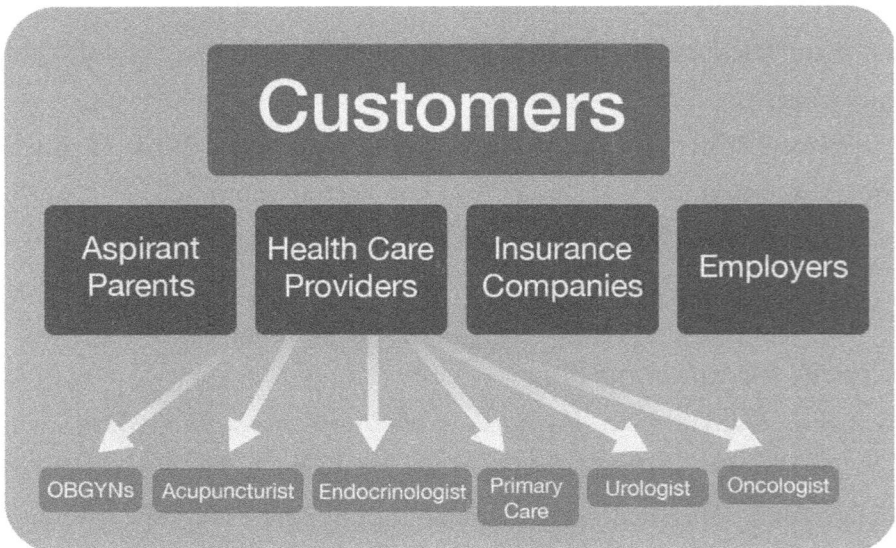

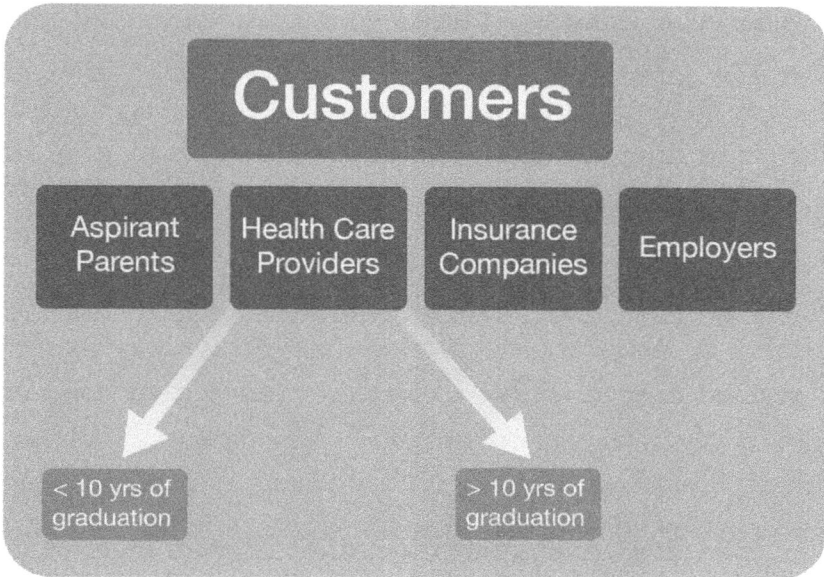

Customers

| Aspirant Parents | Health Care Providers | Insurance Companies | Employers |

< 10 yrs of graduation

> 10 yrs of graduation

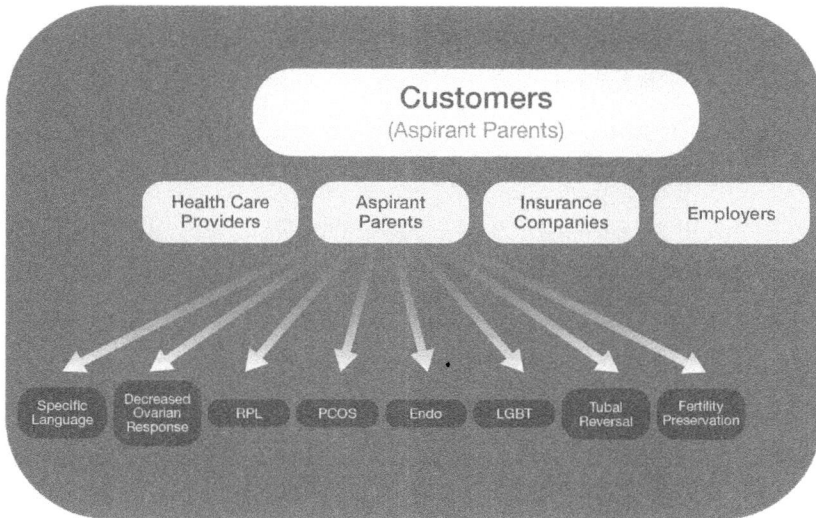

Customers
(Aspirant Parents)

| Health Care Providers | Aspirant Parents | Insurance Companies | Employers |

Specific Language | Decreased Ovarian Response | RPL | PCOS | Endo | LGBT | Tubal Reversal | Fertility Preservation

RPL = Recurrent Pregnancy Loss

PCOS = Polycystic Ovarian Syndrome

Endo = Endometriosis

LGBT = Lesbian Gay Bisexual Transexual

Your Target Market—Who are your ideal patients or clients? Research their demographics: age, education, geographic region, likes, dislikes, hobbies, trends, income, spending habits, values, and priorities. This will help you know where to find them and how to influence them with your marketing to inspire them to take action and seek your services. What percentage of the immediate population, as well as people in surrounding communities, might need your product or service?

If your business is entirely online, your target market can be global, but you still need to know the characteristics of the specific people you're trying to reach. For example, if you help menopausal women get naturopathic remedies for hormonal imbalances, then you'll be targeting women over 50 who prefer natural remedies over pharmaceuticals. You will not market to teenagers or men, but will strategically focus on the social media sites, organizations, clubs, and other places where these women congregate and seek information. You can also contact OB/GYNs to ask for referrals for menopausal women who want natural remedies for hot flashes, mood swings, weight gain, insomnia, and other symptoms.

When you understand your target market, you'll know what language and tone to use when crafting messages for them. For example, when you're speaking with other doctors, you can use medical lingo and they'll understand what you're saying. However, when you're talking with patients, you simplify terms so they comprehend your explanations and instructions. When we speak to different audiences, we tailor our messages accordingly.

At RMA of Texas, our marketing efforts were directed first at OB/GYNs in San Antonio and surrounding cities, asking them to refer patients who needed fertility services. At the same time, we marketed to the public and specifically to women and couples who were having trouble getting pregnant, maintaining healthy pregnancies, and giving birth to start a family. Therefore, we had a good idea about how to market to each of these groups.

It starts by knowing their "pain points," and offering a promise to solve their problem. The OB/GYNs wanted to help their patients finally experience successful pregnancies under the care of a skilled fertility specialist and team. The women in our communities who longed to become mothers had probably endured the sadness, frustration, and hopelessness of failing to get pregnant, losing pregnancies and wondering if they would ever become a parent. We understood the needs of the people to whom we were marketing, and tailored our messages accordingly.

Market Research—Where have your ideal patients and clients been receiving the product or service that you're offering before you went into business? Learn everything you can about these businesses' geographic locations, their products and services, reputations, the atmosphere of their stores or offices, and their pricing. Very importantly, identify what need is *not* being met by those businesses, and determine whether your business can provide that product or service. If your business is online, you can conduct your market research on the Internet.

Get young and enthusiastic help. We always encouraged interns earning marketing degrees and management degrees in our offices to do a rotation. They benefit by working in the real world and making money, and you get great workers, potential future team members, and energetic young people with fresh ideas. And their work with you creates a positive-sum game when they create a marketing plan for your business that can double as a final project or video presentation for their courses.

As you research your market, understand the history, current dynamics, and future projections. For example, if your company provides Personal Protective Equipment for medical workers, the market's past history may have plateaued at a certain level. Then the coronavirus pandemic struck, and the United States experienced a severe shortage of these materials. If you follow projections for how long the pandemic may last, then you can anticipate robust demand and sales for your PPE products and ride that wave to supply goods for the demand and profit significantly. Then you could shift your marketing messages to encourage emergency preparedness by stocking up on PPE in case another wave or pandemic occurs.

Your market research should help you calibrate your business to current circumstances as well as stimulate projections into future demands to plan accordingly.

Your Competition—Similar to Market Research, you need to know who's already doing business in your niche. Who are they? What products and services do they offer? What are their prices? What is their reputation? How can you differentiate yourself with a unique and transformative customer experience?

Check online reviews to see top customer complaints and determine how you can create marketing messages promising to provide that particular service even better. Is your largest competitor about to retire and is he or she looking to sell the business? Could you purchase it and inherit the company's patients and clients? Did one of your competitors get caught in a scandal or experience a public relations problem that leaves their patients or clients seeking products and services elsewhere?

Or is your greatest competitor dominating the market with big budget advertising on television, billboards and bus ads boasting huge numbers of clients at multiple satellite offices? Here's where you can capitalize on the benefits of a boutique experience, personalized service, and an intimate environment, as opposed to a factory production line atmosphere at the competitor's giant—and possibly impersonal—company. Of course you can convey these messages in a way that is 100% professional and appeals to every patient's desire to be seen, heard, valued, and transformed by you as their trusted MedikalPreneur.

Your Budget—Allot a specific dollar amount for advertising, promotions, and materials such as business cards, flyers, brochures, website design and maintenance, billboards, sponsorships of community events, and signage. What percentage of the revenue would be appropriate to spend in marketing? You may also choose to outsource social media marketing, blogging, and public relations. When you first open your business, you may have very little money allocated to marketing. Here's what I recommend:

- Percentage of revenue dedicated to marketing: 5-15% are reasonable numbers in healthcare businesses.

- Goal oriented marketing: what are your goals?

  » Building a recognizable name?

  » Promoting new available services?

  » Increasing the frequency of your audience to see the ad?

- Marketing based on ROI (Return on Investment)

  » If you place an add, do you use an assigned number or website to track the traffic?

Your Goals—Your team should collaborate on setting goals, and understand budget versus percent of revenue versus goal-based, and those goals should follow a metric that guarantees sufficient revenue to keep the business in operation. Therefore, if your operating costs are X number of dollars per month, how many products and services or numbers of patients must you see every day or week to cover those costs? Know these numbers!

Timeline—Your Marketing Plan should include a timeline with specific dates for hitting certain financial goals, number of products and services sold, amount of new customers attracted and retained, etc. You can make a timeline by the day, week, month, quarter, year, decade, or all of the above.

Marketing Strategies—This is the nuts and bolts of your Marketing Plan. It explains exactly what you're going to do, who's going to do it, how they will execute these tasks, and when. Here's where your team needs to know each person's responsibilities and commit to doing them with excellence.

For example, will you have a website, and will one team member write a weekly blog post? Will that person be responsible for posting on your Facebook page, your Instagram account, your LinkedIn presence, and your Twitter feed? Will you use any other social media platforms, such as SnapChat or TikTok? Identify who your customers are and make sure the platform you use is appropriate at the time of the campaign. These platforms are very dynamic and some may not be relevant—or even in existence—when you're reading this book.

Designate these responsibilities to team members who are already acclimated to the platforms and understand how they work, as well as how to optimize your ranking, views, follows, and engagement on each.

Know the demographics of your target audience, and select your social media platforms accordingly. For example, if you're an orthodontist, promote to parents of adolescents where adults congregate online—LinkedIn and Facebook. However, with the right marketing strategy on platforms that attract adolescents, such as TikTok, you could create a fun campaign that inspires pre-teens to tell their parents that they *must* get their braces from your orthodontic office.

Marketing Strategies can also include attending trade shows to promote your products and services, and having team members do direct sales solicitations by visiting places to do presentations about your offerings. The local media is always looking for stories, and you can pitch ideas that showcase your medical business by emailing a press release or simply calling the news desk to suggest your ideas.

You could reap the tremendous marketing power of pitching yourself to local media—specifically to health reporters—to serve as the go-to authority on your area of expertise when they do stories and breaking news on your topic. You can also pitch yourself for feature stories about growing trends in your field; if you're a dermatologist, for example, perhaps you can convince the local TV news station to interview you about how to remove unwanted tattoos. The station could even feature you in a series about "The Dangers of Tattoos: One Dermatologist Warns What You Should Know!"

Don't discount the power of a surprise twist when marketing. For example, perhaps your MedikalPreneurial endeavor is that you're a dermatologist who now owns a tattoo parlor! That would certainly differentiate you from the competition, and automatically engender trust that your customers would enjoy the safest possible experience in your hands. Your marketing platform could focus on safety, hygiene, and low risk, because you're a medical doctor. This unique concept would set you apart from—and above—the competition.

Be creative, and be bold! Media interviews cost you nothing but time and can amplify your authority to millions of people on live television and on the station's website and mobile app. Even better, newspapers, radio stations, and TV news stations are often part of a national or international network. So the local report about you could air nationally or even around the world! That would be extremely beneficial to your business. When that happens, maximize the promotional value by sharing on your networks, and emblazon your marketing materials with "as seen on" the name of the show.

Similarly, write articles and pitch them to national websites such as *HuffPost* or *MindBodyGreen,* or write editorials on trending topics for national newspapers such as *The Wall Street Journal* and *The New York Times*. All of the above provide limitless exposure while amplifying your authority as the respected expert in your field.

Referrals—Satisfied customers, clients, and patients can serve as ambassadors for your business, because they'll tell people about how your company solved their problem. They may sing your praises in conversations, on social media, and in online reviews.

Marketing is ruled by ethical laws that may not be the same as other services. Know your state laws regarding marketing in medicine. Know what your medical licensing board's regulations are, and the Stark Laws to ensure you steer clear of illegalities or ethics violations.

Analytics—Have a system for constantly monitoring what marketing strategies are working and which are failing to attract people to your business. Do this by asking every patient and client how they heard about you, and what inspired them to come to your office for treatments and procedures, or to purchase your products and services.

This invaluable practice helped RMA of Texas understand where to focus our marketing resources. Our advertising and promotions included: our delivery vehicle decorated with sperm, TV commercials, radio spots, a social media campaign, lunches that we hosted, a website, word-of-mouth referrals, and face-to-face introductions. Our analysis enabled us to determine that neither making social media investments nor spending a small fortune on a fancy website are always worth the expense.

For our company, 14% of our business came from the Internet, while 50% of our referrals came from other OB/GYNS! Nothing is more impactful on marketing than face-to-face introductions and meetings. Understanding this market segmentation enabled our team to know where—and where not—to invest our marketing resources.

As you collect data to learn how people heard of your business, take this a step further to determine which type of advertising is attracting patients and clients who are investing in the most lucrative products and services that you offer. You can develop your own system for tracking this information, and it will enable you to decide how and where to devote the most resources for marketing and advertising. Aim to earn the highest Return On Investment—or ROI.

It's imperative that you strategize how to use marketing as a gateway to attract and keep patients and clients so that you can simultaneously execute your mission as a healer while also monetizing your business. The more prosperous your business becomes, the more you can expand and offer new services to help people in larger geographic regions. You can even leverage your increasingly valuable assets to start new companies that fill a void in the market.

On a personal note, your prosperity will enable you to enjoy the freedom to travel and embark on adventures that would not be possible while restricted to a traditional job in the medical field.

SWOT Analysis—SWOT is an acronym for Strengths, Weaknesses, Opportunities, and Threats. You should identify each for your business and perform a SWOT Analysis on a regular basis because factors can shift. Work to strengthen your weaknesses and mitigate or eradicate threats. Sometimes strengths and weaknesses flip; for example, a strength for Blockbuster Video was that most families owned a VCR and rented movies to watch at home. Its weakness was that it offered no online streaming service, so when Netflix and other movie streaming services became available, Blockbuster failed to strengthen its weakness—and went out of business.

How is SWOT Analysis relevant to your Marketing Plan? You need to market to your target customers that you're offering new products and services that address whatever weakness you may have identified. For example, if Blockbuster had advertised "now offering online movie streaming," then perhaps it would still be in business. In addition, knowing your threats enables you to craft marketing messages to address them.

Face-To-Face Marketing Grows Your Business

You can have the most brilliant Marketing Plan written on paper, but it's worthless without aggressive and sustained action. That's why, as a new business, we took to the streets to introduce ourselves and our services to the people who could help us attract our first patients and continue to grow.

Face-to-face marketing is one of the best methods to let people know about your company, and to convince them to invest in your products and services. This method is free, although you will need to provide a business card, and possibly a brochure or packet of information about your products and services. However, the most important element here—which has no financial cost—is the personal touch. Face-to-face interaction shows your prospects that you are an authentic physician with altruistic intentions to help people.

If you're seeking referrals, this creates a win-win situation because it enhances the reputation of the doctor who referred a new patient to you—after that patient receives a positive transformative experience. Likewise, if you're speaking directly with potential patients or clients—perhaps at networking events or conferences—then you can make a personal connection that facilitates trust and comfort. That can lead to the individuals seeking medical care, treatment, and services from you.

My success as a MedikalPreneur began with word-of-mouth marketing. When we opened RMA of Texas, we had zero patients. I did not want to spend a lot of money by purchasing advertising or hiring a public relations firm. So we relied on the tried-and-true, old-fashioned method of marketing: talking with people and telling them about our fertility center.

It's not enough to sit in your office and blast out mass emails, post on social media, or make phone calls. You need to get out and meet people. You make the most powerful impact and best impressions with face-to-face connections with your ideal patients and clients, and referral sources.

That's what our small team did. And it worked even better than we anticipated. We started by visiting every OB/GYN in San Antonio and surrounding cities. Our goal was to ask the physicians to refer patients—specifically women who needed assistance in getting pregnant and starting a family—to our center.

Many doctors' offices did not want to talk with us. However, I knew that persistence would ultimately result in connections with the right physicians who would see the value of how our fertility center could help their patients. They also understood that if they referred patients to a physician who could solve a major problem—such as repeated, failed pregnancies—then their patients would appreciate them even more. This creates a win-win-win experience for the patient, the referring physician, and the MedikalPreneur.

Going for this triple-win outcome through word-of-mouth marketing will require an investment of your time, energy, and travel. First, you'll need to do some research to make a list of ideal referral sources for your business. If you're a psychiatrist, for example, you may want to approach physicians, faith leaders, and college counselors to solicit referrals. If your business makes prosthetics, then you'll want to meet with people at rehabilitation centers who can refer patients to you. Invest time in analyzing the pipeline of information that your ideal patients or clients might follow to find your products, services, and treatments.

After you compile a list of specific people at places that you want to visit, allocate the hours and days of travel to those locations. It's a good idea to call ahead to make sure that each place is open and that the physician, CEO, or other authoritative individuals will be there that day.

If your quest is anything like mine, people will close the door and simply say they're not interested in whatever you're offering. However, this is a numbers game. Do not give up! If you persist, you'll encounter someone who could open a door to a steady stream of people who need exactly what you're offering.

This happened for me one day when I drove to Laredo, Texas. My intention was to visit 25 OB/GYN offices to seek referrals for our fertility center. On this particular day, I arrived at an office at 4 p.m. I didn't know what to expect, and had become accustomed to doors being closed in my face. Thankfully, this physician was kind enough to come into the lobby and ask: "Paco, can you wait for me? I can't take care of you now, because I have patients. Can you meet me at 5:30 in the country club for a glass of wine?"

"Sure," I said.

Ninety minutes later, I was enjoying wine with him at a nearby country club.

"Paco, for the last 18 years, I have been sending all my patients to Dr. X, your competition in San Antonio," the doctor said. "Beginning tomorrow, all the patients are yours. In 18 years, he has never come down to have a glass of wine or visit with me. You showed that hunger." The doctor referred many, many patients to my office as a result, and I am forever grateful.

This story is powerful because it shows that people want to see who you are. They want that human interaction and personal connection. A book called *The Face to Face Book: Why Real Relationships Rule in a Digital Marketplace*[78] by Ed Keller and Brad Fay describes this brilliantly.

In fact, the American Marketing Association called it the best marketing book of the year. It asserts that in this digital age of email, text messages, social media, and automated phone calls, it's easy to believe that online advertising is the solution for a successful business.

Wrong. The majority of sales are not Internet-based. They're still face-to-face. It's more powerful for a doctor to visit another doctor and say, "Let's have a glass of wine or a coffee and talk about it." What will this cost you? An investment of your time. After all, I didn't even pay for the wine; the doctor was so impressed, he treated me. As I said earlier, referrals from OB/GYNs accounted for 50% of our business.

Doctors Are Already In the Business of Sales and Marketing

Physicians are very uncomfortable about saying that they're selling things. But the truth is, in everyday interactions, a doctor is "selling" patients on an idea and an action:

"Take this pill. This is the best remedy for your ailment."

"Follow this treatment plan, and it will ease your acid reflux."

"I promise that when you follow this diet, or have this gastric surgery, you will lose weight."

We as physicians are seeking "buy in" from patients to take a certain medication, undergo a surgical procedure, or get life-altering treatments such as chemotherapy and radiation. So you see, we're already engaged in the act of sales and marketing. We're already very good at using our authority as trained medical professionals to convince people to do what we recommend, and believe that it will have a positive outcome. When you apply that same authority as a MedikalPreneur, you increase your chances for success.

But putting the marketing label on it, and calling ourselves sales-people, can cause panic. Here's where we need to upgrade our mental software and shift into the MedikalPreneurial Mindset.

I recommend that you read the 2013 book, *To Sell Is Human: The Surprising Truth About Moving Others*[79] by Daniel H. Pink. This provided tremendous insights for me as a MedikalPreneur by first explaining that every human being is almost constantly engaged in the act of selling someone to do or think something. A child is "selling" a parent on giving them a cookie. A boss is "selling" a team on performing a task to reach an objective. A spouse is "selling" their partner on the idea of moving to another city. Life is about sales. It's the terminology that injects an intimidation factor into the equation. However, **sales are all about persuasion.**

Master the Art of Persuasion
By Knowing the Science Behind It

Successful leaders must master the art of persuasion, asserts Robert B. Cialdini, PhD, in an October 2001 article entitled, "Harnessing the Science of Persuasion"[80] in the *Harvard Business Review.* To do that, leaders need to understand the science behind this dynamic, and Dr. Cialdini explains it brilliantly in his book, *Influence: The Psychology of Persuasion.*[81] Please read this book that has been instrumental to my success.

My study of the art and science of persuasion—and successful application while creating and leading more than a dozen companies—enabled me to compile **Paco's Persuasion Practices** for you. Some of these principles are rooted in ancient scripture, and are fascinating to understand, utilize, and especially—succeed in business.

Paco's Persuasion Practice #1 —
Utilize the Law of Reciprocity.

This universal and ancient principal been in practice since before 1700 B.C.![82] Today it's a core tenet of cultures around the world, and it's rooted in the idea that if I do something nice for you, you will automatically feel obligated to do something nice for me. It's the Biblical concept that, "You reap what you sow." And that "Givers Gain,"[83] as described in the book[84] with that title by Dr. Ivan Misner, founder of BNI, the world's largest business referral and networking organization. The science behind the Law of Reciprocity relates to Sir Isaac Newton's Third Law of Physics: for every action, there's an equal and opposite reaction.[85]

Reciprocity is a powerful persuasion tactic. It triggers a psychological and scientific response that makes people want to give *you* something after you give *them* something. If you gave them a gift, did them a favor, attended their event, or made an important phone call to recommend them for a job, then they feel indebted to you. This will inspire them to say "yes" when you ask for something. This principle is similar to the Golden Rule, which says, "treat others as you wish to be treated."

This core tenet in relationships should feel good, like a free flow of giving and receiving. When you apply reciprocity as a MedikalPreneur, you can create the best outcomes in business deals, negotiations, marketing campaigns, cooperative relationships with your team, and much more.

Here's one way that I practiced reciprocity: when new OB/GYNS came to the community, I sent them a welcoming letter and a small gift. You could also screenshot a positive report about colleagues, then email or text it with a note such as: "Hey, congratulations, way to go!" This unexpected act of giving is uplifting, because it's true and genuine, and costs you nothing but a few moments. At the same time, it endears the recipient to you, and in a spirit of reciprocity, he or she may feel inspired to help you at some point.

Chris Flynn applied reciprocity masterfully, by saying yes to staff members' requests, hoping that would inspire a trickle-down generosity to patients. "I always try to do everything I can to accommodate them," she said, "because if you do that for them, they will do the same for the people they take care of. You have to set the example. The person's kindness transfers through. It's like 'pay it forward.'"

Reciprocity, according to Dr. Cialdini, inspires people to pay more money. In a YouTube video entitled, "Science of Persuasion," narrated by himself and Steve Martin, he cited a study that showed when a restaurant waiter provided extra mints and compliments with the bill, the diner tended to leave a 23% higher tip than if no candy were given.[86]

Paco's Persuasion Principle #2—Commit to Consistency, and Inspire Others to Do the Same.

Read any success book, and you'll see this word: consistency. People trust and like you more when you demonstrate consistency. If you say that your business opens at 8 a.m., but no one answers the phone until 8:30 a.m., this demonstrates inconsistency. And if the customer can't trust you to honor something as simple as the time that you posted on your door and website, then why should he or she trust—or pay for—anything else that you promise?

At RMA of Texas, our policy was "the patient is always right, and even if we didn't cause the problem, we own it, and we solve it." We committed to practicing this policy with unwavering consistency. We did this, for example, by delivering medication to a patient's home on a Sunday, even if she forgot or failed to pick up the meds from the pharmacy to ensure an adequate supply and not miss a dose, which would jeopardize her fertility cycle. This commitment to making sure our patients enjoyed successful outcomes to their fertility treatments demonstrated our consistency to always provide whatever service was required to meet the patients' needs.

Another example of consistency that we incorporated in our operations was our policy change regarding new patients' requirements. I cannot get credit for this initiative at RMA of Texas, as I was on the "wrong side" of the argument. When a young physician came and challenged the status quo of receiving new patients, even if they had not completed their medical history—which we had developed online so they could complete it before arriving at the office—I objected. I intuitively wanted to draw as many patients as possible into the office, and once there, we would get them into treatment. I was wrong. The secret was in the commitment to consistency principle. We have had a problem with new patients not showing up.

This bright, young physician requested that new patients who did not complete their medical history 48 hours prior to their appointment should be rescheduled while their slot opened for someone on the waitlist. To be honest, I was skeptical and, frankly, not happy. (So even a person who knows the good of change and embraces it is often reluctant to it.)

Wow, what a difference it made! The patients who had completed their medical histories rarely missed their appointments because they wanted to be consistent and committed to their previous action: complete the medical history. In this same way, find in your business ways that you commit your potential customers to something small, to say yes to something insignificant, and they will feel committed to be consistent with their words.

What do the telemarketers ask you right away?

"How are you doing today?" they ask.

And what is the most common answer? "Good!"

Now you have to be consistent with your statement. You have to be good and listen! So this persuasion secret is to ask for a small commitment that can easily be made, then ask for a bigger commitment for them to stay consistent with. Always find ways to inspire your patients and clients to make voluntary and public commitments; then they have to be consistent.

Paco's Persuasion Practice #3 — Let Social Proof Speak for You

Your most powerful marketing machine is comprised of happy patients and clients, a staff with high morale, and peers who sing your praises. Their word-of-mouth messaging about you—along with online reviews, social media posts, and comments—can generate referrals, boost your reputation for the public, and attract new patients and customers.

In today's digital age, the popular term for this is "social proof." It means that people trust positive comments and recommendations about you and your business, when they hear or read them from *other people* who endorse you and your services.

In addition, people are impressed—and encouraged to like, trust, and work with you—if you have thousands or even millions of followers on social media, because that's social proof that you're an influencer in your field. This concept expands far beyond the screens of cell phones and other devices. It makes the powerful impression on people who already know you, and on those whom you hope to attract to your business. Social proof is rooted in human psychology; when many people endorse someone or something, we tend to trust, buy or hire, respect, and want more of the item or the person.

As a MedikalPreneur, leveraging "social proof" can be the gilded frame around your Marketing Plan. At RMA of Texas, we harnessed the power of our patient's positive endorsements as "social proof"— real people candidly telling other people that they had a positive and transformative experience at our fertility center. This inspired others to visit us and utilize our services. You can harness the influence of "social proof" by inviting your patients or clients to provide testimonials in writing and on video. Ask them to sign a release form granting you permission to use their testimonials on social media posts, radio and television advertising, email blasts, your website, in-office signage, and any other platform that you use for marketing. Their authentic endorsements are far more powerful than a paid model or actress who poses or performs in expensive advertising. Social media is the best example of social proof. People want to see who has the most likes, followers, subscribers, and positive reviews. So cultivate all of those.

Paco's Persuasion Practice #4— Have an Appealing Personality.

You've probably heard that we do business with those we know, like, and trust. Getting to know someone engenders trust, the foundation for all relationships. Plus, it's a human urge to crave acceptance and a feeling of being liked. As a result, we're always open to meeting people, whether personally or professionally, whose personalities we enjoy.

So when we connect with someone whom we know, like, and trust, we're more likely to do business with him or her. In fact, Dr. Cialdini cited a 1990 study that people who attended Tupperware parties bought twice as much from the hostess because they *liked* her, regardless of what products she was selling.[87]

At our fertility centers, we created a harmonious atmosphere that cultivated positive relationships between our team and our patients. We did this by applying one of my favorite concepts from Pine and

Gilmore's book, *The Experience Economy:* creating a harmonious environment with images, sounds, textures, scents, spoken words, and actions that make a positive impression.[88] We tailored as many details as possible in our centers to create an atmosphere that filled our patients with hope about starting a family, and that our team would take exquisite care of them through the fertility process. We achieved this through our language, behavior, protocols, décor, and every detail from the moment they entered the lobby until the day they imprinted their babies' footprints on our wall.

We used conversation cues to find similarities that served as launch points for connection. We paid genuine compliments. And we conveyed our desire to collaborate with them for their success.

First, we had a rule that during any interaction, we said a patient's name three times. Other than "pregnant" in our business, the second most important word that our patients wanted to hear was their name. So our staff members would say, "Thank you for calling, Mary. How can I help you, Mary? We'll see you next week, Mary." This is effective because the human brain cannot discern what is real or not. Specific wording can inspire your patient to start thinking positively and imagining herself with a baby during the next year.

We also enhanced personal connections with exercises such as this one that I requested of our team: "From now until Friday, I want you to write down how many people have green eyes, and tell me the results."

On Friday, our team members said, "There were eight people with green eyes. Why are you doing this?"

"I'm forcing you to look people in the eye," I said.

These shortcuts are universal principles that guide human behavior. We all want to be liked, seen, and heard. These subtle psychological cues enhance the patient experience, which inspires the best compliance with treatments, leading to the most positive outcome. At our fertility centers, that was starting a family.

Another persuasive word is "because," harkening back to when we were children, asking: "Mom, can I have a cookie?"

"No."

"Why?"

"Because." That was all she needed to say to convince you that the answer was no. Similarly, when you offer an explanation after "because" when trying to persuade someone, you're more convincing when you share *why* you're asking for the favor or the business.

At the same time, an authentically appealing personality gives you carte blanche in business and in life. I've learned that when we like someone, they have the power to persuade us. First, we gravitate toward people who share similarities, such as a passion for a certain sports team, a specific genre of films, a type of music, and children who attend the same school. The motivational teacher Tony Robbins calls this building "rapport" with people, which lays the foundation for a relationship, opens a gateway to collaborate, do business, and create mutually beneficial experiences. When we discover similarities and people like us as a result, they are more likely to do business with us.

Second, when you compliment someone, you increase your ability to influence their decision-making. So praise a genuine smile, compliment a person's clothing, say something nice about the décor of an office when you enter, and always look for ways to share kind words. Third, if we feel we can collaborate with someone—such as contributing to a certain charity—we win their approval, which may inspire them to utilize our products and services.

Paco's Persuasion Practice #5—Flex Your Authority

As a physician, you automatically have authority as a medical expert. The patients or clients are coming to you for a product or service because they already believe you're the authority in your specialty. So flex that same authority in your marketing materials. Showcase your education, experience, and any accolades or special honors that can help your patients trust you to solve their medical problem. Post your diplomas on the walls where patients can see them, and frame any magazine articles or covers that feature you.

This is not braggadocious. People automatically defer to you as an authority because you have MD after your name. However, they may not know that you are Board Certified, or that you did a fellowship that further honed your skills in the specialty they require, or that you were featured in the local lifestyle magazine as one of the region's "Top Docs" for your product or service. The credential that you promote may be the factor that differentiates you from the competition and brings new business through your door.

Baby Boomers may be impressed by your diplomas, trophies, and awards, but younger generations perceive authority differently. So craft the best messages for each audience. When you market to younger generations on social media, know who they are and what impresses them. They may actually be turned off by traditional credentialing if you showcase your credentials and awards on your website and social media posts. Instead, Millennials and Generation Z members are more impressed by your validation on social media by bloggers, Instagram influencers, and popularity on platforms as ranked by your numbers of likes, shares, comments, subscribers, and followers.

It's crucial to understand each segment of your target market. Invest time every week to follow trends so you can invest your marketing time and dollars in places where your messages resonate with each audience, then be as bold as is appropriate for each audience.

Paco's Persuasion Practice #6—
Understand Scarcity as a Motivator.

Something in human nature makes people want what they cannot have. If they want a procedure, and you only offer 10 per month, people desire it more; getting access to goods and services that are in high demand creates an exclusive club feeling around what you're offering.

Plus, when people hear about limited supplies, or restricted access to something, they want it more. One example was the perception created at the start of the coronavirus pandemic about a toilet paper shortage. People flocked to stores and bought huge quantities of toilet paper to stock up. Likewise, in my field of fertility, women are facing something very scarce due to time: oocytes. It's important to clarify that their limited supply of eggs will run out at a certain time. That scarcity and urgency often motivates them to proceed with fertility treatments.

Understanding this psychology can boost your marketing power, as long as you're honest. For example, you can use words such as: "Act now. Only 10 appointments are available each week," or "This 50% off coupon expires on Friday."

Unfortunately, scarcity marketing can also create such demand and competition that people resort to mob-like behavior and violence, as demonstrated during Black Friday sales when customers fight over televisions and other sale items.

Be Bold! Be Innovative! Blaze a New Trail!

You're already exhibiting a trailblazing spirit by embarking on a journey to become a MedikalPreneur. The best way to differentiate yourself from the competition is to be bold and innovative, and to ignore people who warn you to play it safe.

Our "sperm mobile" exemplifies this. When I proposed the idea, people called me crazy, but I followed my bold vision. As a result, this delivery vehicle became one of our greatest marketing tools. The story boils down to having two competing needs in the budget. On the one hand, we needed the logistics to move the blood from one office to another one. On the other hand, our marketing team member wanted to fund a highway billboard to promote the clinic. The transportation was going to cost $30 per day and the billboard would be $5,000 a month.

"Aha! I said. "We will have both for the price of one." How? A car and a wrap cost us only about $17,000. It would create a moving billboard while fulfilling the need of a team member driving to get the blood to the other office. This was a positive-sum game: we had two needs and created a few things to utilize these endeavors with less money.

Never underestimate the power of your words as a marketing tool to persuade your team to endorse your innovative ideas. Likewise, the most persuasive words and images can boost the effectiveness of your marketing. I decided to invest in our own delivery vehicle rather than paying another company to pick up and deliver samples to the lab and provide transportation for our center's needs. I gathered our team together and said, "I want everybody to look at the different wraps for the car."

Tony Anderson was in the meeting when I proposed the orange paint job that would show sperm swimming toward the wheels as if they were eggs, along with "RMA of Texas" and our phone number.

"I'm sitting here looking at the car," Tony recalls. "And he wanted to wrap it and it would have sperm all over it, advertising RMA of Texas and the donor egg program. The paint is orange, and it just glows down the road with sperm going around the wheel like the wheel is the egg."

Tony and others thought my idea was a foolish waste of money—until his wife proved my point by photographing the car, posting it on Facebook, and starting a trend for people to continue—more than a decade later—to post pictures of our sperm mobile on social media sites. This free advertising exemplifies the power of bold marketing, even when people disagree with your ideas until they see your innovation getting positive results.

Our sperm mobile became a moving billboard. When people stop at a traffic light, the orange color and unusual design attract their attention. Then, with a simple glimpse, they see our center's phone number.

I share this to show that your Marketing Plan should include old-fashioned, face-to-face meetings, as well as bold innovations. When you follow your hunches, bring your vision to life, and take courageous action as a MedikalPreneur, your marketing strategies can be very successful.

CHAPTER 7

Negotiation: Win-Win Strategies for the MedikalPreneur

"Let us never negotiate out of fear. But let us never fear to negotiate."

– John F. Kennedy

DOCTORS NEGOTIATE WITH PATIENTS every day, seeking the best outcome. But sometimes less fortunate results occur, as described in a *Harvard Business Review* article on October 21, 2013. In "Negotiation Strategies for Doctors—and Hospitals,"[89] writers Deepak Malhotra and Manu Malhotra described a 54-year-old man who was having a heart attack when he arrived in the ER. The doctor recommended a heart catheterization and said the man would probably need a stent placement.

Though the patient understood the grave risks of refusing treatment, he left the hospital. Hours later, an ambulance transported him back; he was in cardiac arrest. This was not a successful negotiation to convince the patient to undergo a life-saving surgery, and the results were tragic.

A doctor's ability to negotiate with patients can be a matter of life and death. Apply this mindset to your business, because your financial survival will depend on it. Unfortunately, many physicians don't like to negotiate; some may find it frightening. And it may be uncomfortable as you shift from the power position with patients who ask, "Hey Doctor, can I have this medication or that treatment?" Now is the time to learn how to *not* care how people respond—and be prepared for them to say no—as you proceed in the best interest of your company.

Good Negotiation Skills Create A Winning Outcome For All Parties

As a MedikalPreneur, your negotiation skills—or lack thereof—can make or break your business. From the beginning, you'll need to finesse negotiations with: the person who is loaning you money to open your company; your team members regarding their salaries and benefits; vendors; potential partners regarding the terms of your partnership; possible shareholders about their role in governance and their portion of profits; and patients and clients.

In every situation, you want the best possible outcome for you, the other party, and the people and situations impacted by the decisions. Negotiations are *not* about getting the best deal for yourself and leaving the other person feeling cheated. Yes, you'll have to do some give and take, but each side should leave the negotiation feeling satisfied that the deal is fair and beneficial. Usually, one person may walk away with a slight advantage, and hopefully that person is you. But again, negotiations set the stage for a relationship that you want functioning smoothly—untainted by resentment or distrust. Any inequality or unfairness can taint the relationship and outcome as you move forward.

Lawyers are considered very good negotiators. Physicians can be excellent negotiators, if they're willing to learn how to negotiate.

"Paco," a lawyer on my side once told me during a negotiation, "a good lawyer and negotiator is when, after the negotiation, both parties agree and both come out a little dissatisfied and unhappy; that is the proof of a good negotiation."

"I have never heard such complete bulsh&*t!" I responded. "So if you do a negotiation and everyone comes happy, you are a bad lawyer?"

This prevailing idea that negotiations are always a zero-sum game is not accurate. We have to think positive-sum game, and know that **creativity** and **patience** are the most important ingredients in a negotiation.

Negotiations: Play a Positive-Sum Game

In negotiations, you can play a zero-sum game where someone takes advantage of the other person, creating an unfair deal. You can play a negative-sum game where you both end up in a worse place. Or you can play a positive-sum game where both parties benefit in positive ways that help more people.

Here's an example of a positive-sum game when you negotiate. Let's say we have nine test tubes for an experiment. Two departments need the test tubes to do the experiments. In a negative-sum game, people will say, "Give me four test tubes, and we cut one in half, so each of us gets four-and-a-half test tubes." This limits us to doing four experiments each, because we cut one in half. That is a negative-sum game!

Next, if we negotiate and I take advantage of you—keeping five test tubes for myself while you only get four—that is a zero-sum game. Now I can conduct five experiments, and you can only do four. I may think I'm a winner, but wrongdoings can backfire and cost you more in consequences than any perceived benefits of "winning."

So how can you create a positive-sum game? By looking at a situation from all angles and strategizing a plan that maximizes the benefits for everyone. For example, I know that you like to work in the mornings, and I am an evening person. During negotiations, I could say, "Why don't you use the test tubes in the morning, and I use the test tubes in the evening? That way, both departments can do nine experiments!"

That's the best explanation for how a MedikalPreneur should apply innovative thinking to create a positive-sum game and resolve every challenging situation. Taking more than a fair share, or destroying assets (such as the test tubes), does not benefit everyone. Being creative and having a positive attitude leads you toward finding the best solutions.

Negotiations are not all about money; they involve an exchange of time, talent, resources, and valuable assets between two or more parties. Therefore, think more holistically and consider all those levers in your negotiation rather than focusing on the money or price.

When Negotiations Fail, Find Your Batna

BATNA is an acronym for the Best Alternative To a Negotiated Agreement. This is your walkout point and what you leave with, if your negotiation is unsuccessful. You MUST know this before entering a negotiation. Knowing your BATNA empowers you, provides you with leverage, and guides your decision-making.

Imagine that you want to rent space for your office, and in your town, a landlord has agreed to lease a good space to you for $8,500 a month. However, you find another space with similar characteristics and the landlord wants $10,500. You as the tenant know that your BATNA is $8,500 and *ideally* would like to rent it at $6,500. The landlord knows his/her numbers and it makes no business sense to rent this space for less than $7,000, because he has other prospects who have offered that amount. Therefore, the landlord's BATNA is $7,000. The range of a possible deal is between $7,000 and $8,500.

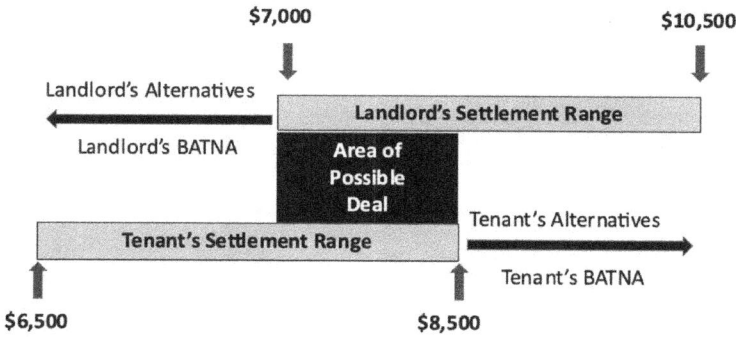

Think outside the box! Sometimes when a negotiation fails, it forces you to conceive a better alternative. Identify potential gains and losses on each side, and ask, "What is the alternative if you don't enter into a negotiation? Or what is the alternative if you don't formalize a negotiation?"

Prepare Before You Begin—Do Your Research

Preparation can help ensure the best outcome when you're negotiating. This means doing research on the issue and the people involved. For example, if you're negotiating to purchase a building to set up shop as a MedikalPreneur, you should know the property's history, the comparative values of nearby buildings, the area's demographics, and local real estate trends. In addition, learn about whoever is coming to the negotiating table with you and your real estate agent, attorney, and team. Research their history, their strengths and weaknesses, and what factors might motivate them to sell the property to you at the lowest price. Investigate the years of the contract. Is it a personal guarantee or a company guarantee? What is the average amount of money you could get for tenant improvements? What is your average triple net? Can you put a sign outside or not?

Feature	Details	Record Your Research
Objectives	What is your objective and the other party's objective?	
What do they want?	What specific things are you and the other party requesting?	
Motivations	Why do they want what they are requesting? What are your motivations and interests?	
BATNA	What alternatives do you have if this does not work?	
Walk-out points and trade-offs	What are your non-negotiable points and what can you concede?	
Interpersonal Relationships	Do you need or want a relationship with this person? What are others' experience negotiating with them? Find common ground. What do you have in common?	
Creative Solutions	How can you create a positive sum game? Think differently.	

In addition, when you negotiate, consider the following:

Know what everybody wants. Listen very carefully and watch for nonverbal cues during initial meetings. Also, ask a lot of questions. When you're treating a patient, you ask questions to determine a diagnosis and treatment. Likewise, when negotiating, ask questions to evaluate the strengths, weaknesses, and objectives of every person involved.

When you see the negotiations from each person's point of view, you can pitch your ideas and craft convincing conversations about why the other person or team should agree to your terms. In addition, when you know what they want in the deal, you'll be able to propose your plan in a way that highlights benefits for them. Also, remember that the *why* is more revealing than the *want*. What they want is one thing. Why they want it is much better! This will help guarantee their support and agreement.

Very importantly, use language that frames your proposal in the most positive terms. For example, let's assume you're negotiating with an organization that owns and operates eight clinics. Your goal is to convince the company to hire your business to manage the clinics. You could enter the negotiations and say something like, "The decision-makers are over there, too far away from the front lines to make good decisions about how to manage each clinic, so the service is inconsistent and chaotic, and the employees are overwhelmed, which results in poor and sometimes tragic outcomes for the patients." How you say it is as—or more—important than what you say.

The above statement is negative and accusatory, so the managers at the negotiating table will become defensive. The mood of the meeting could deteriorate further if you say something like, "You should decentralize the power, and the decision-makers should be down here on our level." Those decision-makers will accuse you of attempting to usurp their power or take something away from them, and they will not be agreeable to anything you propose.

However, if you use positive language and make people feel like they're winning, then they will concede to your ideas. For example, you could say, "Why don't we regionalize the decision-making? This way, we can reduce your load and streamline operations in a way that better serves the patients and creates bigger profits for the company."

When you said "reduce your load" instead of "take away your power," that sounds beneficial to the managers, as do the promises of better patient care and bigger profits. And by replacing "decentralize" with a more positive-sounding word such as "regionalize," you change the tone of the dialogue. And that boosts your chances for successful negotiations. Keep an emphasis on wording; it's powerful!

Know your walk-out point. The most important thing to know before you start the negotiation is, "What is my walk-out point?" That means you should know the parameters of what you will and will not agree to. Always keep this in mind, and do not bend; you will regret it. Your walk-out point may be that, "I will not pay more than six dollars for this orange." The seller may say, "I'll sell it for ten dollars," but you'll respond, "No, I'll buy it for two dollars." Then the seller may offer it for eight dollars. The two of you go back and forth, but the seller won't budge, nor will you. Your walk-out point is six dollars, so you end the negotiation by saying, "You can keep your orange."

Your boundary must be very clear. Do not let emotions take over. And do not allow desperation to dictate decisions. Early in your business, if you're overly eager to complete a deal that lowballs your value, you will regret it—and possibly suffer financial consequences.

Know that you won't get everything you want. Trade-offs are an inevitable reality of negotiations. Physicians are competitive and want everything on their list. But you cannot have it all. It's okay to not get everything you want, and this does not put you in a losing position. It's simply part of the process. Focus on interest, motivations, and whys. Do not focus on positions or wants. Say you're trying to convince a new physician to do Saturday clinics, but he does not want to see patients on the weekends. This is **what** you want, but **why** you want it is to increase revenue. He might say, "You know what, I don't want to come on Saturdays. But why don't I open a clinic in an area where nobody has a fertility clinic?" He's focusing on **why** I want it, not **what** I want. This is the reason that it's important to understand the **why.**

Be creative. Here's an example of how a MedikalPreneur might successfully negotiate employment terms with an ideal candidate for your team. Because you've already done your homework, you understand that she wants a good position to contribute with her skills, and to spend more quality time with her family. When you discuss compensation, she asks for $35 per hour. You can only offer $30, and your walk-out point is $33 per hour.

"No, I want $34.50," she counters.

"Okay, what if I pay you $30 per hour," you respond, "but give you one more week of vacation? Or what if I put your car under the practice and make it tax deductible for me, but you get the car and you get the gas?"

Another example could be that if you know this person wants to take a one-week course in Orlando, you can offer to pay for her to take the class—with her kids tagging along for a five-day family vacation—and you pay for it. Her training will enhance her job performance in the business, and her gratitude will boost her morale, which radiates to the team, your patients, and clients.

Creative negotiation is not based on money; it's inspired by the question: "What do you want?" To know what the person wants, you have to ask, and set a tone where he or she feels comfortable telling you an honest answer. This way, you both win. The result is that you have a happy employee with a cheerful demeanor while doing her best work. Creativity is the key to successful negotiations.

Use the "Hoe vs. Rake" Concept to Balance the Workplace

As a business owner, keep in mind the "hoe vs. rake" concept while interacting with your team. You want to keep a healthy balance between the human and business sides of your workplace environment. Therefore, when you design and operate the company, think of a hoe and a rake in relation to tilling the soil, which symbolizes your profits. Don't always use a hoe, which has a long handle with a flat piece of metal that drags everything along with it. The hoe takes as much soil (profits) as possible and pulls it all toward you. That leaves no soil behind to grow other plants. Instead, you should always use a rake. The rake has space between the metal "teeth" that allows for some soil to remain for others, so you're not taking all the soil for yourself. Your team members should feel that they have a stake in the company's well-being and future success, and they should profit accordingly.

Use evidence-based negotiation. Before you begin negotiations, do research to collect evidence to bolster your offer. This evidence could include recent sale amounts for similar properties in the area where you're attempting to buy a building for your medical business. Evidence could also be demographic details about the communities from which you will attract patients and clients. This will enable you to conclude that, "Hey, this person is doing this for this prize, and the other person is doing X-Y-Z." You have evidence on how something should be done.

You're always in a stronger position when you come to the conversation well-prepared with credible facts. Say you're negotiating a salary. You research the national average of that salary in the area with X years of experience. This gives you a way to start a discussion that is not argumentative. The data facilitates evidence-based negotiation that does the leveraging for you to say, "I'm worth more than that because of A-B-C-D."

The person who is motivated to do the research prior to engaging someone else's time and attention demonstrates self-motivation and wins respect during negotiations. Therefore, be the impressive and authoritative person who comes to the negotiation as fully informed as possible.

The Methodology of Negotiation Is as Important as the Terms and Elements Negotiated

One of the first things that all the parties involved should agree upon is the process of negotiations. It's important to set the rules of the negotiation prior to discussions and bargaining.

A) Both parties need to know who is making the final decision, because you do not want to use all your tools and trade-offs when something can arise to alter the deal.

B) What time frame are you working with? Do you or the other party have specific dates in mind to accomplish something?

C) Who will be in the meetings and what decision-making authority do they have?

The methodology and process should be outlined before the negotiation begins. It's like playing a game: Know the rules before starting to play. Otherwise, people can change the rules as they go; that is not good for negotiation.

Understanding Two-Party and Multi-Party Negotiations

Negotiations that involve you and another person are called two-party negotiations. When they involve multiple people or entities, they are multiparty negotiations. Each situation involves unique dynamics. Consider a tennis game, where the objective is very clear: hit the ball over the net and the other side will respond. However, multiparty negotiations are more like a three-ring circus where each ring orchestrates performances to please different audiences. Chaos can result! It's like having too many chefs in the kitchen, or too many surgeons in the operating room: everyone has an agenda, and reaching an agreement that satisfies everyone can be elusive. So how can you proceed in an orderly fashion?

Create a strategy. This should include researching the goals and desires of each entity, knowing your walk-out point, and campaigning to achieve your objectives. Anticipate fast-moving changes. Three things typically happen to complicate multi-party negotiations, according to the Program on Negotiation at Harvard Law School,[90] and these are:

People form coalitions. Ally with like-minded members of each negotiating party. Convince them of your ideas by using persuasive language that emphasizes the many benefits of your proposal.

Challenges arise. Miscommunication, competition, even deceit can wreak havoc on multi-party negotiations. Be patient and discern fact from fiction, as well as reality from rumors. If the experience feels like you've stepped into a hornet's nest, getting stung from multiple directions, then it's probably best to withdraw from these negotiations.

Each party wavers on their BATNA. People inevitably clash over details and non-negotiables. Evaluate each situation and decide whether you're seeing red flags that could cause major problems later. You can always walk away from a negotiation.

While we're on the topic of multiple negotiators, let's discuss MESOs: Multiple Equivalent Offers Simultaneously. This means you can craft several offers with differing trade-offs, and submit them at the same time. This gives the other party the opportunity to accept or reject one of the offers. If rejection occurs, ask why, and use this knowledge for future reference.

Use the Ackerman Bargaining Method

The extremely effective Ackerman Bargaining Method[91] will spare you the angst of walking away from the negotiating table feeling like you could have gotten a better deal. This technique involves making counteroffers that become increasingly smaller, until you reach your intended offer.

Let's demonstrate the Ackerman Bargaining Method with the example of purchasing a building for your business. Here are the factors to consider.

Know your target price. This is the amount that you want to spend to purchase the property. Don't pull a number out of thin air. Research the market values of buildings that are best suited for medical businesses, and understand the varying factors that impact price, such as location and local demographics. Then, let's say you're willing to spend $500,000.

Set your "anchor price," which is about 65% of your target price. This makes your anchor price $325,000. Offer this to the seller. Chances are, the low amount will shock them. Your intention with this tactic is to devalue the property in their minds.

They will respond by touting all the positive and valuable aspects of the building, and they will come back with a counteroffer. Keep in mind that the seller may also have set an anchor price, and this may be the figure they're presenting at this stage of the game. It will be too much for you. Don't be discouraged. Just move on to the next round of negotiations. Offer the seller 85% of your target price: $425,000. This will indicate your willingness to negotiate to find a dollar amount that's closer to what they want. They will counter-offer this amount.

Your response should be 95% of your target price: $475,000. They will counteroffer again. Stay confident, ask for a break to leave the room and think, but never give in to pressure or feel that you're stuck and desperate. Stay in control. Here's your opportunity to make your final offer—your target price—$500,000, or 100% of the dollar amount you're willing to spend to purchase the real estate.

Remember this formula: 65%, 85%, 95%, and 100%. During each

of the four rounds of negotiations, convey a sense of good will, empathy, and feeling that "this is the absolute most I can afford right now."

Another tip: your final target price should not be a round number. It should be something like $499,875. This shows the seller that you've carefully calculated a precise amount of money for your final offer. The seller may also make non-monetary offers to tempt you to lower your price, such as including lab equipment that's already inside the building.

Remember that you did your research and your numbers are solid. Stay confident in knowing that you're making a solid offer, and that you want the best deal to lay a strong foundation for your company's long-term financial viability. Also keep in mind that you can always end the negotiations if you feel the seller is unreasonable or any other factors give you a gut feeling that this is not the best situation for you. You have the power to decide, speak up, and stand your ground; flex your buying power, or you'll regret conceding to a deal that does not serve your best, long-term financial success.

If these negotiation techniques make you nervous, ask a colleague or mentor to practice with you, and tell them to simulate tough situations riddled with unexpected twists. This will help you learn and master the art of negotiating as a MedikalPreneur.

More Points to Remember About Negotiating

1. Look at the forest. What is the broad view? Ask your counterpart(s) about their perspectives and goals.

2. Investigate. Find ways to cooperate. Understand everyone's motivations, not wants! Put many options on the table and let the other party or parties criticize them or improve on them.

3. Use evidence-based negotiation to reach agreement. Avoid

pressure and coercion. How will they save face with X or Y decisions with the people they report to?

4. Pay attention to details, logistics, and operations.

5. Focus on interpersonal relationships and build rapport. Find common ground and cooperation elements. Understand how politics will influence decisions.

6. Use mirroring: repeat back in a sentence the key words of what your counterpart just said. This promotes clarity and cooperation, and helps you explore hidden points.

7. Remember that no matter what you want to implement, you need three things: operations, finances, and political will. How are you going to do it, who is going to pay for it, and are the stakeholders willing to do it?

   » Manage emotions for yourself and the counterparts. This is difficult, because negotiations are an interpersonal exercise.

   » Studies show that caffeine improves focus and quickens thinking, which can enhance persuasion.

In summary, apply the confidence you feel as a physician negotiating with patients, along with the tools in this chapter, to ensure your success as a MedikalPreneur.

CHAPTER 8

Decision-Making: Wisdom + Evidence = Success

"Decision-making: Evidence is your tool, not your rule. Wisdom is king!"

— Paco

AS A PHYSICIAN, YOU'RE constantly making decisions about how to care for patients. What medication should you prescribe? What surgery should be performed? What procedure should be used to stop the bleeding and save the patient's life? Some choices have life-or-death consequences. You make these decisions in a split-second with confidence that's rooted in your medical training, along with the instincts that you have cultivated over the years. The ability to make decisions, many times with imperfect information, is one reason why physicians can be great businesspeople.

While your decision-making skills and confidence will improve with practice, understanding the psychology and science behind decision-making can help you avoid making wrong and/or inconsistent choices that hurt your company.

Your decision-making method may involve composing a list of pro's and con's, discussing choices with our trusted confidants, crunching the numbers, praying, meditating, and imagining the best- and worst-case scenarios with each choice, and reviewing the outcomes of past choices. Then you make a decision and aim for positive results.

The challenge is finding the sweet spot for ourselves and people affected by our decisions. We need to know their preferences, risks, threats, gains, and the price of decisions made. This constant juggle of quantitative objective data and subjective preferences shifts with our assumptions on risks, benefits, preferences, and costs. We also need to distinguish between wants, needs, and non-negotiables.

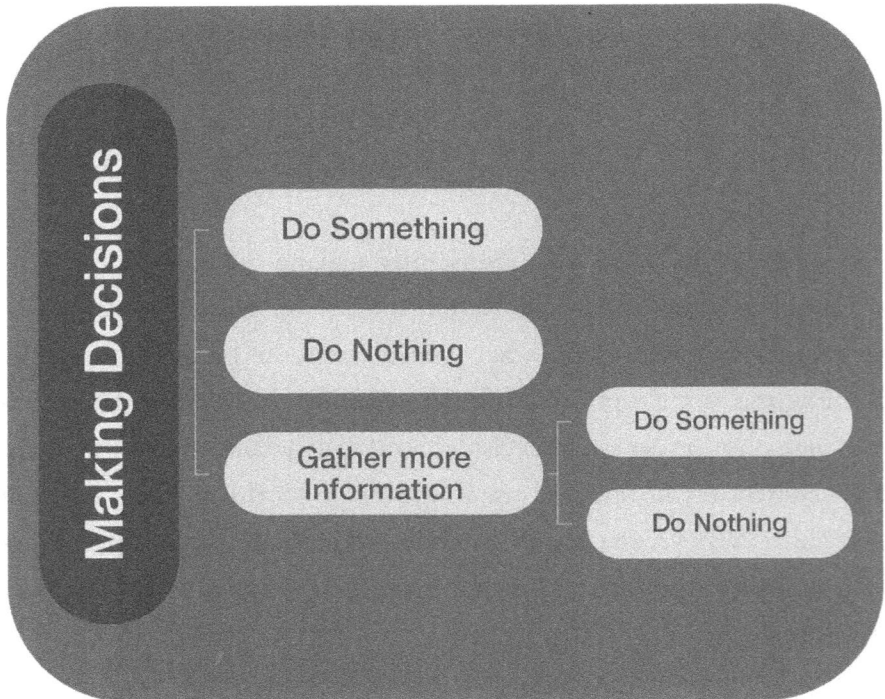

Evidence-based decision-making relies on objective data, but you need to incorporate subjective preferences. For example, the patient wants a pill, not an injection, so you make decisions accordingly. But sometimes we take too long to decide, or we make no decision, which is actually deciding to do nothing. That can cost you the time, money, and success that awaits if you make the most beneficial choice. That's why you should implement processes that utilize as much data as possible to make the most informed decisions to ensure your success.

From Evidence-Based to Wisdom-Based Decision-Making

- **Evidence:** the available body of facts or information indicating whether a belief or proposition is true or valid.[92]

- **Wisdom:** the quality of having experience, knowledge, and good judgment; the quality of being wise; the soundness of an action or decision with regard to the application of experience, knowledge, and good judgment.[93]

—Google/Oxford Language

As physicians, we're trained to use evidence as a tool to provide the best medical care for our patients. With experience comes wisdom, and this forms a foundation for our methods of care. So which one—evidence or wisdom—should most influence decision-making? And how can we translate this into best practices as MedikalPreneurs?

First, let's define Evidence-Based Medicine and Wisdom-Based Medicine.

Evidence-Based Medicine integrates "the best research evidence with clinical expertise and patient values," according to Johns Hopkins Medicine.[94] It requires a commitment to continuing education about the newest research, treatments, and studies that provide guidance for the best medical care. This endless quest for learning involves reading multiple periodicals and integrating new ideas into daily practices.

Wisdom-Based Medicine is the practice of using your experience and expertise to make decisions that increase your chances of the optimal outcome for your patient or client.

In medicine and in business, a vast gray area extends between these two concepts. Every situation is different, and you can manifest the greatest success by utilizing these concepts as tools, not rules.

In an article entitled, "Wisdom based and evidence based medicine" in *Diabetes, Obesity and Metabolism: A Journal of Pharmacology and Therapeutics,*[95] author D.R. Matthews explains that evidence and wisdom sometimes clash. He cites Dr. Archie Cochrane—known as the father of Evidence-Based Medicine—who worked at a World War II prisoner of war camp, where he realized that the conventional treatment for tuberculosis might cost soldiers' lives; that motivated him to advocate for the medical community to rely on scientific, evidence-based medical protocols to provide the best treatments.

Fast forward to the 21st century, and we need to incorporate evidence as our north star while considering our patients' values and preferences, as well as the physician's expertise, and the resources available to implement a given therapy. At the same time, we need to glean wisdom from transparent conversations with our patients about their desires, wants, wishes, fears, circumstances, and financial resources.

His point underscores our mission as physicians to cultivate health in our patients and the population at large. And health is not merely the absence of illness or injury, or a listing of numbers defining resting heart rate, blood pressure, blood sugar, height, weight, Pulsox, etc. Health is defined as a comprehensive state of physical, mental, and social wellness. As we apply this same principle to our work as MedikalPreneurs, let's look at factors that influence whether men, women, and children are healthy or unhealthy:

- Income and social status
- Social support networks
- Education and literacy
- Employment/working conditions

- Social environments
- Physical environments
- Diet and physical activity
- Personal health practices and coping skills
- Healthy child development
- Biology and genetics
- Health care services
- Gender
- Culture

When we treat a patient, we must consider all of the above. The process, as the diagram below illustrates, requires us to merge Evidence-Based Medicine with the Patient's Set of Values (rooted in and influenced by the above health factors) with our expertise as a healthcare provider.

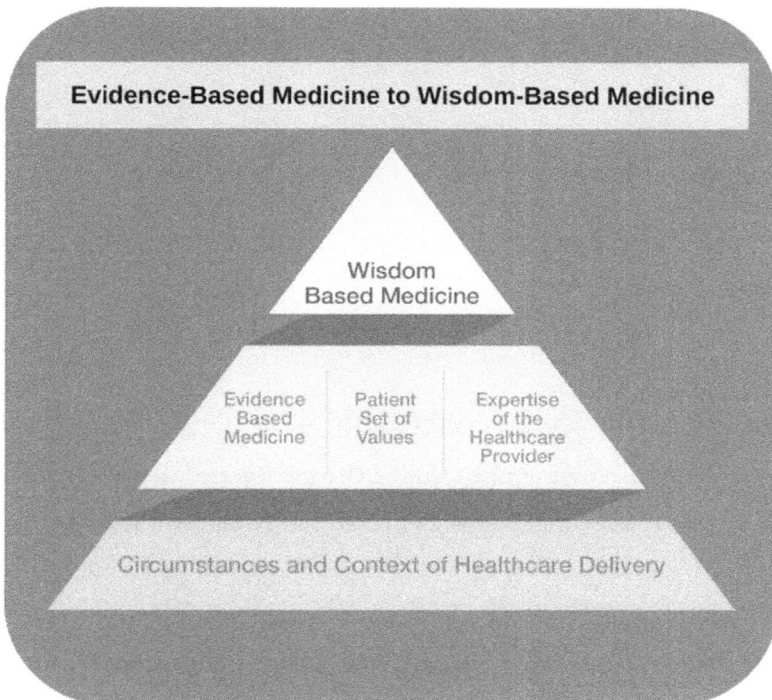

Evidence-Based Medicine to Wisdom-Based Medicine

Wisdom Based Medicine

Evidence Based Medicine | Patient Set of Values | Expertise of the Healthcare Provider

Circumstances and Context of Healthcare Delivery

You can interpret the bottom line as evidence that a particular medication works and the patient knows how to use it, but they can't pay—or lives in a region where that med isn't available. Those three pillars depend upon the circumstances and context of where and how we provide care. These three pillars of Wisdom-Based Medicine form, as the diagram shows, the foundation of Circumstances and Context of Healthcare Delivery. Their impact will depend upon the circumstances and context of where and how we provide care.

As a MedikalPreneur, when you make a decision, consider: the evidence of best business practices; variables presented by your company and your patients or clients; and your wisdom and knowledge of your particular product, service, and industry. Also recognize that:

- Evidence is the concept of clarity, where we think in a binary way: right or wrong.

- Effort in attaining evidence can come with the price tag of not achieving wisdom.

- Evidence should be your employee, not your boss.

- Evidence is like money. It should be your servant, but it cannot be your master.

Evidence Is Your Tool, Not Your Rule

Evidence-Based Medicine is a tool for the greater good, but it's not your rule. Remember this phrase that I coined: **It's your tool, not your rule.**

Nobody questions that evidence is the best guide because it's rooted in research, experience, and proof of the best outcomes. However, can you apply it all the time? This depends upon: the healthcare provider's experience; the circumstances and values of the healthcare; and how it's delivered to the patient. Ask yourself, "How confident am I in delivering this care?" The values come from the patient and his or her preferences.

For example, a woman is bleeding to death in the emergency room. The evidence says that the best way to save her life is to do a blood transfusion. However, as a Jehovah's Witness, her religious values prohibit this type of medical intervention. What should you do? Another example is a woman with a tubal disease who comes to me for fertility treatments. The evidence tells me that the best option is to remove the tube and do IVF. But she's in rural Kentucky and has no money. The circumstances and healthcare delivery tell me that the procedure is the best option to enable her to start a family. What decision should be made? One more example: a woman has only enough money for one IVF cycle. Evidence says transfer one embryo; two would increase the risk of twins.

"Doctor, this is the only chance I have," she says. "I cannot pay another cycle. I understand my risk. I need two embryos."

As the physician, are you going to tell her no? This is a dilemma. Can you impose your values as a physician on the patient? Or are you going to respect her judgment call?

Now let's revisit the "drill and hole" analogy, about the guy who goes into the hardware store and asks for a quarter-inch drill. The employee tells him that he doesn't need a drill to make holes to hang frames; several other options would solve his problem. The lesson is that sometimes people are asking for the wrong thing, because they don't really know what they need.

In business, sometimes patients (or customers) don't know what they need. And what they know is limited. For example, if our patient said, "I want a baby!" we responded by saying, "Wait, you want to plan a family. If you want one baby and you're 25, we have time, so I can start you with a simple procedure. But if you're 38, and you want three children in your family, then we need to freeze your embryos. Do you want a girl first, or a boy?"

Then we helped the patient understand that many options were available, depending upon her circumstances and what she wanted. Many times the patient had not considered or learned about options beyond desiring a baby. An important aspect of this fact-finding conversation is watching the patient's or the client's nonverbal cues. Sometimes an expression or gesture can speak volumes about what the patient or client truly desires. Pay attention and ask questions accordingly.

In terms of Evidence- and Wisdom-Based Medicine, how do these concepts apply? This 38-year-old patient wants to get pregnant. She may get pregnant with artificial insemination. That is not wisdom-based. Why? Because I'm treating a problem, not the patient. Instead, I have to ask the best question: "How many children do you envision in your family?"

"Three," she answers.

"Then you need IVF," I respond, "and we will store the three."

Good doctors use evidence to treat the disease. Great doctors use wisdom to treat patients. Or, as Sir William Osler said, "The good physician treats the disease; the great physician treats the patient who has the disease."[96] Being a great physician means asking questions, listening, and learning the patient's story and circumstances, then tailoring a treatment plan accordingly. If all the factors involved are perfect and known, and all information is absolute, then it's not a decision. Decisions are made when you have imperfect information. And you make some mistakes and undesired outcomes. Here's where wisdom comes into play.

Wisdom-Based Medicine Is Your Rule

Wisdom is the next frontier of medicine because everybody is so focused on Evidence-Based Medicine, which provides comfort and security, but is only a fraction of the equation involving many shifting parts.

"Change is the only constant in life," said the ancient philosopher Heraclitus of Ephesus,[97] so we sometimes have to apply something less idealistic and more practical than the black-and-white, rigid application of the evidence. We can best do this in collaboration with our patients, by assessing their values, preferences, possibilities, wants, and needs.

This epitomizes the idea of the "prosumer," which is "a prospective consumer who is involved in the design, manufacture, or development of a product or service,"[98] according to the Google Dictionary. Your patients or clients can help you deepen your knowledge about your practice by providing real-life evidence of innovative ways to resolve major challenges.

Wisdom-Based Medicine is your rule. Wisdom! Use the tool of Evidence-Based Medicine, combined with the patient's wants, desires, and limitations. Then consider this in the context and circumstances of the healthcare delivery where you are—whether you're practicing medicine in a war zone, the jungle, the suburbs, an urban setting, or a rural area where patients have no insurance. You have the same evidence and the same tools, which you tailor with your wisdom to individualize your decision-making in the context of each patient's circumstances.

Remember, evidence should be your employee, not your boss. Wisdom is your boss. What's the difference between knowledge and wisdom? Nobody summarized it better than British journalist Miles Kington: "Knowledge is knowing that a tomato is a fruit; wisdom is not putting it in a fruit salad."[99]

Evolving From a Sick Care System to a Health Care System

Your expansive thinking as a MedikalPreneur should include challenging the status quo and seeking innovations that lead to better outcomes for your business and your patients or clients. Be forward-thinking, while conceiving new ideas to improve and advance the current state of medical care and/or any other industry. We can do this by transforming our "sick care system" into a "healthcare system," as this diagram illustrates:

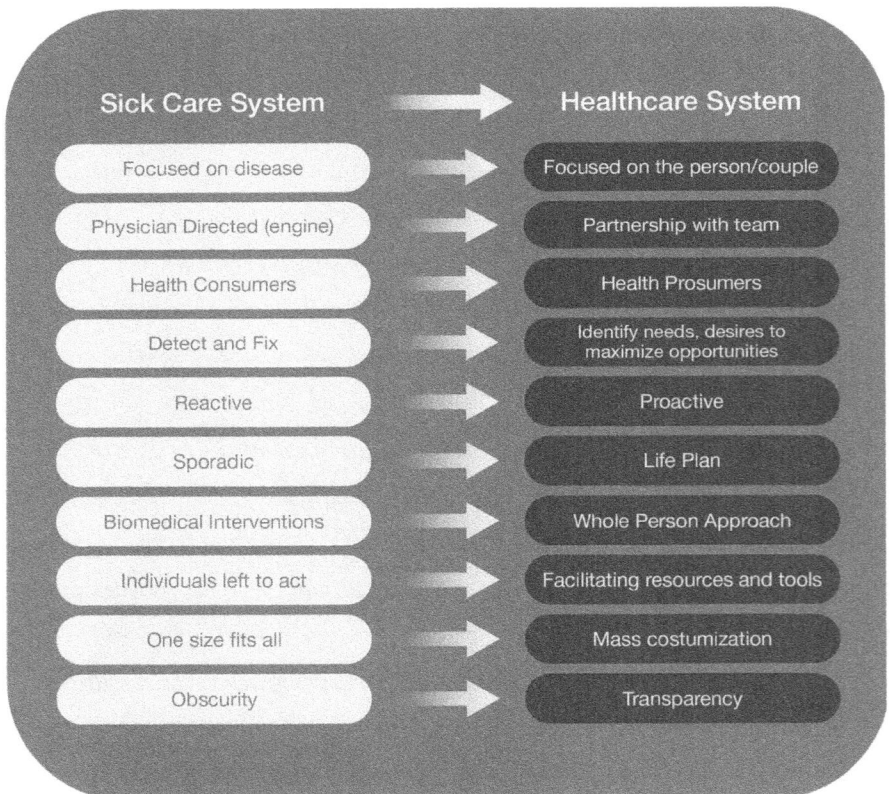

Sick Care System	→	Healthcare System
Focused on disease	→	Focused on the person/couple
Physician Directed (engine)	→	Partnership with team
Health Consumers	→	Health Prosumers
Detect and Fix	→	Identify needs, desires to maximize opportunities
Reactive	→	Proactive
Sporadic	→	Life Plan
Biomedical Interventions	→	Whole Person Approach
Individuals left to act	→	Facilitating resources and tools
One size fits all	→	Mass costumization
Obscurity	→	Transparency

The right column is based on big-picture, long-term thinking with comprehensive analysis, as well as openness. These concepts help you think beyond the current problem and step into a realm of prevention and mass application. Review each point and notice the collaborative dynamics of each concept on the right, in contrast to the outdated practices on the left that result in many of the problems and criticisms that our healthcare industry faces today. Understanding and applying the concepts in the "Health Care" column will serve you well as a MedikalPreneur.

Triads Help You Make Decisions

A triad is a group or set of three connected people or things. For example, a triad of medication, diet, and exercise can help treat high blood pressure. We're constantly using triads to make decisions in our families and in our workplaces. Triads come into play with every decision because, before you take action, you need to consider three factors:

- How you're going to do it;

- How you're going to pay for it; and

- How you're going to get stakeholders to give you the green light.

For example, when my friend received a bonus, I asked, "What are you going to do with the money?"

"I'm going to rent an apartment on a beach close to my parents' house and drop my two kids there," he said, "then take my wife to the beach."

I pointed out that he had the money and the total operational implementation for his idea, but he lacked the third requirement of the triad. "Have you asked your wife and kids if they agree to your plan?" I asked.

A week later, he said he had asked them, and shared his plan with a way to pay for it. However, they wanted to go to Disney World. In the end, the family's political will prevailed. So guess where they went? To see Mickey.

You can have the money to pay for it, but without the political will, it won't happen. You can apply these same dynamics to a family, business, city, or country—anywhere that involves people. His family's buy-in was the "political will" required to execute a plan. Political will is the agreement of everyone before you can spend the money and implement your strategy. Without political will—the support of your stakeholders—nothing happens.

As an entrepreneur, when you're trying to disrupt something—a marketplace, a competitor's business, the status quo, etc.—you will have enemies. The political will is going to oppose you. Find allies to help you implement and pay for what you want. For example, if you have a medical office and want to open on Saturdays, you have the plan and the money to make it happen. But the employees do not like your idea. They're the third aspect of the triad, and without their support, you will remain closed on Saturdays.

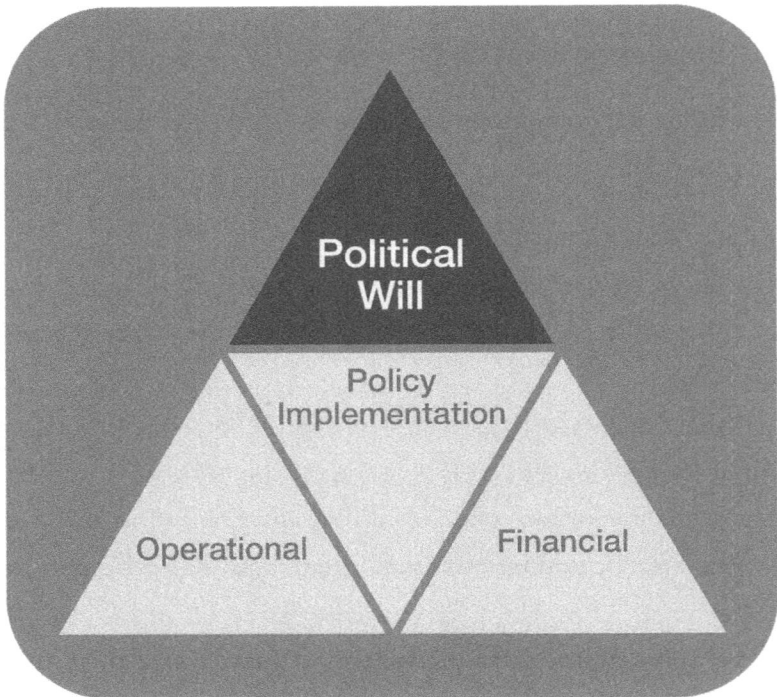

It's Better to Make a Decision Than to Not Make One

Making a big decision can keep you up at night, scanning the ceiling in the darkness for clues on how to make the right choice. Indecision can gnaw at you. Fear of selecting the wrong option can paralyze you, then cause anxiety that you're losing out on opportunities, patients, clients, and money. So, how do you combat the angst of decision-making?

I highly recommend that you read *DEAL! Discovery, Engagement, and Leverage for Professionals* by Dr. Jeff Belkora. As a faculty member at the University of California, San Francisco School of Medicine, he founded and directs the Patient Support Corps, which helps patients and families navigating important medical decisions. In his 2015 book, Belkora presents five "drivers" that can help you make decisions: physical and emotional cues; considerations about social trends; spiritual guidance; self-awareness; and data.[100]

The goal is to implement these ideas with such finesse that you actually put yourself out of business. That means the bariatric surgeon helps so many people lose weight that her surgery is no longer needed. That means that I help every woman get pregnant and fertility services are no longer needed. Then I can move into a new realm of being a MedikalPreneur, by providing products and services that meet unmet needs and offer preventive healthcare programs. Likewise, lawyers and teachers should be creating the architecture for improving behaviors and outcomes so they are no longer needed. Striving for this ideal will result in the best business practices and outcomes. And next business ventures will evolve as a result.

"Paco, why are you sharing the secrets to success?" people ask me.

"Because it stimulates me to create something different," I answer.

This MedikalPreneurial mindset focuses on improving our current ways of doing things by conceiving and applying creative ideas and innovations that radically disrupt and revolutionize health care, and our collective wellness, in the best ways possible. As the writer William James said: "The greatest discovery of my generation is that a human being can alter his life by altering his attitudes."

Apply the 80-20 Rule

If 80% of the factors favor your decision-making, that's enough to make a decision. This is the 80-20 rule, not to be confused with the Pareto Rule, which is totally different. Say you sell books. You have 100 customers. You earn $1,000. From those 100 customers, 20 will be responsible for $800 of your $1,000.

This concept was born when an Italian economist Vilfredo Pareto looked at all the land in Italy and saw that 20% of the families owned 80% of the land. Similarly, if you see the movie *The Founder,*[101] about the man who created McDonald's, he talked to the two men who created the first McDonald's in California. Their business made tacos, tamales, burgers, hot dogs, shakes, sodas, and fries. They realized that 80% of their income came from three products: burgers, fries, and soda. This prompted McDonald's to remove every other product and serve only burgers, fries, and colas, because that was 80% of their revenue. That is the Pareto Rule.

Don't confuse 80-20 with the Pareto Rule. It's a good way to make decisions, by identifying 20% of your activities that represent 80% of the whole. This means that the majority rules. If 80% of people say it's a good decision, and 20% disagree, then 80% agreement is sufficient support to take action.

For example, if 80% of your patients and customers agree that you should discontinue providing a certain product or service that is expensive and time-consuming for your team, while 20% of your patients and customers still want it, then you're justified in discontinuing the product or service.

Consider "Complementarity" In Decision-Making

"Complementarity" means accepting the contradictory nature of some experiences and situations. For example, you can take identical data and come up with completely opposite conclusions about how to make your decision based on that data. The term usually applies to quantum physics, but is useful when applied to business.

Complementarity fuels the imagination and fosters innovative thinking, wrote MIT Physicist Frank Wilczek, recipient of the 2004 Nobel Prize in Physics and author of *A Beautiful Question,* in an article entitled "2017: What Scientific Term or Concept Ought to be More Widely Known?"[102] on the Edge.org website. He said that complementarity inspires the ability to consider other people's perspectives while maintaining our own convictions.

Complementarity is very common in medicine and sometimes in business; it's somewhat dense, but useful for making decisions. The concept was conceived by quantum mechanics innovator Niehls Bohr, a Danish physicist who preceded Albert Einstein and who created the Bohr model of the atom. Bohr also created his own coat of arms that contained a red and black yin-yang symbol inside a purple and gold oval. It contains a motto in Latin: *Contraria Sunt Complementa* which means "opposites are complementary."[103]

At my fertility center, complementarity manifest in the dilemma that arises when seeing 40 patients each day; this heavy workload can cause overwhelm and fatigue amongst employees, which can potentially threaten quality services, and increase the risk of error, inefficiency, and less than superior attention to every detail. Efficiency and customer experience are not always a trade-off.

No, You Cannot Have It All

The goal is to obtain clarity and provide it to your patient. Unfortunately, a lot of times you cannot provide clarity. The same occurs in business.

"Every virtue carried to the extreme, is a vice," Aristotle said. For example, being disciplined and organized is good, but taken to an extreme can become Obsessive-Compulsive Disorder. So ask, "What are you looking for: clarity or truth?" Because this concept involves an inevitable trade-off.

What is the complement of truth? It's clarity. They are opposites. You cannot have both 100%. If you make something so clear, it's going to compromise the whole truth. If you try to explain the truth, it gets complicated and loses clarity. Tobacco is the best example. If you ask any physician, or any person for that matter, if tobacco is good or bad, everyone will tell you that, "Tobacco is bad for your health."

If you want the truth, the answer is more complex. In general, tobacco has been a disaster for global health and is the culprit of many public health issues. However, tobacco and nicotine can sometimes be beneficial. A November 2004 paper from Tabitha M. Powledge in *PLoS Biology*[104] establishes the therapeutic potential of tobacco and nicotine to treat Alzheimer's disease, Parkinson's disease, Attention- Deficit/ Hyperactivity Disorder (ADHD), schizophrenia, obesity, pain, anxiety, depression. Another study linked cigarette smoking with reduced risk of endometrial cancer.[105]

So, are you looking for clarity or truth? The answer will help you have it all. Like the triad, the 80-20 rule, the use of evidence as a tool, and wisdom as a rule, every decision comes down to finding balance that results in the best outcome.

Eric C. Sinoway, co-founder and president of Axcess Worldwide, a partnership development company, and the author of *Howard's Gift: Uncommon Wisdom to Inspire Your Life's Work*, wrote an October 2012 article for *Harvard Business Review* about work-life balance entitled, "No, You Can't Have It All."[106] He said that with every decision, you have to consider factors that include: your family, social and community engagement, wellness, environment and possessions, hobbies and activities, and career.

This also applies when you're evaluating the best course of action for each patient or client. The reality is that some areas of the list take priority and override other factors. Here's where evidence as a tool, and wisdom as your rule, determine your ultimate decision.

The Science of Decision-Making

"Decision Science is the collection of quantitative techniques used to inform decision-making at the individual and population levels," according to the Center for Health Decision Science at the Harvard T.H. Chen School of Public Health.[107] It aims to help you make the best choices with the information you have available.

Relying on science to help us make ideal choices based on data and calculated outcomes is important because many mysteries remain about the actual decision-making process as it happens in the subthalamic nucleus in the brain.[108] Emotions, fatigue, hunger, and even the weather can cloud our thoughts and decisions. Researchers call these mental influences "noise,"[109] and the best way to mute it is to apply the science of decision-making. First understand that biases and judgment amplify the mental "noise." And know that many studies have found that shifting circumstances can inspire different decision-making when the data remains the same, according to an October 2016 article in *Harvard Business Review*, called "The Big Idea: Noise—How to Overcome the High, Hidden Cost of Inconsistent Decision-Making," by Daniel Kahneman, Andrew M. Rosenfield, Linnea Gandhi, and Tom Blaser.[110]

The article cites a study of software developers who varied by an average of 71% when estimating time to finish a work assignment, while other research exposed pathologists making consistent biopsy reports—and therefore diagnoses—only 61% of the time. Unfortunately, researchers cited inconsistent decision-making as a problem afflicting professions that include the criminal justice system, real estate, financial audits, stock valuation, and other realms that make weighty decisions about the freedom, financial status, and health outcome for individuals and organizations.[111]

The results can be disastrous, and for a MedikalPreneur, inconsistent decision-making can lead to financial losses and even failure. So what's the solution? How can you create a system to guarantee consistent decision-making?

- Assess sources for noise and quiet them. Evaluate where you're experiencing interference. It is fear? Naysayers? Bias? Worries about repeating a past failure? Mitigate these influences as much as possible.

- Create an algorithm to analyze the data. Use check lists, spread sheets, and a computerized system to process the numbers and predict the best possible outcomes. If you need help with this, ask an analyst, an accountant, or other professional who is astute with data to help you customize an algorithm for your specific needs.

Remember, not making a decision is actually making a decision to do nothing. It's better to make a decision than to not make one, and you need to feel comfortable and confident with your choice.

The second element in decision-making is that negative consequences are two-dimensional. Evaluate them before making the decision.

Let's talk in terms of COVID-19 and the decision to take the vaccination. The probability of having a side effect after getting the Pfizer vaccine has a high probability: 74.2 %. However, the consequences are manageable and transitory, since these people will have one or several symptoms that include redness in the injection site, swelling, fever, fatigue, headache, cold-like symptoms, diarrhea, and joint pains. On the other hand, if you do get the disease, the probability of having a severe magnitude has a low probability; however, the magnitude of the negative impact could be death for up to two- to three percent.

Therefore, this matrix is useful to keep in mind to make the best decisions for ourselves and our companies.

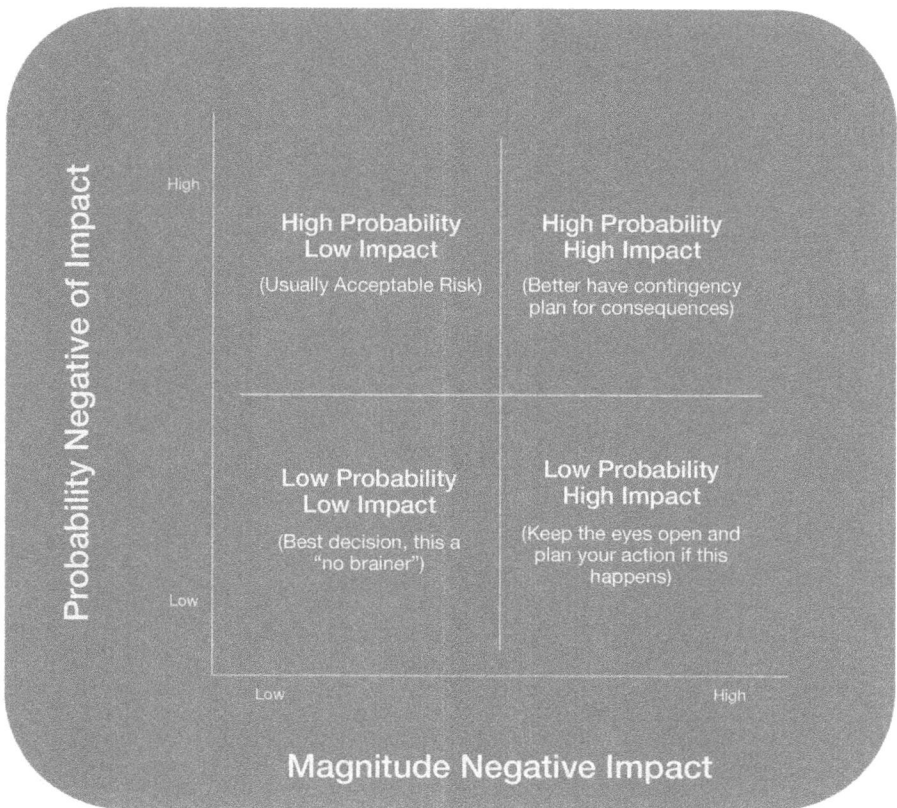

High

High Probability Low Impact

(Usually Acceptable Risk)

High Probability High Impact

(Better have contingency plan for consequences)

Low Probability Low Impact

(Best decision, this a "no brainer")

Low Probability High Impact

(Keep the eyes open and plan your action if this happens)

Low

Low   High

Probability Negative of Impact

Magnitude Negative Impact

CHAPTER 9

Autopoiesis: Creating More Businesses to Meet the MedikalPreneur's Needs

Autopoiesis

the property of a living system (such as a bacterial cell or a multicellular organism) that allows it to maintain and renew itself by regulating its composition and conserving its boundaries[112]

Merriam-Webster

As you grow your business, you'll probably notice voids in the marketplace where you need a particular product or service, but it's not available. Why? Either it has yet to be invented, or it's not offered in your region.

This is a golden opportunity! As you shift into the MedikalPreneur's Mindset, you'll pursue new ways to create and offer products and services to fill marketplace voids—often to serve your own needs first. If your company needs these products and services to operate at optimum capacity, then other businesses will also benefit when you pioneer new ground and launch innovative new companies.

Your constant assessment of your industry and marketplace for unmet needs will help you expand, succeed, prosper, and assist more customers and clients. Stay aware of market trends, as well as what is—or is not—happening in your realm. Listen to customers and clients when they express a desire for a certain treatment, device, medication, or program. Is it something you can offer?

By upgrading your thinking beyond your daily business activities, you'll conceive new ideas to implement now. At the same time, think long-term. View the current business landscape as your forest: what furniture can you create from it? What are the veritable businesses you can create from the core company?

If you're opening a dental or a dermatology clinic, what can you do laterally to provide revenue? As a dentist, will you sell the Invisilign tooth-straightening product? As a dermatologist, will you offer Botox injections? Perhaps you'll cater to Millennials, who love tattoos so much that half of them in their early thirties have a tattoo.[113] The process of removing tattoos is lengthy and expensive, so by offering tattoo removals for those Millennials who regret that the name of a former boyfriend or girlfriend is emblazoned on their skin, you could create a booming business.

As you explore new ideas to increase your revenue and help more people by offering additional products and services, assess what bottlenecks or obstacles might stop you from expanding. How can you remove those obstacles?

Don't stay so focused on the daily grind of being an entrepreneur, which requires long hours and tremendous stamina, that you limit yourself. Constantly analyze the big-picture potential for your company by asking, "How can this business generate from within? What insights do I have from my day-to-day business operations that tell me what's missing in our field?" You know your niche better than everybody, so take advantage of opportunities to offer innovative new products, services, and programs.

The concept of Autopoiesis was a major success secret for RMA of Texas. For example, we created a program to train our nurses, embryologists, and administrators. The next program will be a "brainery" to train embryology nurses, embryologists, and embryology personnel, thereby instilling our philosophy in the way they operate. This business trajectory includes producing your own human resources, and training your individuals with your unique values. Yes, it's important to learn from other systems and enrich your values with other values. However, it's clever to create your own that are infused with the DNA of your company's mission.

When you think of this in terms of biology, "a cell is a network of reactions which produce molecules such that (i) through their interaction [they] generate and participate recursively in the same network of reaction which produced them, and (ii) realize the cell as a material unity," according to the book, *Autopoiesis and Cognition: The Realization of the Living* by H.R. Maturana and F.J. Varela.[114]

As we repeatedly identified and filled marketplace voids—often to serve our company's needs first—our single fertility clinic expanded into a multimillion-dollar network of 13 businesses. We accomplished this by applying the process known as Autopoiesis.

Autopoiesis: Birthing New Companies

As you apply Autopoiesis to your business, think of it as "self-creation or self-production." It creates infinite possibilities!

At RMA of Texas, our first offshoot company was Reconceive, which evolved from the success of our patient experience program that was developed by our team member Lisa Duran. Reconceive enabled her to provide patient experience training for other fertility centers and women's health practices.

A few years later, we noticed that improving the customer experience required us to *bundle the pricing* and minimize the stress of the patient, who was receiving multiple bills from the anesthesiologist, the lab, the pharmacy, the doctor, and more. We needed to create a package for bundle billing, so the patient could pay us. We managed payouts to the various parties involved in the fertility process. To facilitate that, we created a software that provided a menu of financing options for our patients. Due to the expense of fertility treatments, this was a tremendous relief for our patients.

Our team members, Adrian Elorza and Bob Hoff, created the software package for fertility financing, and we called it Imagine Fertility. We were the first—and remain the only—company providing that service of packaging the pricing of fertility services and the medications. I still own 50% of the business. In addition, we created: a couple of real estate companies: PolePole LLC and APR LLC; an investing business, Fertility Holdings LLC; and a management company, Ataraxy, which managed the RMA of Texas offices in San Antonio, Austin, and McAllen.

Tony Anderson, our lab director, had his own company, Embryology and Andrology Training Institute at EmbryoDirector.com, which trained embryologists for fertility centers around the world. My daughter, Paula, took Tony's embryology course at his Institute and learned to do semen analysis, semen washes for inseminations, and other fertility-related procedures. We also developed KAR affordable maintenance solutions to provide cleaning and maintenance services to our real estate properties.

The Ultimate Autopoiesis: Aravind Eye Hospitals In India

Blindness from cataracts is an epidemic in India. Four million or more Indian people are diagnosed with cataracts every year, causing almost one quarter of the world's blindness.[115] Poverty and lack of transportation have exacerbated this problem and prevented people from getting the simple, quick surgery that removes cataracts and restores their vision.

This deeply troubled Dr. Govindappa Venkataswamy, a retired eye surgeon. To help rural poor people who were blinded by cataracts—and were so ashamed that they wanted to die because they could not work and felt burdensome to their families—he created a clinic in the southern Indian temple city of Madurai in 1976. Though lacking money and a business plan, he and his family embarked on a mission to end curable blindness.

With only 11 beds in a world of 45 million blind people, he learned how to help more people during a visit to the United States during the 1980s, when he witnessed how McDonald's restaurants used assembly-line production to provide consistency, affordability, and a scalable, standardization of selling burgers and meals.[116]

"He would say, over and over again, 'If we can provide eye care the way McDonald's provides hamburgers, the problem of blindness would be gone,'"[117] said Pavithra Mehta, author of *Infinite Vision*, which chronicles her grand-uncle's story, while speaking at The Institute for Health and Healing Mini Medical School. To achieve this, he implemented assembly-line techniques that systemized the process of diagnosing and treating cataracts to restore vision. He created "eye camps" that took medical teams into villages for assessments, bussed patients to the hospital, provided food and housing, and returned them home. The hospitals provide this service 40 or 50 times a week, more than 2,000 times a year, Mehta said, treating 76,000 people.[118]

Dr. V's vision for assembly-line surgeries resulted in world-class hospitals equipped with rows of operating beds where a doctor performs a surgery in as little as 3.5 minutes, while a nursing team preps the patient in the next bed. The quality—based on the frequency or rate of complications—is considered the best in the world. About half the surgeries are free; the other half are paid with non-government subsidies.

Today, the Aravind Eye Care System is the world's largest and most productive eye care conglomerate, overseeing more than 65 million outpatient visits and more than 7.8 million surgeries, according to Aravind.org. It includes 14 eye hospitals, six outpatient eye examination centers, and 80 primary eye care facilities in South India, as well as a postgraduate institute, a management training and consulting institute, a research institute, a transportation company, a manufacturing unit that exports $10 intra-ocular lenses used during cataract removal to 120 countries, a suture company, eye banks, and The Aravind Center for Women Children and Community Health, which provides preventive healthcare to help reduce nutrition-related blindness in children.[119]

The city of Madurai is also a success story; Dr. V's first clinic helped establish the city as an international mecca for patients and their families. Its economy benefited from the need for hotels, restaurants, transportation, and other businesses providing services for patients and their families.

This multimillion-dollar network—founded by a physician motivated by altruism, not money—exemplifies Autopoiesis. Dr. V's legacy highlights many ideals that you as a MedikalPreneur can emulate. His successful business model and exceptional impact inspired me when I went into business, and he taught me the importance of using Autopoiesis to expand and help people in ways that continue to evolve.

As you embark on your business, apply Dr. V's wisdom: "Aravind Hospital aims at bringing higher consciousness to transform mind and body and soul of people. It is not a mechanical structure repairing eyes. It has a deeper purpose. It is not about buildings, equipment, money or material things, but a matter of consciousness."[120]

The Biological Nature of Autopoiesis

The concept of Autopoiesis in business is rooted in the idea that organisms are in synchrony or desynchrony with their own environments and their behaviors are dependent upon the environment where he/she/it inhabits. In business terms, it means that companies should respond to what they learn from their environment and act accordingly to those needs.

The best explanation of this idea was first presented in the 1980 book, *Autopoiesis and Cognition: The Realization of the Living* by Humberto R. Maturana and Fransciso J. Varela.[121] These Chilean biologists expounded on how the chemistry of living cells creates an environment of self-preservation and growth. Their concepts have since been applied to many fields. They've helped me as a MedikalPreneur, and they can for you as well.

The Autopoietic Story of Monterrey, Mexico

The Institute of Technology and Higher Studies of Monterrey (ITESM in Spanish), where I attended medical school, is Mexico's largest private university—and grew from the vision and autopoiesis of entrepreneurs who literally built a city, and the powerful economical epicenter of Mexico.

During the early 1890s, when Monterrey had about 50,000 residents, Jose Muguerza-Crespo, Francisco Sada-Gomez, Isaac Garza-Garza, and Joseph Schneider founded the Moctezuma Brewery, creating its landmark, globally celebrated "Carta Blanca" beer. In 1919, after studying engineering at MIT, Isaac Garza's son, Eugenio Garza-Sada, worked at the brewery as a statistician and began the Autopoiesis of the company and the city, sparking one of history's most impressive vertical and horizontal integrations. They created Fabricas Monterrey S.A. de C.V., dominating the market for bottle caps, then creating aluminum bottles and other products.

This company evolved in 1943 into HYLSA (Hojalata y Lamina, S.A.) when World War II made it difficult to obtain raw materials. During the Korean War, in 1957, it created, patented, and exported a pure, porous iron that is easier to handle during steel manufacturing. Its holding company, Vidrios y Cristales de Monterrey, SA manufactured its own glass bottles. This company evolved into Vidriera Monterrey and finally Grupo Vitro. Today Grupo Vitro is Mexico's largest glass producer, as one of the global glass industry's most important organizations, with 15,000 employees and revenues of $2.1 billion USD.[122] Their business units encompass architectural glass, automotive glass, glass containers, chemicals, machinery, and equipment.

Boxes used to transport the beer birthed Titan Company, now part of Biopappel,[123] Latin America's largest corrugated fiberboard, paper, and box company, producing 2500 million pounds per month of corrugated fiberboard for thousands of companies. Another company created in 1929 was Malta, S.A., supplying the malt for beer; it expanded to sell other seeds. Like these enterprises, the Brewery offered a comprehensive welfare system that spanned healthcare, retirement, and education.

Now let's return to my alma mater. The founder's son, Eugenio Garza-Sada, once paid for his high-end executives to earn master's degrees at MIT—until his son, Eugenio Garza-Laguera, created his own university: Monterrey Institute of Technology, ITESM, in 1943. Today the Monterrey metropolitan area—with 11 towns and more than six million residents—is considered the industrial heart of Mexico.

So you see, Autopoiesis is a great biological theory that, as a MedikalPreneur, can help you expand by creating new, independent businesses.

Real Estate Provides a Foundation for Success

As a MedikalPreneur, you're providing an experience to transform your patient's life. You do this by creating a story around the experience, and your story needs a setting that conveys hope, and an environment most conducive to a positive conclusion.

Therefore, research and carefully select the location, design, and décor for your business. Are you leasing? Are you purchasing a building? Either way, make sure that the building or buildings are located close to your customer base, with easy access and parking. The area around the building should be safe, well-lit, inviting, attractive, and clean. Prominent signage should convey the name and function of your company. Work with an interior designer to create a warm atmosphere with colors, music, aromas, textures, and lighting.

In terms of Autopoiesis, owning real estate can blossom into many other businesses. First, if you have extra space, you can lease units to other companies. Second, you can create businesses that provide services for MedikalPreneurs who own real estate: insurance, janitorial services, parking lots and ramps, an interior design firm that specializes in decorating dental offices, or pediatricians' clinics, or spas, and more. Be creative, innovative, and dare to do what's not been done!

Chapter 10

Paco's "Microbrewery vs. Budweiser" Theory: How to Keep a Personal Touch as You Expand and Franchise

Becoming a successful MedikalPreneur can create a dilemma. You may struggle with maintaining the intimate, personalized connections that you've created with your patients or clients while you expand to serve more people, potentially on a global platform. As you increase in quantity, how do you maintain quality?

Consider this in terms of the unique and flavorful tastes from beers created in a microbrewery. How do you mass-produce the microbrewery beer taste on the scale of the world's top-selling Budweiser,[124] which Anheuser-Busch distributes to more than 80 countries? As a medical entrepreneur, how do you preserve that personalized patient or client experience that has been the secret to your success, as you grow?

Consider Paco's Microbrewery vs. Budweiser theory to keep a personal touch as you grow and franchise. This idea is rooted in the concepts of quality vs. quantity, and the systems that McDonald's and Avarind Eye Hospitals use to ensure high quality products, services, and results with consistency and uniformity—even while serving millions of people worldwide.

You want to master the Microbrewery vs. Budweiser concept by keeping the microbrewery taste and avoiding the uniform, comparatively regular beer flavor of a mass-produced beer. The formula for achieving this is the secret for how big companies seem small, globalization feels local, and worldwide enterprises deliver a neighborhood feel to your town.

The coronavirus pandemic has been a great catalyst for local economies and deglobalization, which began in 2008 when the world reached "peak globalization" and began a phase of "slowbalization"[125] that reverses a trend since global trading began increasing in 1945. The pandemic has increased the focus on regional, neighborhood, domestic, provincial, denizen, and family. Therefore local firms and small companies will have a stronger impact in the economy in the near future than global, transnational firms. We're moving into an era where local is king! That means the time is ripe for more microbreweries rather than huge global beer companies.

This is valid for medical companies. As more private equity firms enter healthcare, opportunities expand for providing personalized, concierge medicine.

Take advantage of this trend by creating a strong brand and culture, along with a detailed prototype for your business model that you replicate each time you expand. Every aspect of the business should be consistent in each office, clinic, website, customer service experience, product, and service by adhering to the language, culture, and personalized attention that patients and customers desire. As you design these customer experiences, think of McDonald's; walk into any franchise anywhere, and the food, atmosphere, and experience are identical. Customers expect the same menu, prices, and bright decor at McDonald's, whether they're in Los Angeles or DuBuque. Likewise, if you enter an Apple store in Manhattan or Middle America, the experience, atmosphere, prices, and products are the same.

So, master the art of creating a transformative customer experience in one business as your prototype, then replicate that as you expand. The key word is individualization: no matter how big your company grows, every person is treated like a family member. They are seen, heard, and understood, enjoying an individualized transformational experience through programs or products that meet their needs. Whether you plan to remain the equivalent of a small microbrewery, or grow as large as a huge corporation like Budweiser, you'll need the same strategy. Everything hinges on your company's management, culture, and brand.

The best example is Apple Computers. Remember its first Macintosh commercial[126] in 1984 when Apple was competing with IBM, a huge, global corporation dominating the computer business. The commercial directed by Ridley Scott evokes George Orwell's futuristic book and movie, *1984*, when the "Big Brother" of technology controls everyday people; with a David vs. Goliath nuance, it shows an athletic woman running with a sledgehammer past rows of zombie-like people to smash a huge screen showing a man representing the tech giant. The prophetic message that Apple's quest for eventual dominance wouldn't be like Orwell's eerie movie.[127]

Similarly, Samuel Adams beer was a microbrewery and started developing a plan to dominate Budweiser. The only way to compete with Budweiser and Anheuser-Busch is to create a microbrewery.

Do not be intimidated to confront big firms just because you're small. Being small has strength; being big has weaknesses. So study your strengths and your opponent's weakness. David was small and Goliath was big; he had gigantism, a condition triggered by a pituitary tumor that spiked a growth hormone in Goliath. The tumor on his optic nerve affected his vision by causing hemianopsia, so he only saw in the middle of his visual line. David, though smaller and weaker, used this knowledge to slay Goliath with only a sling and a stone. Even against seemingly impossible odds, you can succeed as a small business competing against giant companies.

So, what do you want as a MedikalPreneur? Do you want to be a local, small, personalized concierge doctor? Or part of a university healthcare system? Do you want to create a David vs. Goliath phenomenon like Apple did with IBM? Do you want to be a microbrewery, or the world's biggest beer company? Know where you want to go. And if you change your mind, adjust your strategy. You can do this, and enjoy great success.

CHAPTER 11

The MedikalPreneur's Business Plan

As a physician, you assess a patient's injury, illness, or condition, then you create the best treatment plan for him or her to heal, recover, or achieve a certain outcome, such as lowering blood pressure or facilitating conception. This individualized treatment plan addresses every aspect of care. It specifies what medications you're prescribing, as well as the doses and schedule for administering them. Your treatment plan may include checking vitals and conducting follow-up tests or assessments at prescribed times. And you may even refer the patient to specialists to evaluate, treat, and monitor specific areas of the patient's needs.

All the while, you can quantify the patient's status with numbers—such as steady blood pressure or a healthy white blood cell count. You can also measure progress—or lack thereof—with tests such as x-rays, MRIs, and urine analysis. Then your patient will follow your treatment plan for as long as necessary. As a MedikalPreneur, think of your business plan as the treatment plan for your business. It lays the foundation for every aspect of what you do, and it's required by banks and investors if and when you seek financial backing to start your company.

So what is The MedikalPreneur's Business Plan?

Let's start by defining a standard business plan: a written document that explains the purpose of the business, as well as its sales and marketing strategy, financial background, and a projected profit and loss statement.

If the native language of MBAs sounds foreign and intimidating, I'm here as your trusted guide to navigate a new realm of understanding. Now consider a medical treatment plan: a documented plan prescribed by a physician describing the patient's condition and treatment(s) required, expected outcome and duration of the treatment.

When you combine the definition of a business plan and a medical treatment plan, the result is The MedikalPreneur's Business Plan, which I define as a document describing how your business will provide medical products and services, along with your marketing strategy, financial analysis, a profit and loss statement, and every detail required to start and succeed as an entrepreneur.

This builds the framework to create a thriving company. Without it, you're doomed. As Benjamin Franklin said, "If you fail to plan, you plan to fail." We're very fortunate to live in an era where the internet provides free, instant access to everything we need to know to write an excellent business plan and understand the many aspects of being an entrepreneur.

Present a Persuasive Story to Your Audience

Before we dissect the anatomy of a business plan, consider the intention of this document. It's far more than facts and figures. Your business plan should tell a story. It should evoke emotion, and inspire the readers—investors in particular—to see your vision so vividly that they eagerly provide financial support to bring your idea into reality.

To do this, adopt a mindset that's similar to creating a transformative experience for your patients and clients. The key is to find common ground, present a promise, and cultivate emotional connections with the people you're working with, then back that up with solid material. In the case of your business plan, you need to appeal to stakeholders' interests. Therefore, know who they are, what they're looking for, and how to showcase the most persuasive information to inspire their investment in your business.

As you assemble your business plan, tell a story that appeals to your stakeholders' emotions while illustrating what your target patients or clients want and need, and how your business can satisfy their desires with high-quality products and services. Your investors want to avoid as much risk as possible; make them see your business concept as a solid investment with strong potential for success.[128] Your storytelling can make or break your MedikalPreneurial dream, so invest significant work into creating a captivating business plan.

Before your presentation, research the people who will hear your pitch. Know each person's role in the decision-making process, and understand the perspective that they bring to the table. For example, your idea may thrill the marketing professional on the team, but it may scare the accountant and fail to impress the HR person. You want everyone to support your idea; understanding what will impress each person will enable you to tailor your presentation accordingly.

Likewise, prepare a short pitch and a longer one.[129] You may attend expecting to talk for 20 minutes, only to learn you have five minutes to present your idea, and vice versa. Be prepared and be flexible. Consider presenting a colorful slide show, providing hand-outs that stakeholders can review in advance, or even writing on a white board as you talk. You could even make a video featuring music, graphics, and narration to illustrate your idea. Here are some tips for presenting your business plan:

It's Best to:

- Engage and persuade your audience to endorse your business idea by telling a story that appeals to their emotions.

- Clearly explain why people need your product or service.

- Use an energetic and enthusiastic tone of voice and body language—if you're bored by your idea, others will be also.

- Show video, graphs, slides, and drawings to enhance your storytelling.

- Extend or shorten your presentation to accommodate the time you're granted.

It's Best to Not:

- Disregard stakeholders' issues. Research each person at the table so you can present your content accordingly.

- Ramble or oversaturate your talk with too much information. When you confuse, you lose people.

- Bore your audience by reading from a document or PowerPoint.

The MedikalPreneur's Business Plan:

"A document describing how your business will provide medical products and services, along with your marketing strategy, financial analysis, a cash forecast statement, and every detail required to start and succeed as a Medikal-Preneur."

—Francisco Arredondo, MD, MPH

Anatomy of a Business Plan

In medical school, we learned human anatomy. We memorized every bone that creates the physical framework of the body. We learned about the vital organs that keep life pulsing through this body. Our professors taught us about how the body thrives on oxygen and nutrition. And they emphasized the physical conditions required to keep humans healthy.

Now think of your business plan as the skeleton of your company; it's the foundation upon which everything is built and sustains its existence. The vital organs are you and your staff, your physical location, your customers, your products and services, and your cash flow, without which you cannot function. Your company thrives on excellent service for a steady stream of patients and customers, and the financial sustenance they provide. And just as people need the right temperature, hydration, nutrition, and shelter to survive, your business also requires that you regulate the physical environment, the morale, and company culture that creates harmony and positive outcomes for you and your patients and customers.

Now let's look at the anatomy of a business plan. It contains nine essential parts:

The Executive Summary provides a clear, concise snapshot that highlights the key points of your business. **The Company Description** explains your products and services. **The Market Analysis** presents research on your industry that explains why your business is needed. It also describes your competitors, potential allies and collaborators, and cooperative competition, and what service or product gap you'll fill. **The Organization and Management** area reveals the names and credentials of the owner (you), as well as your managers and board of directors (if applicable), and what expertise they bring to the company. **The Service, Product, and/or Experience** section showcases your services and products, and how they benefit customers. **The Marketing and Sales** portion presents your marketing strategy and your plan for ensuring sales and growth. **The Funding Request** explains your funding requirements now and for the next three to five years. **The Financial Projections** forecast revenue based on financial documents from the past several years. **The Appendix** is a separate document that provides additional information, such as reference letters, credit reports, resumes, and permits.

The MedikalPreneur's Business Plan 101

Here's a more detailed explanation of every component of The MedikalPreneur's Business Plan.

The Executive Summary provides a clear, concise snapshot of your business. Summarizing your proposed company in as few words as possible can be challenging. So, talk it out with a trusted person such as your mentor, partner, colleague, or friend. Chances are, you'll capture that person's attention and speak with conviction as you describe your idea; record the conversation, or write down what you say. Then tweak the words to best describe your concept.

Think of your Executive Summary as your "elevator pitch." You want to capture attention and inspire action. If it's dull, your potential business partners, investors, or bank loan officers may glaze over and stop reading. Then you fail to secure the partnership and/or financing. Be bold and get results!

The Company Description explains your products, services, experiences, and/or transformations. This starts with your company's name. Use appealing words and sounds that make you feel proud to announce and promote the name of your company. Think big and long-term. Many physicians name their practice after themselves. Name recognition is valuable, but can be limiting if you want to add partners. You can also choose a name that conveys a positive spin on health, or some other desired outcome for the problem you're solving.

Be aware of how your company's name translates on billboards and on the Internet. Is it short and easy to understand? Is it something people will remember so they can Google it and contact your business?

Is the URL available? How will your company name perform and rank in Internet searches, or SEO—Search Engine Optimization? If you're unfamiliar with these concepts, read articles and watch videos on SEO before you make your name official.

Next, is your company name easy to trademark? Consult with a lawyer to confirm the name is not already trademarked. If someone already owns the name, you could receive a "cease and desist" letter from a lawyer saying you're infringing on a trademark. Do this before you invest in signage and branding. At first, I considered naming my fertility center "RMA of San Antonio." But I wanted to expand across the state. Naming my center after the city would limit its appeal and brand it to San Antonio. So I named it RMA of Texas. Likewise, putting USA in your company name may limit your future. Words such as "global" and "worldwide" convey your intention to provide products and services for patients and customers everywhere.

Consider my friend, a San Antonio entrepreneur who started an independent coffee house called Local Coffee. The goal was to compete with Starbucks by differentiating the business by utilizing local coffee roasters and bakery goods in a neighborly environment.

"What if you become a brand that grows outside San Antonio?" I asked.

"Naah!" he responded. "I just want my nice coffee place." Fast forward six years, and he had five "Locals" in San Antonio, and expanded to open shops in Austin, Dallas, Houston, and Atlanta. Now more than a decade after opening, it's the Merit Coffee Company, a chain whose branding value shifted with expansion.

This reminds me of a story about a father who held up an acorn and asked his son, "What do you see?"

"I see a tree," the boy answered.

"Tell me when you see a forest," his father said. One acorn can produce one tree that produces enough acorns to create a forest.

Think big! Even the smallest concepts have infinite potential. Apply this mindset to your business name, to appeal to the broadest range of customers in the largest geographical area possible. Even if you only plan to open one location for now, lay a foundation that enables future expansion. Sometimes you may have no idea what the future holds, so don't limit your growth before you even get started.

The naming of Apple computers is a great example. It evolved from a moment in 1976 after co-founder Steve Wozniak picked up Steve Jobs from a commune in an apple orchard in Oregon, according to his 2006 book, *iWoz: Computer Geek to Cult Icon*.[130] Jobs was on a fruit-only diet and the men loved how the name differentiated them from other computer companies' cold-sounding names. The problem? The Beatles-owned Apple Records sued them in 1989 for trademark violations. Wozniak and Jobs paid the fines and kept the name. Ironically, years later, Apple's iTunes platform transformed the music industry as an online music store that evolved to include TV shows, movies, and podcasts.

Before you can describe your company, you need to know what products and/or services you'll provide. Think big, know that anything is possible, and no idea is outlandish. Would you have ever imagined that it's now acceptable—even vogue—to take your dog into a restaurant? Or, that we'd see huge stores—even salons!—catering to our pets? Values and cultural practices change—sometimes quickly and radically. So if you see a void, a gap, or an untapped niche, fill it with your MedikalPreneurial products and services.

Another way to explore medical business ideas is to look at what's happening around the globe. Stay abreast of trends in the medical field and the business world. Pay attention to lifestyle shifts. The pandemic has dramatically changed how we think and live. For awhile, classrooms went online; jobs became remote. More people started online businesses. Divorce, dating, and wedding trends evolved. Fear prompted people to avoid medical procedures. More people cooked.

How can these shifts inspire your MedikalPreneurial venture? For example, say you ascribe to Hippocrates' philosophy to "Let food be your medicine and medicine be thy food." Perhaps you could start an internet company that delivers meals whose medicinal properties promote healing for people with specific ailments. In addition, how could you address the heightened need for mental health services in the midst of tumultuous times that include economic disruptions, anxiety and grief in the wake of the pandemic, political conflicts, and global protests for racial equality and justice?

The pandemic also illuminated the life-saving power of the medical industry, along with the grueling and dangerous realities of being a medical professional. It sparked shifts in protocols and a boom in telemedicine. How can you provide solutions for these new problems? When you consult your Ikigai diagram, you may pinpoint what to do.

Consider starting your company on a small scale while maintaining your primary job. You could begin a YouTube channel, offer online classes and seminars, and host retreats to showcase your expertise and build a brand that later expands into a full-time enterprise.

The Market Analysis section presents research on your industry that shows: the need for your business, your competitors, and the service or product gap you'll fill. Now let's look at each item in detail:

• **Industry Analysis**—Describe your industry, such as geriatrics, pediatrics, obstetrics and gynecology, oncology, etc., or industries unrelated to medicine where your innovative ideas create an advantage. As a MedikalPreneur, you can expand into any field, such as real estate and transportation. Showcase your industry knowledge with statistics from trusted sources.

For example, if I were opening a fertility center today, I would cite these 2018 statistics from MarketResearch.com: the American infertility services market spiked 21% since 2016, reaching $5.87 billion, while 500 fertility clinics, 100+ sperm donor banks, the egg donors market, fertility drugs, and 1,700 reproductive endocrinologists compete for the business.[131] I would also refer to predictions from credible sources about the future of the fertility industry to prove that this is a thriving field that analysts see growing and generating impressive revenues. You'll also want to list the key players in your industry. In addition, describe trends, areas of growth and decline, and new innovations that are transforming how consumers use a particular product or service.

What's happening in your industry in your geographical region, or online if your business is virtual? Use as much solid information as possible. You can glean valid statistics and facts from: government agencies such as the Census Bureau; industry websites, magazines, and databases; trade associations; media reports; and data from Standard & Poor's Financial Services, a credit-rating agency that publishes financial research and analysis on stocks, bonds, and commodities. Your Industry Analysis should provide a convincing case that your industry is financially sound and projected to grow, making your business a wise investment. A business plan is an excellent learning tool; it forces you to learn and think about things you have not yet considered.

Target Market Analysis—Who is your ideal patient or client? Here you need to show that your market includes enough people who want or need your product or service. So create an ideal customer profile, also known as a persona or avatar. If you already have a business, gather information about your current customers, including demographic data. This would include occupations, income, education, geographic area, family composition, political affiliations, preferences for recreation and entertainment, cultural traditions, and anything else that's relevant to your industry.[132]

It's helpful to know their location, purchasing habits, average age range and socio-economic status. Also ask, who has the power to encourage, interrupt, or stop your sales? These can include:

Cynics: People who have persuasive power over your patients or clients—such as the husband who tells the wife they cannot try IVF to have a baby because he believes it's too expensive, or the media personality who's always sharing a horror story about the service you provide.

Influencers: Individuals whose endorsement of your products and services can prompt people to do business with you. This can be a neighbor telling another to get plastic surgery at your clinic, or someone on social media who tells thousands of followers to seek your services or buy your products.

Anti-avatars: People who are not your ideal patient or client. You won't be marketing to them, or trying to woo their approval to make an investment. It's just smart to understand, for example, that you won't be marketing the latest menstrual cycle products to men or to post-menopausal women.[133]

As you research your target market, your focus may shift. For example, if you consider opening a pediatric clinic in a certain area, but you discover a large population of Baby Boomers there instead, it would be wise to cater to geriatric patients and clients.

A Competitive Analysis—Who is your competition? How are they succeeding and failing at serving your target market? The answers will help you fill gaps and create your unique niche. When I was conducting my market analysis before opening RMA of Texas, I learned that no fertility center in San Antonio catered to the large city's Spanish-speaking population. That automatically set me apart from the competition of other fertility specialists in my market.

The Organization and Management area reveals your name as the owner, along with your managers and board of directors (if applicable).

This tells lenders and investors *who* will operate your company. Describe your management team, including: names; descriptions of positions and responsibilities; compensation; credentials such as education, certification, employment history, unique talents, and past career triumphs illustrating skills that could help your medical enterprise. Emphasize that your team can efficiently operate a prosperous business.

Next, describe the company's legal structure—LLC, PLLC, etc. ToryBurchFoundation.com recommends that you describe each persons' ownership in the company, and in what form, such as limited partner, stockholder, etc., as well as how much they're involved with the business.[134]

Create an organizational chart to lay a strong foundation for your company's future. Architecture generates behavior. So when you establish a structure from the beginning, your employees' behavior conforms accordingly. The chart and the rules you establish also help you operate with maximum efficiency.

If you have a board of directors, include their names, positions on the board, biographical information, key career triumphs that are valuable to your business, and other distinguishing characteristics that show your lenders or investors that your team will ensure the company's success.

The Service, Product, and Experience section showcases how you help people. Describe your products and services to convey how you're filling a void in the market or providing something specialized that elevates you over your competition. If you're creating a first-of-its-kind company, and you have no comparison, then explain exactly what you're offering. List patents or trademarks that you have secured for your products and services.

Also explain pricing and availability for your product. When can people buy it, and will enough inventory be produced to supply the demand that you'll create? Explain your supply chain, distribution, and other factors that could impact availability.[135] Next, use storytelling skills to describe the transformational experience you'll create for your patient or customer.

The Marketing and Sales portion presents your marketing strategy, as well as your plan for ensuring sales and growth. Get creative! Be innovative! Everything should cater to what your ideal patient or client wants. So research your target market to become an expert on how to attract them with the most alluring words, images, pricing, products, services, and messages.

Investigate how your competition markets their businesses, and figure out how you can do better, or offer an irresistible variation that convinces people to patronize your company instead. Can you differentiate yourself by providing hours when your competition is closed? Can you offer prices or another feature that nobody else can? How can you convert your service into an experience?

Can you cultivate relationships with local media personalities who will feature you on the radio, television, or newspaper websites? Can you start a podcast or be a guest on popular podcasts that address your target audience? Can you participate in events and organizations where your ideal patients or customers congregate?

If you have a sales force, describe each person, along with their credentials and sales histories. Likewise, if you plan to hire a publicist or public relations firm, describe their campaign to boost your brand awareness and draw customers to your website or doorstep. Share your PR team's past successes while promoting a medical business. Also, include a marketing budget that itemizes how you'll spend money to make money.

The Funding Request explains your funding requirements during the next three to five years. Many medical professionals have great success securing traditional bank loans to open a practice. If you take this route, you'll need to present a business plan to the bank's loan officer.

You'll also need to submit your business plan to obtain three other forms of funding: an angel investor, a venture capitalist, and private equity. These examples are more useful for ventures such as a medical device, a software program, or a company providing a unique service or experience. Understand the following terms; they're easily confused because often they can overlap.

• **Angel Investor—(also called Seed Investors)**—This affluent individual has the desire to invest in you and your idea. This could be a friend, a relative, or a stranger. On a somewhat playful note, Angel Investors are often "The Three F's: Friends, Family, and Fools." When you're in the early inception of an idea, and you lack money to research your idea, you need cash to get started. Who will believe in you enough to lend you money? Most likely, your friends, family, and fools.

If you secure funds from an Angel Investor, then he or she may provide a lump sum of money to help you launch your enterprise; the angel investor may also provide ongoing financial support as you open and build your business. They usually invest in an early stage of the process.

You may pitch an idea that impresses the angel investor, who may say, "Here's ten thousand dollars." You have agreed to the terms in a written contract, and if your business is successful, then the angel investor is entitled to the agreed-upon portion of profits. MedikalPreneurs typically work one-on-one with an angel investor. Some prefer to be involved and may say, "Here's your check; let's meet in one month so I can see your progress." He or she may also offer to connect you with affluent individuals.

Some angel investors are certified by the Securities and Exchange Commission (SEC) as an "accredited" investor if their net worth includes: having $1 million or more in assets (not including personal residences); earning $200,000 in income for the previous two years; or reporting a combined income of $300,000 as a married couple.[136] Angel investors typically use their own money, which they invest through an

LLC, a trust, a business, or an investment fund. If the startup fails, the angel investor loses their investment entirely.

On the other hand, say the angel investor helps you develop a salve that heals minor wounds quickly. The product sells fast, but distributing it to stores would require a significantly larger investment. Here's where a venture capitalist could help.

• **Venture Capitalist**—Because you've already established the success of the salve, your product is attractive to a venture capitalist. The difference between a venture capitalist and an angel investor is that the angel investor provides financial support *before* you launch your MedikalPreneurial endeavor, whereas the venture capitalist comes on board with funding *after* you've proven you have a successful product or service. Now you want to expand, but you lack the finances to do so. The venture capitalist does.

They typically want to see your Proof of Concept, which I will explain later in this chapter. Proof of Concept essentially means that you've launched a small-scale version of your MedikalPreneurial enterprise, and proven that it's successful.

In the case of the healing salve that the angel investor helped you create, the venture capitalist will help you finance the efforts to manufacture it and distribute it to 30 stores, for example. The venture capitalist could invest the funds required to do research on what stores can sell your product, where and how you can mass-produce the salve, and how you can distribute it to the best retail outlets. This would result in a huge return on their investment as sales multiply exponentially. Typically, venture capitalists invest a half-million dollars or more.

Venture capitalists—comprised of affluent investors, investment banks, and other financial institutions—prefer to invest in small businesses that are already operating, demonstrating success, and proving their potential. These venture capitalists may provide monetary backing or supply assistance in other forms, such as technical support or guidance with your management.[137] Venture capital usually involves a group of investors who form a limited partnership whose members pool their capital and decide how to invest it. They prefer companies that have a solid management team and sell a product or service that outshines the competition. If the venture capitalists have experience with your type of company, it will be an especially attractive investment.[138]

Venture capitalists seek opportunities that are too high-risk to secure traditional bank loans, but promise the potential for a significant return on their investment. For this, they receive a significant portion of equity, or ownership, in your company. Beware: they often want to help run the company, which could conflict with your vision and management style. Decide whether the funding is worth relinquishing some control over how you operate your business.

• **Private Equity**—When a high net worth individual or firm invests in your entrepreneurial endeavor, that investor owns a stake in your company. The investor's motivation is to secure an interest in or ownership of a business enterprise that is privately owned and thus not publicly listed or traded.[139]

Your decision about whether to seek funding from private equity sources will depend upon whether you want to share ownership of your company, and how much power and control your stakeholders may have in how you operate your business. Many entrepreneurs want to be captain of the ship and steer it in the direction that they desire. Sharing ownership with investors can sometimes hamper your vision as a MedikalPreneur.

So who are private equity investors? Private equity usually refers to a group of wealthy individuals and investment firms who use their combined resources to purchase shares of privately-owned companies. They typically want to see your Proof of Concept, which shows the success of your product or service thus far.

Once the private equity firm sees that your business has the potential to explode with success, they will invest in your company, gain control of it, then help improve it, streamline operations, and grow the business over five to seven years. After that, the private equity firm will help sell your business, possibly with an IPO, or Initial Public Offering, on the stock market.

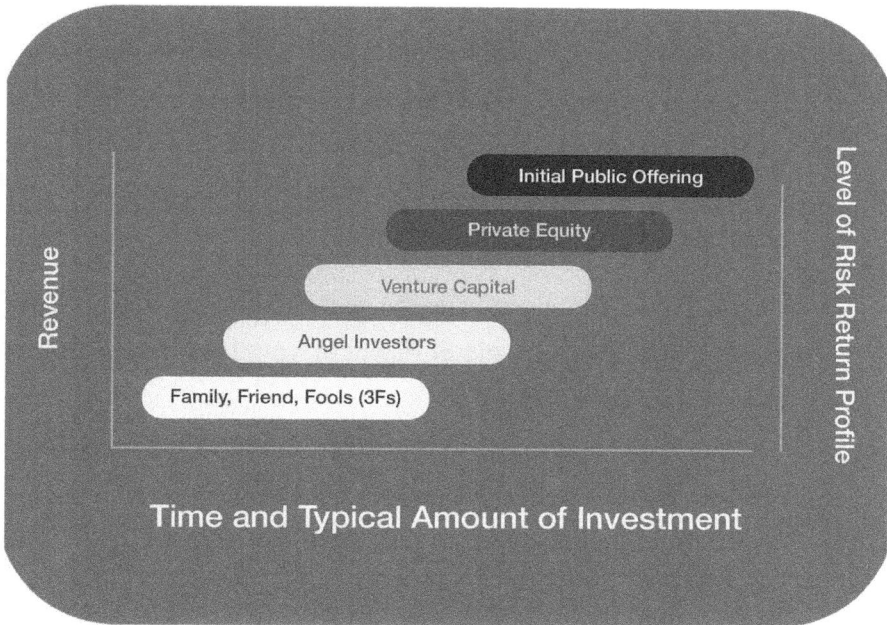

Once you have your business in a box and you want to replicate the box, you're a desirable investment for private equity, because they want to sell the box and reproduce as many boxes as the market can bear, which results in you and everybody making money.

Private equity can be tricky, so establish everything in writing. However, I have discovered that the longer the contract, the more likely it will fail, because length reflects distrust. And relationships thrive on trust.

The **Financial Projections** provide a forecast of revenue based on financial documents from the past several years. But if you're starting a new business, you will not have these documents. So how do you project your future finances? By providing the following five documents:

1. **A Sales Forecast**—Research what you're offering, how much you're charging, and how many customers or patients you can expect to purchase your products and services each month. Then create a grid showing how many of each product and service you're selling, how much they cost, and the number you expect to sell. This creates your sales forecast. Then, when you write your sales forecast for years following the initial 12 months in business, you can provide figures that reflect quarterly sales, units sold, and money earned.[140]

2. **A Cash Flow Statement**—This financial document shows all the money that comes into, and flows out of, your company. It reports what money comes from sales, investments, and other sources. This very important financial statement shows the proverbial bottom line and illustrates the financial viability of your business. You can find Cash Flow Statement templates online.

3. **Balance Sheet**—This financial statement is a snapshot of your company's assets, liabilities, and shareholders' equity at a specific point in time. Think of it as a freeze-frame or status check of your business's financial wellness; you'll record its vital signs that include assets and debts.

4. **Profit and Loss Statement—aka Income Statement**—This shows your company's financial health over the past year. Consider it as your MedikalPreneurial annual check-up that shows your financial struggles and well-being during the previous 12 months. As the name suggests, this document shows your profits and losses. Also known as an income statement, your P&L illustrates

whether your company can stabilize its finances by earning more money or lowering costs.

5. **Expenses Budget**—You need to know how much money will be required to open and operate your business. You can do this with a budget, which summarizes your income and expenses over a specific time.

When you create your Expenses Budget, research how much money will be required to launch and sustain your enterprise for three years or longer. Create your budget on an excel spreadsheet, or a template that you can find online. If you're not savvy with accounting, budgeting, and financial calculations, invest in the services of a trusted accountant. Your Expenses Budget will require research to assess costs of the following categories:

Real Estate—Will you lease office space or purchase a building? Does it require renovations to accommodate your ability to provide medical products and services? Do you need to make any changes to bring the building up to code? What licenses and permits are required? How much is the owner going to provide for tenant improvements?

Interior Design—Consider the costs of: building renovations; paint, carpeting, flooring, rugs, wall art, light fixtures, furniture, lobby/welcoming room furniture; and perks such as snacks and beverages. If you need help from an interior designer, then add that cost to your budget.

Equipment—What machines, if any, will you need? Will you equip an on-site lab or will you outsource lab services? Do you need x-ray machines and protective gear? Itemize the quantities and costs of machinery and technology; this includes computers and a software program designed to assist you in your medical niche. Does your business require a vehicle or a fleet of vehicles for pick-ups and deliveries of products and services, or to transport patients or customers?

Human Resources—How many people will you hire? How much will you pay your employees in salaries or hourly wages? What benefits will you provide? Will you pay for their uniforms? Quantify each expense and include it in your budget.

Insurance—Speak with your insurance professional about what kind of coverage, and how much coverage, your business will require.

Signage & Branding—The exterior of your building will require at least one sign to let everyone know that this is your place of business. If you have multiple entrances, or several offices, you'll need more signs. Have your sign custom-made to reflect your branding, which is a color scheme, logo, font, and specific verbiage for all messaging. This includes signs, stationery, business cards, your website, pamphlets and brochures, email templates, packaging, and patient/customer correspondences such as instruction sheets for procedures. You may want to hire a graphic designer to create a logo that reflects your unique style. Websites such as 99designs.com and fiverr.com enable you to hire talented graphic designers to create your logo for a low cost.

Advertising—Your promotional costs could include: hiring a public relations firm; creating a website and social media campaign; and paying for advertising via radio, television, newspapers, magazines, websites, billboards, and bus ads. You could also sponsor community events such as health fairs and charitable efforts relating to your products and services.

Outsourcing Services—What services will you outsource? Calculate costs for couriers, lab work, and other services. Be conservative to keep your costs low. The less you borrow, the less you owe.

The **Appendix** provides information such as reference letters, credit reports, resumes, and permits. These items are more private and sensitive, and should only be provided upon request. Here is a list of possible items to include in the Appendix.[141]

- Images of your products, prototypes, and store (if applicable)

- Your marketing materials, including logos, website, branding colors and fonts, and advertising templates

- Your market research analysis

- Credit reports and tax returns for the company and its owners

- Resumes and CVs for the owners and managers

- Recommendation letters from professional colleagues and leaders

- Financial projections

- Descriptions of your competition

- Media reports about you, the business, and your industry

- Legal documents pertaining to your shareholders, incorporation, etc.

- Documentation for your patents, permits, and licenses

- Copies of your property and equipment leases or rental agreements

- Contact information for your professional staff, including your accountant and attorney

- Contracts for business

Legalities are an important aspect of creating your business. Consult with a lawyer and tax professional to understand which type of business structure is best for your needs, and why it's imperative to select one to protect your personal assets from business debts and lawsuits. Here are the choices:

PA—Professional Association—is a business entity for companies that offer a professional service. Because certain states restrict the use of a

PA to particular industries, such as lawyers and physicians, some doctors choose PA status for their businesses.[142] Your state may require you to appoint a board of directors for your PA. In certain states, PA owners can only practice in the profession the PA represents. This matters because if you want people unrelated to that specific profession to buy into the business, you would be required to change the structure and incur future costs that could have been avoided by considering this beforehand.

LLC—Limited Liability Company—allows you to classify your company as a separate entity from yourself personally. The benefit is that you can maintain separation between your personal assets and your business assets. Very importantly, you can shield your personal assets from your professional debts and liabilities.

Whether you're a solopreneur or in partnership with others, you can perform all business transactions in the name of your LLC. That includes signing contracts that may include a lease for your business, opening bank accounts, hiring staff, and securing the permits and business licenses required to operate your company.[143]

PLLC—Professional Limited Liability Company—is a specialized LLC for specific professions that include physicians. A PLLC operates the same as an LLC, except it does not protect individuals from malpractice lawsuits, so malpractice insurance is required for each member.[144] If your state prohibits the formation of a PA, then a good alternative is a PLLC.

Corporation S or "S Corp"—enables owners to pay themselves salaries and receive dividends from the corporation's additional profits. Like an LLC, an S Corp protects your personal assets from creditors seeking payment from your business. They're also similar because an S Corp enables you to avoid paying both personal and corporate taxes.[145] Another similarity is that LLCs and S Corps can deduct expenses that include advertising, healthcare premiums, phone bills, computers, uniforms, and travel.[146]

Other Points to Consider About Your Business

Once you select a business entity and file paperwork with your state, you'll probably need to file an annual report and pay a fee every year for your LLC to remain in good standing. The IRS website provides links to every state's licensing department, so you can obtain specific requirements for filing your company's paperwork, operating as a business, filing taxes, and more. Here's the link: https://www.irs.gov/businesses/small-businesses-self-employed/state-government-websites.

In addition, you'll also need to contact the IRS to obtain an Employer Identification Number, or Federal Tax Identification Number. Your EIN is the government's identification for a business entity, just as your Social Security number and Driver's License number are used for your personal identification. You can apply for your EIN here: https://www.irs.gov/businesses/small-businesses-self-employed/apply-for-an-employer-identification-number-ein-online. The IRS provides this free service to immediately obtain your EIN.

Should You Create a Management Company?

The business entity that you select will protect you and your company as you operate and expand. In addition, you may want to create a management company that oversees two or three medical businesses that include a laboratory and your company. As you start growing, your management company owns all the assets. If a lawsuit bankrupts one company, your other business assets are protected.

As you know, anatomy forces physiology. Likewise, architecture forces behavior; it determines the direction and limitations of the ship, not the captain. Remember the concept of seeing a forest in a seed? Once you create the legal architecture for your business, and it limits you to grow only one tree, you're doomed; you cannot grow your forest in terms of additional offices, patients or clients, products and services, or more profits and people you can help. Focus on the forest, not the seed.

Invest the Time and Energy to Brainstorm and Research

Before you write your business plan, brainstorm what kind of company you want to create. What product, service, and experience do you want to provide? What's unique about you that will differentiate your company from the competition? Who is your target customer or patient, and what is the best geographical location—if you're opening a brick-and-mortar business—to set up shop?

Your business plan is important, so discipline yourself to write it within three months. Take action and tweak your business plan as you proceed. As you'll see later in this chapter when I talk about Proof of Concept, you will be building the airplane as you fly, but on a small scale. Consider it a model airplane; you can launch the jet after you gain experience, just like your medical training may have enabled you to operate on a hernia before working your way up to performing open heart surgery.

Likewise, limit your business plan to 20 to 25 pages. Writing a formal business plan makes you more likely to succeed compared to entrepreneurs who do not commit their plans to writing.[147] Your investment in time and energy to contemplate every aspect of your MedikalPreneurial enterprise will prepare you to tackle problems while building and sustaining a successful business.

Tools & Resources to Help You Write a Business Plan

You can learn more about how to create your business plan from YouTube videos and websites such as Forbes.com, Inc.com, Entrepeneur.com, and *Harvard Business Review.* The Small Business Association provides an abundance of information about how to write a business plan. Learn more at https://www.sba.gov/business-guide/plan-your-business/write-your-business-plan.

You can also get help at SCORE.org, a nonprofit organization and U.S. Small Business Administration partner that provides a template that guides you through creating your business plan. The template, available at https://www.score.org/resource/business-plan-template-startup-business, provides fillable worksheets for each section.

Paco's Proof of Concept:
Validate Your MedikalPreneurial Idea

proof of con·cept

noun

evidence, typically derived from an experiment or pilot project, which demonstrates that a design concept, business proposal, etc., is feasible.[148]

—*Google/Oxford Languages*

The best way to launch your idea as a MedikalPreneurial is to test it on a small scale. You can create a pilot project of your larger vision to ensure that it's viable. This experiment will save you time, money, and effort, and will enable you to revise your idea and make adjustments as you learn from mistakes and observations.

You can validate your idea with Paco's "Pistol First, Cannon Next" philosophy. In a battle, you may begin fighting with a pistol. If you fail at the first shot, you can try again and again, adjusting your aim until you consistently hit your target. Then you can bring the canon. The problem is, if you don't make a simple start on a company, then you don't adjust. You spend all your money, then regretfully realize that you made mistakes.

If you start lean with a small concept and prove that it works, then you can invest significant amounts of money. Now that you know where to aim, you can progress to firing a cannon. If you start with the cannon and fail, you may run out of gunpowder and can't really hit your target. Similarly, when you're learning how to perform surgeries, you remove an appendix before learning how to perform the more complex procedure of an organ transplant. The idea is to start small, and work your way up to the bigger, more complicated procedures that have risks and consequences.

The same philosophy applies to starting your business. Here are some pointers:

Put Creativity over Certainty. Have the courage and confidence to try bold new ideas that may revolutionize your business or industry.

Start lean. Begin with a small project, the minimum amount of effort and expense. If you fail, it's okay; you can include the expense to your education budget.

Create a Proof of Concept. This—the scaled-down, simplest version of your idea—is the pistol. You point it at your target, which is launching a successful business as a MedikalPreneur. You miss your target market. As a result, you also miss the target of making money. So you adjust your aim. You hit the target. You replicate and replicate. Then, boom! Bring the cannon. The cannon is the full-scale launch of your business. If you do not follow this method, you will spend all your gunpowder.

Another example is a soccer coach in Argentina who trained his players to perfect every move slowly, many, many times. Only then did he allow them to worry about speed. His philosophy was that if the players learned the moves the wrong way, then applied speed, they would fail miserably. So he forced them to pass the ball, then shoot, slowly, 20 consecutive times, until they mastered the move. Practice makes perfect.

But if you want to do something fast and perfect, you will mess it up. When you do a small project, slowly with the focus on learning and perfecting the actions, then you can speed up and expand the process. I used this method with doctors, and we perfected our methods. Within one year, we started applying it to nurses, embryologists, administrators, and clinics.

Start now. It's much better to start, even if you have it wrong, than trying to get it perfect before you begin. I'd rather make a decision and correct my decision, than not make a decision. Procrastination is horrible for entrepreneurs. When you have an idea, you have to take action. That's why academia is not a good milieu for entrepreneurs. Academics encourage mental gymnastics. It may make you feel good at first, but there's a good chance that you may regret it later.

Entrepreneurs take action. We hypothesize and somebody presents. Our attitude is, "Have you done it? Do it!" That's an entrepreneur. An entrepreneur does it! An entrepreneur is 80% taking action and 20% thinking! Similarly, we devote 10% of our time to dreaming, 10% to thinking, and 80% to doing.

Entrepreneurs are idea transformers. You implement. You execute. Your product or service as a MedikalPreneur could save lives!

CHAPTER 12

The Simple Business Model™ for MedikalPreneurs

This chapter is written in collaboration with Adrian Gonzalez.

My good friend Adrian Gonzalez created an Education Program for Company Leaders that can help MedikalPreneurs. He calls this program The Simple Business Model because it condenses everything you need to know while earning a Master's in Business Administration without going back to school for years to earn a formal degree. I am very grateful that he, as the owner of the business model, gave me permission to share this concept with you.

The Simple Business Model describes the core principles that apply to everything you do when starting and operating your medical business.

This concept ties together every aspect of your business plan. Even better, the following diagram of Adrian Gonzalez' business model shows a very clear picture of the cycle that you will use as a MedikalPreneur.

The Simple Business Model shows a transaction, the core act in business. Everything you do leads up to the transaction. If you sell a product, a service, an experience, or something else, you're engaging in transactions every time a client or customer compensates you for the item.

Look at the left side of the diagram. Your business endeavors begin with promotions—your marketing efforts—which cover a wide circle of actions aimed at bringing in potential patients or clients. A smaller number of those who contact your business encounter your sales team, which includes everyone from the receptionist who answers the phone, your website, and every employee in the office. They are "selling" the product, service, or experience through their communications and action. As your company becomes more complex, you may have several individuals doing sales. At the beginning, an individual may perform several of these tasks. Sales lead to your "delivery," where the patients or clients experience whatever product or service you're providing. And that results in "billing and collecting."

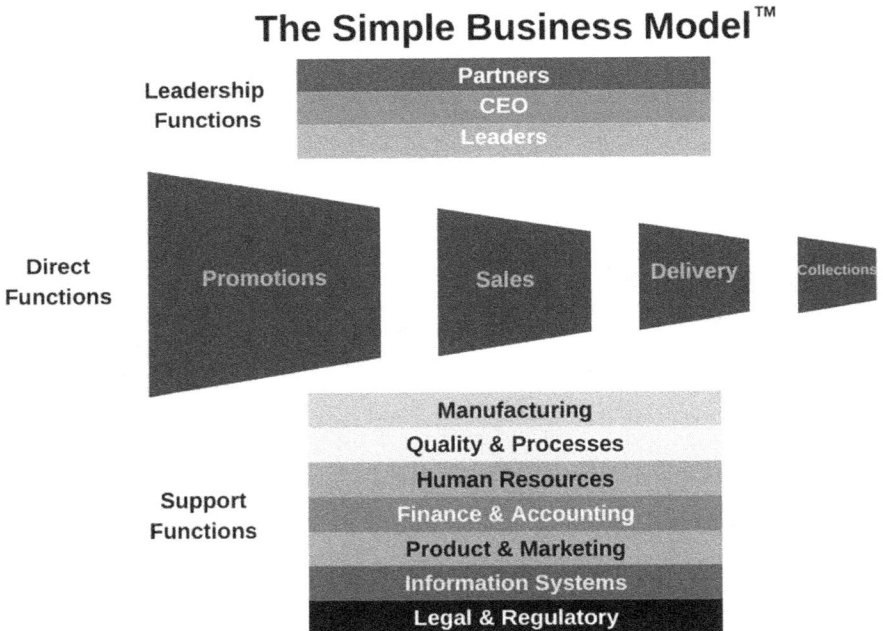

The Simple Business Model™

Leadership Functions
- Partners
- CEO
- Leaders

Direct Functions
- Promotions
- Sales
- Delivery
- Collections

Support Functions
- Manufacturing
- Quality & Processes
- Human Resources
- Finance & Accounting
- Product & Marketing
- Information Systems
- Legal & Regulatory

It's important to note that the diagram resembles a funnel; each segment gets smaller as it approaches the financial compensation that results from operating your business. It's imperative that you as a salesperson for your business understand every aspect of the diagram. Typically, people in each area of your business are busy doing their specific tasks each day; so the technician in the laboratory (operations) isn't monitoring what the promotions team is doing. However, if the promotions team fails to attract new patients or clients, the business will fail, and the technician will no longer have a job.

Therefore, it's important for you as a MedikalPreneur to create a culture in your office that helps everyone understand the interconnectedness and cross-pollination of every aspect of the company. Each person plays an important role that affects every other person on the team, and this enables the business to thrive by providing the best experience for a growing number of patients and clients.

Author Bio

DR. FRANCISCO ARREDONDO GRADUATED *summa cum laude* from the Monterrey Institute of Technology and Higher Studies School of Medicine in Mexico. In 1991, the Mexican president honored him as "one of the best medical students in the country."

Two years before that, Dr. Arredondo found his passion in fertility while collaborating with Mexico's first successful In Vitro Fertilization team. His determination to become a fertility specialist led him to do: research at the World Health Organization's Reproductive Biology Center in Mexico City; an internship at Icahn School of Medicine at Mount Sinai in New York City; an OBGYN residency at University of Texas Health Science Center of San Antonio, Texas; a Fertility Fellowship at Hospital of the University of Pennsylvania; and a Master's in Public Health at Harvard University, where he focused on international health and business management.

He practiced as an OBGYN in rural Kentucky and later became an Assistant Professor of Reproductive Biology at Case Western Reserve University in Cleveland, Ohio.

Dr. Arredondo's 40th birthday inspired him to combine his medical, entrepreneurial, and management skills to follow a new path as a "MedikalPreneur"—a term he coined—which led him back to San Antonio to open his own fertility center. Over 13 years, he and his three-member team grew a network of fertility centers and entrepreneurial ventures with more than 80 team members. In 2018 and

2019, some of his corporations underwent two mergers and made him the Chief Medical Officer of America's largest network of fertility centers, overseeing more than 50 fertility specialists.

After achieving his professional and financial goals, Dr. Arredondo sold his interest in many of his companies and embarked on a new venture: Social Entrepreneurship to democratize fertility services by applying lean management, Six Sigma and Toyota Production systems to fertility services, thereby simultaneously increasing safety, affordability, and quality.

A member of the medical advisory board for various American companies, he also advises national and international private equity firms that focus on health investments.

Dr. Arredondo shares his success secrets so you can become a MedikalPreneur to transform your medical practice, achieve your greatest professional fulfillment, and maximize your financial potential.

Recommended Reading

The Experience Economy: Work is Theatre and Every Business a Stage by B. Joseph Pine II and James H. Gilmore

The Dream Society: How the Coming Shift from Information to Imagination Will Transform Your Business by Rolf Jensen

The Renaissance Society: How the Shift from Dream Society to the Age of Individual Control Will Change the Way You Do Business by Rolf Jensen

To Sell Is Human: The Surprising Truth About Moving Others by Daniel H. Pink

Influence: The Psychology of Persuasion by Robert B. Cialdini, PhD

DEAL! Discovery, Engagement, and Leverage for Professionals by Dr. Jeff Belkora

Range: Why Generalists Triumph in a Specialized World by David Epstein

Purple Cow, New Edition: Transform Your Business by Being Remarkable by Seth Godin

Words That Work: It's Not What You Say, It's What People Hear by Frank Luntz

On Caring by Milton Mayeroff

Grit: The Power of Passion and Perseverance by Angela Duckworth

The Checklist Manifesto: How to Get Things Right by Atul Gawande

The Face to Face Book: Why Real Relationships Rule in a Digital Marketplace[149] by Ed Keller

Endnotes

1   Jorge Bucay, *El elefante encadenado,* (Mexico: Oceano Travesia, 2014), last accessed September 15, 2021, https://www.amazon.com/Elefante-encadenado-El-Nueva-edici%C3%B3n/dp/6077350613/ref=sr_1_1?dchild=1&qid=1624480583&refinements=p_27%3AJorge+Bucay&s=books&sr=1-1

2   "Krav Maga," Wikipedia, last modified September 15, 2021, last accessed September 15 2021, https://en.wikipedia.org/wiki/Krav_Maga

3   "Imi Lichtenfeld," Wikipedia, last modified August 7, 2021, last accessed September 15 2021, https://en.wikipedia.org/wiki/Imi_Lichtenfeld

4   "Thomas Merton," Wikipedia, last modified September 7, 2021, last accessed September 15 2021, https://en.wikipedia.org/wiki/Thomas_Merton

5   David Epstein, *Range: Why Generalists Triumph in a Specialized World,* (New York: Riverhead Books, 2019), last accessed September 15, 2021, https://www.amazon.com/Range-Generalists-Triumph-Specialized-World/dp/0735214484/ref=asc_df_0735214484/?tag=hyprod-20&linkCode=df0&hvadid=344057888328&hvpos=&hvnetw=g&hvrand=14628316044637504074&hvpone=&hvptwo=&hvqmt=&hvdev=c&hvdvcmdl=&hvlocint=&hvlocphy=9033109&hvtargid=pla-750234669981&psc=1&tag=&ref=&adgrpid=69543898472&hvpone=&hvptwo=&hvadid=344057888328&hvpos=&hvnetw=g&hvrand=-14628316044637504074&hvqmt=&hvdev=c&hvdvcmdl=&hvlocint=&hvlocphy=9033109&hvtargid=pla-750234669981

6   B. Joseph Pine II and James H. Gilmore, *Experience Economy,* (Boston: Harvard Business School Press, 1999), last accessed September 15, 2021, https://www.amazon.com/Experience-Economy-Joseph-Gilmore-Hardcover/dp/B009O2HB8E/ref=sr_1_1?dchild=1&keywords=The+Experience+Economy+by+B.+Joseph+Pine+II+and+James+H.+Gilmore.&qid=1631742365&s=books&sr=1-1

7   B. Joseph Pine II and James H. Gilmore, *The Experience Economy, With a New Preface by the Authors: Competing for Customer Time, Attention, and Money,* (Boston: Harvard Business School Press, 2019), last accessed September 15, 2021, https://www.amazon.com/Experience-Economy-New-Preface-Authors/dp/1633697975/ref=sr_1_3?dchild=1&keywords=The+Experience+Economy+by+B.+Joseph+Pine+II+and+James+H.+Gilmore.&qid=1631742365&s=books&sr=1-3

8   "Roger Bannister," Wikipedia, last modified September 3, 2021, last accessed September 15, 2021, https://en.wikipedia.org/wiki/Roger_Bannister

9   Arlen Myers, "What Makes Doctors Great Entrepreneurs," *The T,* March 9, 2016, last accessed September 15, 2021, https://thetranslationalscientist.com/outside-the-lab/why-doctors-make-great-entrepreneurs

10 "Active Physicians with a U.S. Doctor of Medicine Degree by Specialty, 2015," AAMC, last accessed October 7, 2021, https://www.aamc.org/data-reports/workforce/interactive-data/active-physicians-us-doctor-medicine-us-md-degree-specialty-2015.

11 Georgia McIntyre, "What Percentage of Small Businesses Fail? (And Other Need-to-Know Stats)," *Fundera by Nerdwallet,* November 20, 2020, last accessed September 15, 2021, https://www.fundera.com/blog/what-percentage-of-small-businesses-fail

12 Ben Harder, "America's Best Hospitals: the 2021-22 Honor Roll and Overview," *U.S. News & World Report,* July 27, 2021, last accessed September 15, 2021, https://health.usnews.com/health-care/best-hospitals/articles/best-hospitals-honor-roll-and-overview

13 James K. Stoller, Amanda Goodall, and Agnes Baker, "Why the Best Hospitals are Managed by Doctors," *Harvard Business Review,* December 27, 2016, last accessed September 15, 2021

14 "About: Dr. Robert Kiltz," Doctor Kiltz, last accessed September 15, 2021, https://www.doctorkiltz.com/about/

15 Alison Wood Brooks, "Get excited: reappraising pre-performance anxiety as excitement," *Journal of Experimental Psychology: General* 143, no. 3 (June 2014): 1144-58, last accessed September 15, 2021, https://pubmed.ncbi.nlm.nih.gov/24364682/

16 Elizabeth W. Dunn, Daniel T. Gilbert, and Timothy D. Wilson, "If Money Doesn't Make You Happy, Then You Probably Aren't Spending It Right," University of British Columbia, Harvard University, University of Virginia, November 2010, last accessed September 15, 2021.

17 B. Joseph Pine II and James H. Gilmore, "Welcome to the Experience Economy," *Harvard Business Review,* July-August 1998, 97-105, last accessed September 15, 2021, https://www.researchgate.net/publication/11783228_Welcome_to_the_experience_economy_It's_no_longer_just_about_healing_patients_want_a_personal_transformation

18 "Home: Jungle Roots," Jungle Roots Children's Dentistry & Orthodontics, last accessed September 15, 2021, https://www.jungleroots.com

19 Hillel M Finestone, MD, and David B. Conter, PhD, "Acting in Medical Practice," *The Lancet, University of Western Ontario* 344, no. 8925 (September 1994): 801, last accessed September 15, 2021.

20 Tina Mermiri, "The transformation economy," in *Beyond experience: culture, consumer, and brand,* (London: Arts & Business, 2009), 19.

21 "Prosumer," Wikipedia, last modified September 8, 2021, last accessed September 15, 2021, https://en.wikipedia.org/wiki/Prosumer

22 Rolf Jensen, *The Dream Society: How the Coming Shift from Information to Imagination Will Transform Your Business,* (New York: McGraw Hill Education, 2001), last accessed September 15, 2021, https://www.amazon.com/Dream-Society-Information-Imagination-Transform/dp/0071379681

23 Rofl Jensen, *The Renaissance Society: How the Shift from Dream Society to the Age of Individual Control will Change the Way You Do Business,* (New York: McGraw Hill Education, 2013), last accessed September 15, 2021, https://www.amazon.com/Renaissance-Society-Individual-Control-Business/dp/0071806059/ref=sr_1_2?keywords=The+Renaissance+Society+Rolf+jensen&qid=1627759412&s=books&sr=1-2

24   "Customer Service: Consulting & Training" The DiJulius Group, last accessed September 15, 2021, https://thedijuliusgroup.com

25   B. Joseph Pine II and James H. Gilmore, *The Experience Economy: Work is Theater & Every Business a Stage,* (Boston: Harvard Business School Press, 1999), last accessed September 15, 2021, https://www.amazon.com/Experience-Economy-Theater-Every-Business/dp/0875848192

26   James Allen, Frederick F. Reichheld, Barney Hamilton, and Rob Markey, "Closing the delivery gap," *Bain & Company,* 2005, last accessed September 15, 2021, https://media.bain.com/bainweb/PDFs/cms/hotTopics/closingdeliverygap.pdf

27   Seth Godin, *Purple Cow: Transform Your Business by Being Remarkable,* (New York: Portfolio, 2009), last accessed September 15, 2021, https://www.amazon.com/Purple-Cow-New-Transform-Remarkable/dp/1591843170

28   Dr. Frank Luntz, *Words That Work: It's Not What You Say, It's What People Hear,* (New York: Hatchette Books, 2008), last accessed September 15, 2021, https://www.amazon.com/Words-That-Work-What-People/dp/1401309291

29   Sonja Lyubomirsky, Lorie Sousa, and Rene Dickerhoof, "The costs and benefits of writing, talking, and thinking about life's triumphs and defeats," *Journal of personality and social psychology* 90, no. 4 (April 2006), last accessed September 15, 2021, https://escholarship.org/content/qt93k8b43s/qt93k8b43s.pdf

30   Alison Wood Brooks, "Get excited: reappraising pre-performance anxiety as excitement," *Journal of Experimental Psychology: General* 143, no. 3 (June 2014): 1144-58, last accessed September 15, 2021, https://pubmed.ncbi.nlm.nih.gov/24364682/

31   Milton Mayeroff, *On Caring,* (New York: William Morrow Paperbacks, 1990), last accessed September 15, 2021, https://www.amazon.com/Caring-Milton-Mayeroff/dp/0060920246

32   "Home," Carmen Martinez Jover, last accessed September 15, 2021, https://www.carmenmartinezjover.com

33   "As You Like It," Wikipedia, last modified September 11, 2021, last accessed September 15, 2021, https://en.wikipedia.org/wiki/As_You_Like_It

34   "Accounting Basics: Debits and Credits," Patriot Software, last accessed September 15, 2021, https://www.patriotsoftware.com/blog/accounting/debits-and-credits/

35   "Accounting Basics: Debits and Credits," Patriot Software, last accessed September 15, 2021, https://www.patriotsoftware.com/blog/accounting/debits-and-credits/

36   "Examples of operating expenses," *Accounting Tools,* April 12, 2021, last accessed September 15, 2021, https://www.accountingtools.com/articles/what-are-examples-of-operating-expenses.html

37   "Examples of operating expenses," *Accounting Tools,* April 12, 2021, last accessed September 15, 2021, https://www.accountingtools.com/articles/what-are-examples-of-operating-expenses.html

38   "Examples of operating expenses," *Accounting Tools,* April 12, 2021, last accessed September 15, 2021, https://www.accountingtools.com/articles/what-are-examples-of-operating-expenses.html

39   Alicia Tuovila, "Non-Operating Expense," *Investopedia*, August 25, 2021, last accessed September 15, 2021, https://www.investopedia.com/terms/n/non-operating-expense.asp#:~:text=A%20non%2Doperating%20expense%20is%20an%20expense%20incurred%20from%20activities,or%20costs%20from%20currency%20exchanges

40   Adam Hayes, "EBITDA – Earnings Before Interest, Taxes, Depreciation, and Amortization," *Investopedia*, February 4, 2021, last accessed September 15, 2021, https://www.investopedia.com/terms/e/ebitda.asp

41   Claire Boyte-White, "The Difference Between Cash Flow and EBITDA," *Investopedia*, May 31, 2021, last accessed September 15, 2021, https://www.investopedia.com/ask/answers/012015/what-difference-between-cash-flow-and-ebidta.asp

42   "Anna Karenina principle," Wikipedia, last modified March 2, 2021, last accessed September 15, 2021, https://en.wikipedia.org/wiki/Anna_Karenina_principle

43   "Miracle (2004 film)," Wikipedia, last modified September 2, 2021, last accessed September 15, 2021, https://en.wikipedia.org/wiki/Miracle_(2004_film)

44   "Miracle (2004 film)," Wikipedia, last modified September 2, 2021, last accessed September 15, 2021, https://en.wikipedia.org/wiki/Miracle_(2004_film)

45   Stuart Heiser, "New Findings Confirm Predictions on Physician Shortage," *AAMC*, April 23, 2019, last accessed September 15, 2021, https://www.aamc.org/news-insights/press-releases/new-findings-confirm-predictions-physician-shortage

46   Tam Recruiting, "Top 7 Strategies for Healthcare Recruiting," *The Applicant Manager*, August 8, 2019, last accessed September 15, 2021, https://www.tamrecruiting.com/healthcare-recruiting/

47   "Home: JAMA Career Center," JAMA Network, last accessed September 15, 2021, https://careers.jamanetwork.com/

48   Patrick Monaghan, "Passing the Baton," *Nothing Ventured*, August 22, 2016, last accessed September 15, 2021, https://nothingventured.rocks/passing-the-baton-3f10d945745f

49   Angela Duckworth, *Grit: The Power of Passion and Perseverance,* (New York: Scribner, 2018), last accessed September 15, 2021, https://www.amazon.com/Grit-Passion-Perseverance-Angela-Duckworth/dp/1501111116/ref=sr_1_1?dchild=1&qid=1596839620&refinements=p_27%3AAngela+Duckworth&s=books&sr=1-1&text=Angela+Duckworth

50   "Niki Lauda," Wikipedia, last modified September 14, 2021, last accessed September 15, 2021, https://en.wikipedia.org/wiki/Niki_Lauda

51   Marilyn Rogers, "Eight Signs That You're Highly Empathetic Even If You Don't Notice It," *Lifehack,* last accessed September 15, 2021, https://www.lifehack.org/345721/8-signs-youre-highly-empathetic-even-you-dont-notice

52   "Patient Experience Summit 2020," Empathy and Innovation, last accessed September 15, 2021, http://www.empathyandinnovation.com/cleveland/2020/one-question-inspired-international-movement-toward-more-empathetic-care

53   "Patient Experience Summit 2020," Empathy and Innovation, last accessed September 15, 2021, http://www.empathyandinnovation.com/cleveland/2020/one-question-inspired-international-movement-toward-more-empathetic-care

54   James I. Merlino and Ananth Raman, "Health Care's Service Fanatics," *Harvard Business Review,* May 2013, last accessed September 15, 2021, https://hbr.org/2013/05/health-cares-service-fanatics

55   James I. Merlino and Ananth Raman, "Health Care's Service Fanatics," *Harvard Business Review,* May 2013, last accessed September 15, 2021, https://hbr.org/2013/05/health-cares-service-fanatics

56   Toby Cosgrove, MD, "One Question That Changed Our Organization (Video)," *Cleveland Clinic,* July 1, 2016, last accessed September 15, 2021, https://consultqd.clevelandclinic.org/one-question-changed-organization-video/

57   James I. Merlino and Ananth Raman, "Health Care's Service Fanatics," *Harvard Business Review,* May 2013, last accessed September 15, 2021, https://hbr.org/2013/05/health-cares-service-fanatics

58   Rhett Power, "Instill Empathy Into Your Culture – It Could Save Your Business," *Inc.,* March 21, 2019, last accessed September 15, 2021, https://www.inc.com/rhett-power/instill-empathy-into-your-culture-it-could-save-your-business.html

59   Atul Gawande, *The Checklist Manifesto: How to Get Things Right,* (London: Picador, 2010), last accessed September 15 2021, https://www.amazon.com/Checklist-Manifesto-How-Things-Right/dp/0312430000

60   Brett Munster, "Why A Honduran Bridge Is a Perfect Metaphor For Disruption," *Road Less Ventured,* April 22, 2018, last accessed September 15, 2021, https://medium.com/road-less-ventured/why-an-honduran-bridge-is-a-perfect-metaphor-for-disruption-2a2d7c910535

61   "John Lubbock – Earth and sky…" BrainyQuote, last accessed September 15, 2021, https://www.brainyquote.com/quotes/john_lubbock_122570

62   "Sully Sullenberger," Wikipedia, last modified August 26, 2021, last accessed September 15, 2021, https://en.wikipedia.org/wiki/Sully_Sullenberger

63   Ruth Umoh, "Why Amazon pays employees $5,000 to quit," *CNBC: Make It,* May 21, 2018, last accessed September 15, 2021, https://www.cnbc.com/2018/05/21/why-amazon-pays-employees-5000-to-quit.html

64   Adam Robinson, "Zappos Pays Employees $2000 to Quit. This Superstar CEO Has a Different Approach," *Inc.,* January 12, 2018, last accessed September 15, 2021, https://www.inc.com/adam-robinson/zappos-pays-employees-2000-to-quit-this-superstar-ceo-has-a-different-approach.html

65   Tech 2 News Staff, "Chrome and Firefox users are more committed to work than Safari or Explorer users: Study," *Firstpost: Tech2,* June 7, 2016, last accessed September 15, 2021, https://www.firstpost.com/tech/news-analysis/chrome-and-firefox-users-are-more-committed-to-work-than-safari-or-explorer-users-study-3683233.html

66   Adam Grant, *Originals: How Non-Conformists Move the World,* (New York: Penguin Books, 2017), last accessed September 15, 2021, https://www.amazon.com/Originals-How-Non-Conformists-Move-World/dp/014312885X

67   Jacob Morgan, "New Research: The Top 10 Factors for Employee Happiness on the Job," *The Future Organization,* December 8, 2014, last accessed September 15, 2021, https://thefutureorganization.com/new-research-top-10-factors-employee-happiness-job/

68   Frederick F. Reichheld, "The One Number You Need to Grow," *Harvard Business Review,*

December 2003, last accessed October 7, 2021, https://hbr.org/2003/12/the-one-number-you-need-to-grow

69 "About Amazon in the UK: Our Mission," Amazon UK, last accessed September 15, 2021, https://www.aboutamazon.co.uk/uk-investment/our-mission#:~:text=Our%20mission%20is%20to%20continually,Earth's%20most%20customer%20centric%20company.

70 Rich Allen, "Rich Allen – Why," YouTube video, 07:27, February 24, 2012, last accessed September 15, 2021, https://www.youtube.com/watch?v=ZDE6YIJOkLs&list=UUrV2F VZl3i-GeywNxVPLHSA&index=146

71 Simon Sinek, "How great leaders inspire action," TED Talk, September 2009, last accessed September 15, 2021, https://www.ted.com/talks/simon_sinek_how_great_leaders_inspire_action?language=en

72 Alexandra Twin, "Marketing," *Investopedia,* August 17, 2020, last accessed September 15, 2021, https://www.investopedia.com/terms/m/marketing.asp

73 "What is Marketing – The Definition of Marketing," American Marketing Association, last accessed September 15, 2021, https://www.ama.org/the-definition-of-marketing-what-is-marketing/

74 "Marketing Plan Definition," Entrepreneur, last accessed September 15, 2021, https://www.entrepreneur.com/encyclopedia/marketing-plan

75 Steven Covey, *The 7 Habits of Highly Effective People,* (Free Press, 1990), last accessed October 7, 2021, https://www.amazon.com/Habits-Highly-Effective-People/dp/0671708635

76 "About: Alzheimer's Association," Alzheimer's Association, last accessed September 15, 2021, https://www.alz.org/about

77 Hannah Bae, "Bill Gates' 40th anniversary email: Goal was 'a computer on every desk,'" *CNN Business,* April 6, 2015, last accessed September 15, 2021, https://money.cnn.com/2015/04/05/technology/bill-gates-email-microsoft-40-anniversary/index.html

78 Ed Keller and Brad Fay, *The Face-to-Face Book: Why Real Relationships Rule in a Digital Marketplace,* (New York: Free Press, 2012), last accessed September 15, 2021, https://www.amazon.com/Face-Face-Book-Relationships-Marketplace/dp/1451640064

79 Daniel Pink, *To Sell Is Human: The Surprising Truth About Moving Others,* (New York: Riverhead Books, 2013), last accessed October 8, 2021, https://www.amazon.com/Sell-Human-Surprising-Moving-Others/dp/1594631905.

80 Robert B, Cialdini, PhD, *Influence: The Psychology of Persuasion,* (New York: Harper Business, 2006), last accessed September 15, 2021, https://www.amazon.com/Influence-Psychology-Persuasion-Robert-Cialdini/dp/006124189X

81 https://www.amazon.com/Influence-Psychology-Persuasion-Robert-Cialdini/dp/006124189X

82 "Reciprocity (social psychology)," Wikipedia, last modified May 25, 2021, last accessed September 15, 2021, https://en.wikipedia.org/wiki/Reciprocity_(social_psychology)

83 "The 7 Principles of Givers Gain," Ivan Misner, last accessed September 15, 2021, https://ivanmisner.com/7-principles-givers-gain/

84 Ivan R. Misner and Jeff Morris, *Givers Gain: The BNI Story,* (Colorado: Paradigm, 2004),

last accessed September 15, 2021, https://www.goodreads.com/book/show/2058503.Givers_Gain

85 "Newton's Laws of Motion," Glenn Research Center, last accessed September 15, 2021, https://www1.grc.nasa.gov/beginners-guide-to-aeronautics/newtons-laws-of-motion/

86 influenceatwork, "Science of Persuasion," YouTube video, 11:50, November 26, 2012, last accessed September 15, 2021, https://www.youtube.com/watch?v=cFdCzN7RYbw

87 Robert B. Cialdini, PhD, "Harnessing the Science of Persuasion," *Harvard Business Review,* October 2001, last accessed September 15, 2021

88 B. Joseph Pine II and James H. Gilmore, *The Experience Economy,* (Boston: Harvard Business Review Press, 2011), last accessed September 15, 2021, https://www.amazon.com/Experience-Economy-Updated-Joseph-Pine/dp/1422161978?ie=UTF8&redirect=true&tag=wwwstrategich-20

89 Deepak Malhotra and Manu Malhotra, "Negotiation Strategies for Doctors – and Hospitals," *Harvard Business Review,* October 21, 2013, last accessed September 15, 2021, https://hbr.org/2013/10/negotiation-strategies-for-doctors-and-hospitals

90 "What is a Multiparty Negotiation?" *Program on Negotiation: Harvard Law School,* 2021, last accessed September 15, 2021, https://www.pon.harvard.edu/tag/multiparty-negotiation/

91 Austin Duerfeldt, "Gold Star Negotiations: Applying the Ackerman Bargaining Method," *Institute of Agriculture and Natural Resources: Cropwatch,* February 13, 2018, last accessed September 15, 2021, https://cropwatch.unl.edu/2018/gold-star-negotiations-applying-ackerman-bargaining-method

92 Google/Oxford Language Dictionary, Last accessed October 8, 2021, https://www.google.com/search?q=evidence+definition&oq=evidence+definition+&aqs=chrome..69i57j0i27l2.5524j0j7&sourceid=chrome&ie=UTF-8

93 Google Dictionary, Last accessed October 8, 2021, https://www.google.com/search?q=wisdom+definition&sxsrf=AOaemvIowdq2yQCHdwxrs24XYDfe2Hsdmg%3A1633698644779&ei=VENgYdL9LoSGtQb4wapg&ved=0ahUKEwjS95Db8brzAhUEQ80KHfigCgwQ4dUDCA4&uact=5&oq=wisdom+definition&gs_lcp=Cgdnd3Mtd2l6EAMyCQgjECcQRhD5ATIFCAAQgAQyBggAEAcQHjIGCAAQBxAeMgUIABCABDIGCAAQBxAeMgYIABAHEB4yBQgAEIAEMgYIABAHEB4yBQgAEIAEOgcIIxCwAxAnOgcIABBHELADOgcIABCwAxBDOgQIABBDSgQIQRgAUN2_A1jwwwNg58UDaAFwAngAgAHAAYgBjgWSAQM0LjKYAQCgAQHIAQrAAQE&sclient=gws-wiz

94 "Evidence-Based Medicine," John Hopkins Medicine, last accessed September 15, 2021, https://www.hopkinsmedicine.org/gim/research/method/ebm.html

95 D. R. Matthews, "Wisdom-based and evidence-based medicine," *Diabetes, Obesity and Metabolism,* November 25, 2011, last accessed September 15, 2021, https://dom-pubs.onlinelibrary.wiley.com/doi/full/10.1111/j.1463-1326.2011.01514.x

96 Robert M. Centor, MD, "To Be a Great Physician, You Must Understand the Whole Story," *National Center for Biotechnology Information,* March 26, 2007, last accessed September 15, 2021, https://www.ncbi.nlm.nih.gov/pmc/articles/PMC1924990/

97 "World View: Who Said 'the Only Thing Constant is Change'?" Reference, last modified March 24, 2020, last accessed September 15, 2021, https://www.reference.com/world-view/said-only-thing-constant-change-d50c0532e714e12b

98 Google Dictionary, last accessed October 8, 2021, https://www.google.com/search?q=pr osumer+definition&sxsrf=AOaemvK01x42EhOb6delOfcIpz5q0CJvsQ%3A1633699752 106&ei=qEdgYfH-BYKlqtsPsZOegAo&oq=prosumer+definition&gs_lcp=Cgdnd3Mt-d2l6EAEYATIECCMQJzIKCAAQgAQQhwIQFDIECAAQQzIECAAQQzIFCAAQ gAQyBQgAEIAEMgUIABCABDIFCAAQgAQyBQgAEIAEMgUIABCABDoHCC-MQsAMQJzoHCAAQRxCwAzoFCAAQkQI6BggAEAcQHkoECEEYAFDqm19Y6pt-fYO6rX2gBcAJ4AIABf4gB3QGSAQMxLjGYAQCgAQHIAQnAAQE&sclient=gws-wiz

99 "Miles Kington," Wikipedia, last modified September 1, 2021, last accessed September 15, 2021, https://en.wikipedia.org/wiki/Miles_Kington

100 Jeff Belkora, *DEAL! Discovery, Engagement, and Leverage for Professionals,* (Guidesmith, 2015), last accessed September 15, 2021, https://www.amazon.com/gp/product/B012UG-G0AA/ref=dbs_a_def_rwt_bibl_vppi_i0

101 "The Founder," Wikipedia, Last accessed October 8, 2021, https://en.wikipedia.org/wiki/The_Founder

102 "Responses: What Scientific Concept Would Improve Everybody's Cognitive Toolkit?" Edge, last accessed September 15, 2021, https://www.edge.org/responses/what-scientific-concept-would-improve-everybodys-cognitive-toolkit

103 "Niels Bohr," Wikipedia, last modified August 30, 2021, last accessed September 15, 2021, https://en.wikipedia.org/wiki/Niels_Bohr

104 Tabitha M. Powledge, "Nicotine as Therapy," *PLoS Biology* 2, no. 11 (November 2004): 1707-10, last accessed September 15, 2021, https://www.ncbi.nlm.nih.gov/pmc/articles/PMC526783/pdf/pbio.0020404.pdf

105 Bo Zhou, MD, Li Yang, MD, PhD, Qingmin Sun, MD, Rihong Cong, MD, Haijuan Gu, MD, Naping Tang, MD, Huaijun Zhu, MD, Bin Wang, PhD, "Cigarette Smoking and the Risk of Endometrial Cancer: A Meta-Analysis," *Clinical Research Study* 121, no. 6 (June 2008): 501-508, last accessed September 15, 2021, https://www.amjmed.com/article/S0002-9343(08)00194-0/fulltext

106 Eric C. Sinoway, "No, You Can't Have It All," *Harvard Business Review,* October 2012, last accessed September 15, 2021, https://hbr.org/2012/10/no-you-cant-have-it-all

107 "Approaches: What is Decision Science," Harvard T.H. Chan School of Public Health, last accessed September 15, 2021, https://chds.hsph.harvard.edu/approaches/what-is-decision-science/#:~:text=Decision%20science%20seeks%20to%20make,any%20particular%20ac-tion%20or%20inaction.

108 Anna Powers, "The Science of Quicker Decision Making," *Forbes,* April 30, 2018, last ac-cessed September 15, 2021, https://www.forbes.com/sites/annapowers/2018/04/30/the-science-of-quicker-decision-making/#695122545c9e

109 Daniel Kahneman, Andrew M. Rosenfield, Linnea Gandhi, and Tom Blaser, "The Big Idea: Noise – How to Overcome the High, Hidden Cost of Inconsistent Decision-Making," *Har-vard Business Review,* October 2016, last accessed September 15, 2021

110 Daniel Kahneman, Andrew M. Rosenfield, Linnea Gandhi, and Tom Blaser, "The Big Idea: Noise – How to Overcome the High, Hidden Cost of Inconsistent Decision-Making," *Har-*

vard Business Review, October 2016, last accessed September 15, 2021

111 Daniel Kahneman, Andrew M. Rosenfield, Linnea Gandhi, and Tom Blaser, "The Big Idea: Noise – How to Overcome the High, Hidden Cost of Inconsistent Decision-Making," *Harvard Business Review,* October 2016, last accessed September 15, 2021

112 "Autopoiesis," Merriam-Webster, last accessed October 8, 2021, https://www.merriam-webster.com/dictionary/autopoiesis

113 Will Feuer, "Tattoo removal company seeks to ride a wave of millennial 'regretters,'" *CNBC,* December 21, 2019, last accessed September 15, 2021, https://www.cnbc.com/2019/12/20/soliton-plans-to-make-a-fortune-off-millennials-who-regret-tattoos.html

114 H.R. Maturana and F.J. Varela, *Autopoiesis and Cognition: the realization of the living,* (Holland: D. Reidel Publishing, 1980), last accessed September 15, 2021

115 "Aravind Eye Hospitals," Wikipedia, last modified June 25, 2021, last accessed September 15, 2021, https://en.wikipedia.org/wiki/Aravind_Eye_Hospitals

116 Institute for Health & Healing, "Infinite Vision: The Story of Aravind Eye Hospital," YouTube video, 23:53, November 15, 2012, last accessed September 15, 2021, https://www.youtube.com/watch?v=Jr70IrWM-n8

117 Institute for Health & Healing, "Infinite Vision: The Story of Aravind Eye Hospital," YouTube video, 23:53, November 15, 2012, last accessed September 15, 2021, https://www.youtube.com/watch?v=Jr70IrWM-n8

118 Institute for Health & Healing, "Infinite Vision: The Story of Aravind Eye Hospital," YouTube video, 23:53, November 15, 2012, last accessed September 15, 2021, https://www.youtube.com/watch?v=Jr70IrWM-n8

119 "About Us: Our Story," Aravind Eye Care System, last accessed September 15, 2021, https://aravind.org/our-story/

120 Pavithra Mehta and Suchitra Shenoy, *Infinite Vision: How Aravind Became the World's Greatest Business Case for Compassion,* (San Francisco: Berrett-Koehler, 2011), last accessed September 15, 2021

121 H.R. Maturana and F.J. Varela, *Autopoiesis and Cognition: the realization of the living,* (Holland: D. Reidel Publishing, 1980), last accessed September 15, 2021

122 "Our Company: About Vitro," Vitro, last accessed September 15, 2021, https://www.vitro.com/en/our-company/history/

123 "Home: Biopappel," Biopappel, last accessed September 15, 2021, https://www.biopappel.com/en

124 "Budweiser," Wikipedia, last accessed October 8, 2021, https://en.wikipedia.org/wiki/Budweiser

125 Luca D'Urbino, "The steam has gone out of globalization," *The Economist,* January 24, 2019, last accessed September 15, 2021, https://www.economist.com/leaders/2019/01/24/the-steam-has-gone-out-of-globalisation

126 Mac History, "1984 Apple's Macintosh Commercial (HD)," YouTube video, 00:59, February 1, 2012, last accessed September 15, 2021, https://www.youtube.com/watch?v=VtvjbmoDx-

I

127   Mac History, "1984 Apple's Macintosh Commercial (HD)," YouTube video, 00:59, February 1, 2012, last accessed September 15, 2021, https://www.youtube.com/watch?v=VtvjbmoDx-I

128   William A. Sahlman, "How to Write a Great Business Plan," *Harvard Business Review*, July-August 1997, last accessed September 15, 2021

136   William A. Sahlman, "How to Write a Great Business Plan," *Harvard Business Review*, July-August 1997, last accessed September 15, 2021

129   Carolyn O'Hara, "The Right Way to Present Your Business Case," *Harvard Business Review*, July 21, 2014.

130   Branding Strategy Insider, last accessed September 15, 2021, https://www.brandingstrategy-insider.com/how-did-apple-computer-get-its-brand-name/#.XpY8cNNKg8Y

131   John LaRosa, "Top 6 Things to Know About the U.S. Fertility Clinics Industry," *Market Research Blog*, December 10, 2018, last accessed September 15, 2021, https://blog.market-research.com/top-6-things-to-know-about-the-u.s.-fertility-clinics-industry

132   Mark Williams, "Market analysis for your business plan," *Wolter's Kluwer*, June 1, 2020, last accessed September 15, 2021, https://www.wolterskluwer.com/en/expert-insights/market-analysis-for-your-business-plan

133   Aaron Beashel, "The Complete Actionable Guide to Marketing Personas + Free Templates," *Buffer Marketing Library*, last accessed September 15, 2021, https://buffer.com/library/marketing-personas-beginners-guide/

134   "Resources: Starting a Business," Tory Burch Foundation, last accessed September 15, 2021, http://www.toryburchfoundation.org/resources/starting-a-business/create-your-business-plan-organization-management/

135   Jeff Haden, "How to Write a Great Business Plan: Products and Services," *Inc.*, April 6, 2015, last accessed September 15, 2021, https://www.inc.com/jeff-haden/how-to-write-a-great-business-plan-products-and-services.html

136   Akhilesh Ganti, "Angel Investor," *Investopedia*, July 26, 2020, last accessed September 15, 2021, https://www.investopedia.com/terms/a/angelinvestor.asp

137   Investopedia Team, "Private Equity vs. Venture Capital: What's the Difference?" *Investopedia*, July 30, 2021, last accessed September 15, 2021, https://www.investopedia.com/ask/answers/020415/what-difference-between-private-equity-and-venture-capital.asp

138   Akhilesh Ganti, "Venture Capitalist," *Investopedia*, March 16, 2020, last accessed September 15, 2021, https://www.investopedia.com/terms/v/venturecapitalist.asp

139   Investopedia Team, "Private Equity vs. Venture Capital: What's the Difference?" *Investopedia*, July 30, 2021, last accessed September 15, 2021, https://www.investopedia.com/ask/answers/020415/what-difference-between-private-equity-and-venture-capital.asp

140   Daniel Richards, "Writing a Business Plan – Financial Projections," *The Balance Small Business*, February 10, 2021, last accessed September 15, 2021, https://www.thebalancesmb.com/writing-a-business-plan-financial-projections-1200842

141   "Business Plan Section 9: Appendix," *Accion Opporunity Fund*, last accessed September 15,

2021, https://aofund.org/resource/business-plan-section-9-appendix/

142 Christine Funk, J.D., "PA vs. LLC," *LegalZoom,* last accessed September 15, 2021, https://info.legalzoom.com/article/pa-vs-llc

143 "Business: Business formation: LLC," LegalZoom, last accessed September 15, 2021, https://www.legalzoom.com/business/business-formation/llc-overview.html?_ga=2.126353933.1622684918.1586913273-1162218147.1586913272

144 Brette Sember, J.D., "What Makes an LLC Different from a PLLC?" *LegalZoom,* last accessed September 15, 2021

145 Darren Dahl, "Should Your Business Be an LLC or an S Corp?" *Inc.,* March 17, 2011, last accessed September 15, 2021, https://www.inc.com/guides/201103/s-corp-vs-llc.html

153 Darren Dahl, "Should Your Business Be an LLC or an S Corp?" *Inc.,* March 17, 2011, last accessed September 15, 2021, https://www.inc.com/guides/201103/s-corp-vs-llc.html

146 Darren Dahl, "Should Your Business Be an LLC or an S Corp?" *Inc.,* March 17, 2011, last accessed September 15, 2021, https://www.inc.com/guides/201103/s-corp-vs-llc.html

153 Darren Dahl, "Should Your Business Be an LLC or an S Corp?" *Inc.,* March 17, 2011, last accessed September 15, 2021, https://www.inc.com/guides/201103/s-corp-vs-llc.html

147 Francis J. Greene and Christian Hopp, "Research: Writing a Business Plan Makes Your Startup More Likely to Succeed," *Harvard Business Review,* July 14, 2017, last accessed September 15, 2021, https://hbr.org/2017/07/research-writing-a-business-plan-makes-your-startup-more-likely-to-succeed

148 "Proof of concept," Google/Oxford Languages, last accessed October 8, 2021, https://www.google.com/search?q=proof+of+concept+definition&oq=proof+of+concept+&aqs=chrome.1.69i57j0i512j0i20i263i512j0i512l7.4534j1j4&sourceid=chrome&ie=UTF-8

149 Ed Keller and Brad Fay, *The Face-to-Face Book: Why Real Relationships Rule in a Digital Marketplace,* (New York: Free Press, 2012), last accessed September 15, 2021, https://www.amazon.com/Face-Face-Book-Relationships-Marketplace/dp/1451640064

Index

Index